PAINTING · COLOUR · HISTORY

COLLECTION PLANNED AND DIRECTED BY
ALBERT SKIRA

*A handsome book is not the work
of a single person, but a product of
the collective, well-directed efforts
of all who have contributed to its
success.*

HISTORY OF MODERN PAINTING

MATISSE MUNCH
ROUAULT

FAUVISM

EXPRESSIONISM

VAN GOGH · GAUGUIN
MATISSE · MARQUET · VLAMINCK · DERAIN · DUFY · FRIESZ · BRAQUE
MODERSOHN · KIRCHNER · SCHMIDT-ROTTLUFF · KANDINSKY · JAWLENSKY
MUNCH · HODLER · ENSOR · ROUAULT
NOLDE · WEBER · KOKOSCHKA · CHAGALL · SOUTINE

TEXT AND DOCUMENTATION
BY MAURICE RAYNAL
ARNOLD RÜDLINGER HANS BOLLIGER
JACQUES LASSAIGNE
TRANSLATED BY STUART GILBERT

INTRODUCTION BY GEORG SCHMIDT
TRANSLATED BY DOUGLAS COOPER

ALBERT SKIRA
GENEVA

Our Foreword to the first volume of THE HISTORY OF MODERN PAINTING, " From Baudelaire to Bonnard " (which was also the first volume of our series PAINTING, COLOUR, HISTORY), gave a full description of our programme. Briefly, this was to make each volume of the series an art-book of an entirely new description, one in which colour reproduction was not merely a source of pleasure to the eye, but acted as the guiding principle ; indeed the whole book was built up around it. Needless to say, that programme holds equally good for this, the second volume.

We saw, in the first volume, a memorable era of painting come to a brilliant close with the art of Bonnard ; an era during which the liberation of painting from academic convention was achieved, thanks to the revolutionary drive of the Impressionists. In this second part is illustrated a no less remarkable phase in the evolution of painting, during which the age-old problem of Form and Content came to the fore, and was vigorously tackled by the ' Fauves ' in France and, in the Germanic and Scandinavian countries, by the ' Die Brücke ' group and by Expressionism properly so called. The ' Fauves ' handled their art constructively, centering their activity on the structure of the picture (which they built in ' bricks ' of pure colour) without regard to its psychological content ; whereas Expressionism aimed, above all, at bodying forth human emotions, and paid less attention to problems of technique.

While we have had a flood of literature about Impressionism, less is known of Fauvism ; indeed it has not been seriously studied until quite recent years. As for ' Nordic ' Expressionism, it has remained practically unknown outside the countries of its origin, and we have therefore discussed it in some detail and illustrated it as copiously as space permitted. The interest and considerable influence of this School, never esteemed at its full value, even in Germany (owing largely to the intense and brutally repressive hostility of National Socialism), will receive in the present work an overdue amends for the undeserved obloquy it incurred, involving even the destruction of many of its works.

To ensure the best possible presentation of the subject, we have, for the part of the present volume dealing with Expressionism in Germany and Austria, enlisted the help of writers on art who are not only eminent for their specialist knowledge of the subject but warm admirers of the great modern masters of Expressionism. For, as has often been observed, to write well about a subject one needs to love it.

Thus we would here convey our sincere thanks to Arnold Rüdlinger and Hans Bolliger, who have compiled the documentation relating to ' Nordic ' Expressionism and brilliantly expounded its aesthetic ; to Jacques Lassaigne who has discussed French Expressionism, as illustrated by the work of Rouault and Soutine ; and to Maurice Raynal, a wise adviser and loyal friend, whose close personal contacts with the great Fauve artists and sympathetic comprehension of their aims and achievements enable him to write on them both with authority and complete understanding.

In his preface Georg Schmidt gives a lucid and instructive ' résumé ' of the art movements of the XIXth Century, enabling the reader to make that panoramic retrospect so essential for any just appraisal of modern art.

In selecting the colourplates, we have made a point of choosing less known but highly significant works, so that the reader will not have cause to complain of being shown yet once again those world-famous masterpieces whose appeal has been blunted through over-familiarity. Finally, we have kept to our method of giving all our reproductions in full colour ; for mere black-and-white reproduction is apt to be not merely tame but actually misleading, since it is unable to bring out those ' values ' which are of capital importance in painting.

Once more we express our gratitude to the Directors and Curators of Museums who have both helped us with invaluable advice and so generously made the art-treasures in their keeping available for this book ; and no less warmly do we thank the eminent collectors who, with unvarying kindness, have given us access to their private collections and facilitated in so many ways the long and exacting task of our photographic experts.

A. S.

CONTENTS

THE COLOURPLATES

MATISSE MUNCH ROUAULT

INTRODUCTION

°

FAUVISM

°

DIE BRÜCKE

°

EXPRESSIONISM

IN

NORWAY — BELGIUM — SWITZERLAND
FRANCE — GERMANY
THE UNITED STATES

THE BIRTH OF MODERN ART

LESSONS OF THE PAST

BY

GEORG SCHMIDT

Curator of the Museum of Fine Arts, Basel

The following text by Georg Schmidt links up the present volume with the first of our History of Modern Painting : From Baudelaire to Bonnard. *For those readers who may not have followed the artistic developments described in our previous volume, the present introduction is indispensable to an understanding of the two great movements dealt with : Fauvism and Expressionism. It provides a brief but suggestive panoramic view of the history of XIXth Century art, and deals with the main currents, tendencies, schools and foremost individual figures who made their mark on it, from Ingres to Bonnard, by way of Delacroix, Courbet, Manet, Monet, Cézanne, Gauguin, Van Gogh and Toulouse-Lautrec.*

Without this perspective it is impossible to grasp the true significance of the two main groups with which this volume is chiefly concerned : Fauves and Expressionists.

Classicism : Ingres

In order to survey XIXth Century art one must start at the beginning, with Ingres. From Delacroix to Gauguin the whole of painting was conditioned by the struggle between those for and those against Ingres. And in post-impressionist painting certain elements of Ingres' art reappeared.

From the first to the last brush-stroke, Ingres' pictures were painted in the oblique light of the studio. Every picture began with a drawing, with lines. The tonal values of the chiaroscuro were only added afterwards in order to give an effect of plasticity and modelling. As for colour it was exclusively that of the objects represented.

Ingres composed his pictures in three distinct stages : drawing, colouring, modelling.

Ingres' painting is wholly naturalistic, that is to say it contains all those elements which together make up the idea of ' naturalism ' : 1) the illusion of roundness, 2) the illusion of space, 3) the illusion of solidity, 4) completeness of detail, 5) correctness of anatomical proportions and perspective, 6) accurate colouring of objects.

But though Ingres' artistic means were wholly naturalistic his spiritual approach to painting was strictly anti-realistic. He certainly never thought of painting as the business of making pictures of everyday reality or of revealing the problems of daily life. He thought that art should only concern itself with a loftier, more spiritual picture of reality. Thus, by its very conception, Ingres' painting was idealistic. He may look for form—both linear and plastic—in details, but it is in the whole that he looks for composition, for the rhythm between linear and plastic forms, for the architecture of his picture.

Ingres was born in 1780. His period coincided with that of Napoleon. And it is interesting to note, in this connection, that in refusing to admit ' vulgar reality ' as a fit subject for art, Ingres was adopting an attitude which corresponds to Napoleon's policy of restraining the more radical democratic tendencies of the Revolution. Naturally, then, after the fall of Napoleon, Ingres' art became the art of the Bourbon Restoration.

Romanticism : Delacroix

In 1822 with the *Barque de Dante*, and in 1824 with the *Massacre de Scio*, Delacroix raised the standard of the romantic revolt against classicism. Delacroix was movement as opposed to tranquillity, the dynamic as opposed to the static, the diagonal as opposed to the horizontal. Delacroix was the victory of the brush over the pencil, the victory of direct painting over the classical sequence of drawing, modelling, colouring. This meant that the artist ceased aiming at completeness in every detail and consequently gave up attempting to create an illusion of solidity. For material objects can only be imitated so that they appear palpable if the artist has a draughtsman's approach and applies colours in thin layers. Delacroix already sacrificed accuracy of anatomical proportions to the expressiveness of a body.

Delacroix dealt the first blow at the complete naturalism of academic painting. And what is the history of European painting, from Delacroix to Picasso, but a record of the gradual dismembering of naturalism ?

To the romantics, the *pleinairistes* and the Impressionists, Ingres was the embodiment of their antithesis and the means by which they found themselves. But Delacroix was both a precursor and a guide : to the *pleinairistes* because of his belief in painting directly, to the Impressionists because of his discovery of the law of complementary colours, and to the Expressionists because of his blatant disregard for the accuracy of anatomical proportions. Of the impressionist generation, Degas alone remained faithful to Ingres. Indeed it was not until the period of Impressionism was past that Ingres was once again admired and understood, by Cézanne particularly, by Renoir at the close of his life, by Gauguin, Seurat, Matisse and Picasso. Delacroix was born in 1798, twenty years later than Ingres. His work was an expression of the spirit of the years 1820-1840.

Open-Air Painting : Courbet

Soon after 1840, however, an artist twenty years younger than Delacroix came to the fore : this was Courbet, who too took his place beside Delacroix in the passionate fight against Ingres, whose domination of official art continued until well after the middle of the century. Courbet shared with Delacroix the belief that painting had to be freed from the tyranny of drawing, and followed his example in abandoning the illusory naturalistic representation of objects. But he broke sharply with Delacroix in rejecting absolutely historical or exotic subjects in favour of views of the French countryside and in deliberately choosing subjects from everyday life. Courbet was in painting a radical realist, just as in politics he was a radical democrat. Indeed the doctrine of realism in art— " everything that is natural is beautiful "—corresponds exactly with the doctrine of political democracy— " every man has an equal right to live. " Courbet in fact was the typical 1848 democrat.

Now although he freed painting from the model in the studio, Delacroix was not an open-air painter. His pictures were derived from his imagination. On the other hand, Courbet rejected the idea of painting either studio arrangements or imaginary scenes ; and though his pictures were as a rule finished in his studio, his vision was nevertheless entirely based on nature. Delacroix defied the static objectivity of Ingres with his dynamic subjectivity. But Courbet defied them both with that calm underlying the appearance of mobility, or mobility underlying the appearance of calm, which one constantly finds united in nature, for example in the movement of clouds, in the breathing of a person asleep or in the gradual erosion of rock. It was in order to represent these delicate, persistent yet implacable movements in nature that Courbet invented his particular technique of painting, which consists in spreading over the surface of the canvas with a knife a layer of transparent paint which is broken here and there and which at each break comes to life.

In his use of colour Courbet represents the transition from the romantic medley of Delacroix to the natural and prosaic monotony of everyday life. The very basis of Courbet's art is the relativity of apparent colours ; the local colours of objects are blurred by atmosphere and they are given a relative value depending on effects of light and weather. Courbet, then, became the great master of tonal painting, the master who worked in an infinite gradation of cool greyish and warm brownish tones. In a word Courbet was the great master of the open-air school.

Plein-air painting no longer tried to convey the illusion of tactile values in material objects. The hardness of stone, the brittle rigidity of wood, the softness of a flower's petals were things of the past. Plein-air painting conveyed nothing more of the material properties of objects than what appeared to the eye. All that our finger can feel in a plein-air painting is the mobile surface of colour, the material presence of the coloured pigment. Thorough-going naturalism is based on a harsh contrast between one natural substance and another ; pleinairisme fused this diversity into the single substance of the colour.

In pleinairisme the naturalistic illusion of solid objects was, to say the least, threatened. In the oblique and un-atmospheric light of the studio, forms were modelled with relentless precision. But in the diffused light of the great outdoors, and in the gently caressing atmosphere of daylight, solid forms are noticeably attenuated.

Of the six fundamental elements of naturalism, three were definitely rejected by the pleinairistes : completeness of detail, the illusion of solidity and the accurate colouring of objects. Pleinairisme weakened the illusion of objects in the round ; all it retained was the illusion of space and the accuracy of anatomical proportions and perspective. But in the work of the pleinairistes space is no longer airless as it is in the work of the classical painters ; on the contrary, it is full of atmosphere. And to render space the pleinairiste uses the technique of aerial perspective, just as the naturalists had used linear perspective.

The pleinairistes were less interested in objects as such than in what lay between them, what transformed them : that is to say light which changes hour by hour. Thus for the first time painters began to lose interest in objects, although the interest of the pleinairiste painters in effects of light was still evidence of their concern for objects as such. Now the vehicle of light is atmosphere. Atmosphere alone makes light perceptible through direct contrasts. Pleinairisme therefore was a form of chiaroscuro painting.

The Generation of 1820-1830

After the decade 1810-20, which witnessed the birth of almost all the plein-air painters (Th. Rousseau in 1812 ; Troyon in 1813 ; Millet in 1815 ; Menzel in 1815 ; Daubigny in 1817 ; Courbet and Jongkind in 1819), there was a gap of almost ten years before a new generation emerged to continue and go beyond pleinairisme. Between 1820 and 1830, from the birth of Courbet till the birth of Pissarro, no important realist painter was born in Europe. These ten years gave birth to an idealist reaction : Puvis de Chavannes and Monticelli were born in 1824 ; Gustave Moreau in 1826 ; Böcklin in 1827 ; Dante Gabriel Rossetti in 1828 ; Feuerbach in 1829. Puvis de Chavannes voted for the admission of Night by the young Hodler to the 1891 Salon and openly approved of the symbolist reaction against Impressionism. Gustave Moreau was the master of Georges Rouault.

The Generation of 1830-1840

With the year 1830, the year in which Camille Pissarro was born, there began to appear a new and amazingly prolific generation of painters who have for too long been indiscriminately grouped together under the name of Impressionists : Pissarro born in 1830, Manet in 1832 ; Degas in 1834 ; Cézanne and Sisley in 1839 ; Monet in 1840 ; Renoir in 1841. To-day we can see that only Pissarro, Monet and Sisley were true impressionists. None of the others—Manet, Degas, Renoir and Cézanne—can be classed as Impressionists except with major reservations.

To begin with, that is to say between 1860 and 1870, most of these painters practised tonal plein-air painting. Pissarro and Sisley followed in the steps of Corot (born in 1796), who had created ' intimate ' landscape in the years after 1820 ; Monet followed in the steps of Jongkind and Boudin, Manet and Renoir in those of Courbet. Renoir's Cabaret de la mère Antony (1865-1866) and Manet's Déjeuner (1868) are like a profession of faith in Courbet and his Après-dînée à Ornans (1849). Degas on the other hand derived from Ingres, while Cézanne took as his mentors Delacroix and Daumier.

Now for the true Impressionists-to-be—Pissarro, Monet and Sisley—the years 1860-70 were, significantly enough, only a period of preparation.

They were not to find themselves until tonal painting had been replaced by colouristic painting. On the other hand, Manet, Degas, Renoir and Cézanne already painted works during these years in which the full range of their personality was revealed.

Now what distinguishes the early works of the generation of 1830 from the plein-air painting of the generation of Courbet is not so much a particular use of colour as a far brighter tonality. And this was what struck their contemporaries. For this painting was still entirely tonal and based on chiaroscuro. In order to achieve a greater intensity (which had also been the principal aim of the *plein-airistes*) this new generation of painters distributed light over much wider surfaces, and then set dark surfaces off against these light ones (The *Olympia* of Manet, 1863).

It was at this moment that these painters saw Japanese prints for the first time. Yet they were not immediately struck by the expressive force of the lines, which seems to us to-day the most essential feature. Nor were they struck by the pure colours or the absence of shading. What impressed them was simply the tension between the light and dark areas. Therein lies the significance of the Japanese print that is pinned to the background wall in Manet's *Portrait of Emile Zola* (1868).

From the very beginning, it was Claude Monet who, of all these painters, was the most intoxicated with light. Compared with Manet's picture of the same title painted in 1863, Monet's *Déjeuner sur l'herbe*, painted in 1866, is flooded with light. But Monet was destined to become the creator and the foremost exponent of Impressionism by virtue of the preference he showed from the start for nature rather than for man. For the whole evolution from *pleinairisme* to Impressionism took place in landscape painting.

From their earliest days to their last, Manet, Degas and Renoir on the contrary, were interested above all in man. And that in particular is the reason for which they hesitated to allow human figures to be dissolved first in light then in colour. And that is why fundamentally they were opposed to pure Impressionism.

Now a further contrast between the generation of Courbet (pre-1860) and that of Manet (post-1860) lay in their choice of subjects. For scenes of rustic and peasant life were replaced by scenes of city life. Thus Manet became the first " painter of modern life " ; Monet, after 1866, discovered that a town with its play of light and atmosphere was also a landscape ; and only Pissarro remained faithful to Millet and his love of the countryside.

Impressionism : Monet, Pissarro, Sisley

It was around 1870 that the decisive step was taken from *pleinairisme* to Impressionism, when light as a colourless tonality was transformed into pure colour. While trying to render the intensity of natural light, the Impressionists discovered accidentally that although, objectively speaking, pure colours were darker than white, they were nevertheless more capable of conveying this intensity to the eye than white itself. They also observed something else : that there are no completely black shadows in nature, nor even colourless shadows. And so, gradually, the whole apparatus of classical *pleinairisme*—that is to say pure white and pure black, and the intermediate tones, pale grey, dark grey, light brown, dark brown—was decomposed into its constituent colours.

So it was almost inevitable, under the circumstances, that the law of contrasting complementary colours originally discovered by Delacroix should be confirmed. Now according to this law each of the three primary colours of the spectrum (red, blue and yellow) is intensified optically when it is placed beside its spectral complementary : red beside green (mixture of blue and yellow), blue beside orange (mixture of red and yellow), yellow beside violet (mixture of red and blue). Hence Monet's passion for poppies and red parasols in green fields, for orange sunsets reflected in blue water, and for blue shadows on orange walls.

This use of contrasted complementaries, which became general around 1875, had an important consequence. In order to give the maximum of luminosity to a green field, even when no poppies were visible,

the green area on the canvas was scattered with little dabs of red. As a result the long sweeping brush-strokes of the *plein-air* painters, or indeed of the Impressionists in their early years, gradually became shorter and more fragmentary. And this was the origin of the well-known impressionist ' comma ' brush-stroke.

But there were other equally far-reaching consequences of the transition from *plein-air* tonalities to impressionist colour painting. We have already noted how, by comparison with the pure naturalism of classicism, *pleinairisme*, with its diffused outdoor light, had weakened the illusion of material solidity. The Impressionists dissolved modelled objects almost completely, because they attached most importance to coloured light. For example, a tree painted in accordance with the laws of open-air *chiaroscuro*, still retains, generally speaking, a certain volume, because it is lighter in those parts which face the source of light and darker in those which are in shadow. By breaking up shadows into their constituent colours and transforming the chiaroscuro contrasts into colour contrasts, the Impressionists did away almost entirely with modelling.

Their transformation of pictorial space is noticeable but nevertheless not quite so radical. One of the fundamental principles of *pleinairisme* was the creation, by means of aerial perspective, of a pictorial space ooded with light and atmosphere. Now aerial perspective consists in a gradual increase in light values coupled with a gradual loss of precise detail as things are further removed from the foreground. In a pure impressionist landscape, however, everything has the same luminous value and is equally undefined whether it is situated in the foreground or background. An impressionist landscape is painted throughout in the same little ' commas ' of colour. Furthermore, looked at in terms of aerial or colour perspective, impressionist pictures are more or less without space. But the Impressionists, apparently, felt a strong need for a space to contain their light ; and so foreshortened roads, rivers and river-banks, which are accentuated, by linear perspective to give depth, are a typical element in impressionist landscape paintings.

But perhaps, ultimately, the most important consequence of this transition by means of Impressionism to a universe of colour was the final abandoning of naturalistic colouring. The Impressionists no doubt tried to persuade themselves and their naturalistic critics that they really did see the world entirely in terms of colour. But, objectively speaking, the prosaic tonalities of the *pleinairistes* do render the appearance of nature more faithfully. Nevertheless, this transposition of the visible world into terms of pure colour was the grandest and most revolutionary attempt to escape from naturalism, to free painting from being a slavish imitation of nature, and to make the artistic means independent. Impressionism turned painting into song and made of the artist a musician. From then on, practically the whole development of modern painting has depended on the principle of a pure use of colour.

The Impressionists, however, still had certain things in common with the *pleinairistes*. They denied matter, that is to say they transposed the various natural substances into the single substance of colour. They did not concern themselves with representing every detail but painted straight on the canvas. And, thirdly, they preserved correct anatomical proportions and perspective as well as the illusion of space.

The suppression of these last two elements of naturalistic representation—naturalistic space and correct anatomical proportions—was the decisive step taken by Cézanne, Van Gogh, Gauguin and Toulouse-Lautrec. And practically every subsequent artist has followed their example.

The spiritual attitude of the Impressionists, too, was not different from that of the *pleinairistes*. They followed them in regarding the contemplation of visible reality as the only possible source of art. They all rejected the idea of painting some imaginary vision. Despite their increasing opposition to pure naturalism, they were nevertheless great realists. They looked at visible reality with a genuine optimism and did not flinch before the most prosaic inventions of the triumphant industrial civilization of the XIXth Century—railway trains and stations, steamers and steel bridges.

Near-Impressionism : Manet, Degas, Renoir

It has already been said that some painters of this generation can only be called Impressionists with considerable reservations.

Manet, painter of modern man and city life, was from 1863 to 1870 the leader of his generation. But soon after 1870 he had to give way to Monet, who was by eight years his junior. Nevertheless Manet could not escape the influence of Monet's pure colour. In 1874, the climactic year of Impressionism, Manet even spent a few weeks with Monet at Argenteuil. But right up to his death in 1883 Manet was opposed to the complete dissolution of those lines by which planes are defined ; and he was also opposed to the 'comma' brushwork, because this technique led to the dissolution of the human figure into a number of spots of colour. In order properly to represent man, as Manet saw, some degree of drawing must be retained. On the other hand Manet had not the same passion for depicting human beings as Degas and Renoir, who on this account were carried beyond Impressionism towards a more expressive attitude. There is no link between Manet and post-impressionist painting. His achievement was in itself supreme.

Now *Degas* did not adopt the pure colours of Impressionism until shortly before 1880, and then chiefly in his pastels. Degas' origins lay behind *pleinairisme*, for he derived from Ingres and Puvis de Chavannes. That explains why his large idealistic compositions of the early 1860's are so completely the opposite of *plein-air* realism. And when, in the later 1860's, Degas started seriously to paint scenes of modern life, his debt to Ingres was proclaimed in the need he felt to surround his plastic forms with lines. Indeed the reason why even after he had become a realist painter Degas still continued to reject the dissociation of line and colour, which was common both to the *pleinairistes* and the Impressionists, must be sought in his exceptional sensibility for forms and their definition by line. Unlike the *pleinairistes* and the Impressionists Degas was all his life a passionate draughtsman. Degas never treated painting and drawing as a single simultaneous process ; to him drawing was always the framework of painting.

But in his rendering of plastic and linear elements Degas surpassed the degree of naturalism attained by Ingres. From *pleinairisme* he took only one element : its suppression of detail. So Degas was able to make his forms and outlines more concentrated and to give them a more expressive accent. Although Degas loved silhouette effects, and effects of stage lighting, it is too easy to overlook the fact that in his works the plastic forms, far from being consumed by light, are on the contrary accentuated by it.

Now by this accentuation of forms and accentuation of lines, two anti-impressionist factors, Degas became one of the most important precursors of post-impressionist painting. For post-impressionist painting is a blend of the Impressionists' colour and of Degas' lines and forms. About 1865 Degas also discovered a principle of composition that proved most fruitful : figures and groups are cut by the sides and lower edge of the canvas.

Something of the sort had already been introduced by the *pleinairistes* in opposition to the closed type of composition set, one might say, in a box or on a stage, so dear to the classicists. But where the *pleinairistes* and the Impressionists introduced an atmospheric space between the edges of the picture and the objects which were cut, Degas pushed his figures right up into the forefront of the canvas. His pictures lost in depth accordingly ; but psychologically the fact of bringing these cut figures nearer to the spectator makes them more human and forces us to identify ourselves with them.

Degas also makes use of another trick for emphasizing the flatness of his compositions while still accentuating the plasticity of his forms : he pushes the horizon line far up the canvas and exaggerates the effect of looking sharply down on to a road, a racecourse or a floor. Thus his figures are kept below the horizon line, or at any rate not allowed to stand out far beyond it, and so they look as though they are in a single plane. Here undoubtedly one can trace the influence of Japanese prints, for flat surfaces, a high horizon line and a sharply descending angle of vision are three of their principal characteristics.

The same features, which reappear in the work of Toulouse-Lautrec, Bonnard, Vuillard and Munch, were derived from Degas.

Finally Degas differs from the other painters of his generation in his choice of subjects. He shared the passion of Manet and Renoir for the human figure. However, where Manet was coldly objective and Renoir naïvely gay, Degas was the first to turn his penetrating eye on what goes on behind the brilliant façade of a large city. In this too Degas was the precursor of Toulouse-Lautrec.

With *Renoir* the position is different again. He was not as completely possessed as Degas by the idea of representing human beings. Yet, as with Manet, his landscapes and still-life pictures have not the same fundamental significance as his figures. But where Manet penetrated to the spiritual in man, which is the expression of his unique individuality, Renoir looked at him living, looked at his nature generally and saw how he behaved to other men. Manet observed but Renoir loved man. Manet was the disillusioned city-dweller ; Renoir was naïf, credulous, even candid. Renoir accepted impressionist colour enthusiastically in about 1870, and became the greatest colourist of all the painters of his generation. Indeed from the Impressionists' decomposition of light into pure spectral colours Renoir derived those pearly and iridescent harmonies which distinguished his painting till the end of his life.

Renoir took over the use of pure colour from Monet, but the feeling for plastic fullness was his own. Now we have seen how colour and plastic form are opposed to each other, and this explains why, until 1873, Renoir continued to oppose the dissolution of contour lines. In fact Renoir did not accept the dissolution of contours, as practised by the Impressionists, until he had discovered how to reconcile plastic form and colour by means of reflections, which could be used to emphasize the roundness of objects. All Renoir's late work is based on the use of these reflections. Not only does he model faces and nudes by this means but also tree-trunks, flowers, fruit and vases.

It was in his treatment of bodies, during the years after 1880, that Renoir hit upon a technique which proved to be an important contribution to post-impressionist painting. It has already been stated that despite the Impressionists' tendency to dissolve everything into spots of colour they nevertheless retained one fundamental element of naturalism : accuracy of anatomical proportions. Now Renoir, perhaps as a means of heightening the full-blooded effect of his bodies, took to exaggerating the fullness of the female head, breasts and thighs. Indeed he pushed this tendency to the extent of disregarding normal anatomical proportions. Now this exaggeration of natural forms for the sake of conveying some particular spiritual message was, briefly, one of the principles of *Expressionism*.

At the same time a profound change came over Renoir himself, and this is expressed in his subject-matter. Renoir gave up painting realistic scenes of contemporary life whether of the bourgeoisie, of his fellow-artists, or of the people. Instead he began to depict an ideal, timeless world, a living paradise.

We have already seen how Degas had both anti-naturalistic and expressive tendencies. But in his case they were not, as with Renoir, linked with a rejection of realism. On the contrary, Degas used these tendencies to accentuate and deepen his feeling for realism. This degree of difference which exists between Degas and Renoir is like an anticipation of the differences we shall discover between Gauguin and Van Gogh.

Paul Cézanne

Paul Cézanne is the perfect example of a painter whose deepest instinctive aspirations and whose most cherished convictions were radically opposed to the needs and aspirations of his contemporaries, although they were absolutely the answer to the needs and aspirations of later generations. Cézanne is the most touching example of an artist living in the wrong period. At the start, that is to say between 1858 and 1871, Cézanne's painting was twenty years behind the times ; but after 1872 it leapt three generations ahead. Even in his pictures painted before 1872 one can discover elements which belong more to the XXth than to the XIXth Century.

Cézanne before Impressionism

As with Delacroix, the principal works of Cézanne's early period—compositions remarkable for their wildness and violence—were entirely painted from imagination. *L'Enlèvement, La Toilette funéraire* and above all the key-work of this period *La Tentation de Saint Antoine* betray an almost visionary obsession. And even those compositions which seem to depict actual happenings—*L'Assassinat, Le Déjeuner sur l'herbe* and *Pastorale*—are nevertheless visions of some inner reality.

Technically speaking, Cézanne's use of heavy chiaroscuro and impasto at this date is nearer to Daumier than to Delacroix. This can also be said of the way in which he accentuates expressiveness by playing with anatomical proportions. But whereas even in Daumier's fiercest works one can only speak of an *exaggeration* of forms, in the works of Cézanne's youth it is the dangerous word *distortion* which presses itself upon us for the first time. Beside Cézanne even the most daring liberties that Daumier took with the human anatomy appear more or less naturalistically true. In fact it is only in the work of Van Gogh, and after him in the work of the French and German Expressionists subsequent to 1905 —for example Rouault, Nolde and Kokoschka—that one finds a similar degree of expressive violence, of internal tension, a similar eruption of self-confession.

Cézanne and Impressionism

In 1872 Cézanne went to stay with Pissarro at Pontoise. There he adopted straight away, and apparently without reservation, the decisive element of Impressionism : pure colour. In the work of no other painter was the changeover from tonal painting to painting in pure colours so abrupt ; in the work of no other painter is there such a marked gap between his work before and after 1870. For Cézanne this change meant far more than simply removing white and black from his palette and replacing them by pure colours ; it involved a major decision. Cézanne had to make up his mind what painting is about and what is the artist's purpose. Till that moment he had thought that painting is all a matter of feeling, of sentimental confession, and that the artist's duty is to discover himself. Afterwards he realized—and this realization was to remain the basis of his whole attitude to painting until his death in 1906—that painting only exists as something visible in terms of form and colour, and that form constitutes a sort of rhythmic element while colour is a melodic one. Painting is objective not subjective. And it is the painter's duty to minister, not to rule ; he must not consider himself as being the most important factor but must forget himself in the interest of the objectivity of the work of art he is creating.

In taking this decision Cézanne moved towards the position of Ingres. And this occurred at the very moment at which painting had just been freed from the bondage of academic objectivity and had become the most individual and sensitive calligraphy.

Once Cézanne had made up his mind, he was ruthless in eradicating any trace of the violent subjectivism of his early work. This was not easy. Even until 1877 his repressed eroticism continued to burst out occasionally in pictures with such classic themes as *Le Combat d'Amour* or *La Tentation de Saint Antoine*, although in a greatly toned down form. Later still this repression was sublimated in a more passive and neutral theme, that of *Bathers*, which continued to preoccupy him to the end, though more for its tectonic possibilities than for the subject.

In Cézanne's portraits, however, the expressive element remained, although it became objectified. It is even possible to trace the growth of this objective expressiveness right up to those imposing portraits of his gardener Vallier painted between 1904 and 1906.

But Cézanne found his perfect subject in landscape and still-life, for by their very nature both of these are objective.

One might have expected Cézanne to celebrate his liberation from his gloomy beginning by surrendering completely to Impressionism, then in its first flush. But nothing of the sort occurred. Not one existing canvas by Cézanne can be called purely impressionist. All that he took from Pissarro were his pure colours and his abbreviated brush-strokes. Even in the very first of his so-called impressionist paintings—the *Maison du Pendu* of 1872—Cézanne showed himself to be in every other respect completely opposed to Impressionism.

Cézanne, conqueror of Impressionism

We have seen that, in order to make up for the loss of perspective due to their use of colour, the Impressionists emphasized linear perspective. Cézanne on the other hand, though he gave certain indications of linear perspective (foreshortened roads and walls), nevertheless refused to respect the accuracy of such perspectives. One need not look further than the first of Cézanne's so-called impressionist paintings to see him doing away with the illusion of spatial depth by abandoning the single vanishing point which is the essence of classical linear perspective. By this means Cézanne immediately made his whole image appear as if in a single plane. In the winter of 1873 Cézanne and Pissarro painted the same street at Pontoise from the same spot. Now despite Pissarro's decomposition of every object into colours his picture preserves all the illusion of naturalistic space because he has respected the laws of linear perspective ; in Cézanne's picture each plane conforms to its own linear perspective, but there is no co-ordination between these various perspectives.

We have already stated that the Impressionists, as faithful followers of the *pleinairistes*, virtually abolished the roundness of objects by transposing into colours the shadows by which objects are modelled. Cézanne's handling of volume also was radically different, even in his first so-called impressionist paintings, for he returned to cubic elements. The naturalistic illusion of volume was achieved by the twofold means of linear perspective and modelling with light and shade. Of these Cézanne rejected linear perspective both in the handling of space and objects. The only means left to him therefore was that of modelling with light and shade. But as he shared with the Impressionists the belief that no such thing as a colourless shadow exists, light and shade meant to him simply lighter and darker colours. Therefore colour was Cézanne's only means of modelling.

In order to model by this means Cézanne was forced to invent a technique which was actually the negation of two other basic principles of Impressionism. The Impressionists decomposed the single colour of any surface into particles of complementary colours and broke up the continuity of lines by discontinuous brush-strokes. Cézanne abandoned the Impressionists' little specks of complementary colours and returned once more to surfaces of a single colour surrounded by definite outlines.

With these planes, strengthened by the unity of their colour and their linear contours, Cézanne built up clearly defined volumes, that is to say his cubes. Every colour has its place in a plane and every plane creates a cube. The illusion of solid objects (for no object can be represented as solid on the flat surface of a canvas except by means of an illusion, and Cézanne has been subsequently blamed for preserving this last vestige of naturalism) is produced by juxtaposing a plane of light colour and a plane of a darker colour. But whereas previously the space between objects had been filled by light and shade (the *pleinairistes* achieving luminosity by means of tonalities and the Impressionists by means of colour), Cézanne made light and shade an inherent part of his objects. Then too, whereas with Ingres objects were made to appear round by an imperceptible transition from dark to light, Cézanne used the direct transition from a dark plane to a light to create the facets of an object.

Right from the start Cézanne made use of the abbreviated brush-strokes of the Impressionists in order to achieve the opposite effect. In an impressionist painting the brush-strokes are absolutely free and loose, that is to say they go in no particular direction and therefore have no formative value. On the other hand, Cézanne appeared to take over the impressionist form of brushwork (and he retained it for the whole of his life) but he gave it a special rhythmical value by maintaining it over the whole surface and imposing a uniform direction—vertical, horizontal or diagonal.

Of course Cézanne made no attempt to compromise with two of the fundamentals of naturalism : accurate colouring and the illusion of solidity. Similarly he threw overboard true perspective and accurate anatomical proportions. But whereas before 1872 he used anatomical distortion to heighten expressiveness, between 1872 and 1906 he used the same means to formal and rhythmical ends. Just as the Impressionists took natural colours and transposed them into a pictorial colour melody, so Cézanne took natural forms and transposed them into a formal pictorial rhythm. In the hands of Cézanne, therefore, the art of painting took a great forward step towards objectivity and independence.

Cézanne's paintings are all form, all rhythm. He worked up from the little speck of colour applied by his brush in a certain direction to planes of colour separated from each other by outlines and by coloured volumes composed of adjoining planes ; and so, finally, he established a rhythm between the cubes of colour, that is to say his picture achieved a rhythmic composition. Each of Cézanne's pictures was built up simply with the pictorial elements—lines, planes, cubes and colours.

Between 1872 and 1906 Cézanne's work underwent no fundamental change. All that happened was that his relatively short, free brush-strokes (powerful and already Cézanne-like in form) were replaced by larger more emphatically directed ones. His planes and cubes were simplified and the construction of his pictures became more monumental.

In one respect, however, Cézanne's painting did undergo a transformation : during the last ten years of his life he began to use paint which was liquid and transparent—as unsubstantial, one might say, as water-colour—in place of the opaque impasto which he had adopted from the Impressionists. Thus, when he applied one colour over the top of another, the colour underneath, instead of being concealed, could shine through and produce a new tonality. Compared with the pictures of his second period, in which one opaque colour was set off against another, this new technique of overlaid transparent colours works like an orchestral effect.

There is a direct link between these late works of Cézanne and the Orphism (c. 1912) of Robert Delaunay, just as the early cubist works of Picasso (c. 1908) derive from Cézanne's middle period.

The Post-Impressionist painters : Seurat, Gauguin, Van Gogh

Were we to follow a chronological sequence according to dates of birth, Gauguin (born in 1848) and Van Gogh (born in 1853) would be the first post-impressionist painters. But in fact neither arrived on the scene until rather late. Gauguin began to paint in 1874, but it was not until 1888, at the age of 40, that he found himself. Van Gogh painted his first picture in 1881, but it was not until 1887, at the age of 34, that his years of apprenticeship came to an end. The work of Gauguin and Van Gogh between 1888 and their respective deaths left its mark on the whole of the next generation, which had been born between 1860 and 1870.

The new Ingres : Seurat

Before Gauguin and Van Gogh found themselves, however, a younger painter, Georges Seurat (born in 1859) declared his opposition to Impressionism. As a student at the Ecole des Beaux-Arts during the years 1878-80, Seurat was initiated into the doctrine of Ingres ; yet he did not revolt against it as did Van Gogh at the Antwerp Academy in 1885. Seurat made his mark already in 1884, at the age of 25, with *Une Baignade, Asnières*, which contains the whole of his subsequent achievement, that is to say uniting the colour decomposition of the Impressionists with the feeling for roundness of Ingres.

Seurat made a system out of that very decomposition of colours which the Impressionists had always treated with an empirical freedom. In 1886, the name Neo-Impressionism was given to his method. Seurat himself called it by a more precise name : Divisionism. These two labels however only apply to one aspect of Seurat's art—his handling of colour. His handling of form—and it was in this that Seurat made his greatest contribution—reflects a tendency which was more or less general in 1885 and which we may call the Neo-Ingrist movement.

Degas was especially concerned with the representation of bodies and to this end made use of oblique effects of light (the classic form of naturalistic lighting), of silhouetting and of stage lighting, which he handled with magnificent freedom. Renoir, towards the end of his life, modelled bodies by placing reflected lights on rounded surfaces in the foreground, that is to say he made use of frontal lighting. Seurat made use of an oblique light, which creates a greater impression of space right up to *La Grande Jatte* in 1886. But with *La Parade* in 1887-88 he began to model objects with the same means as Renoir in his late works, that is to say by frontal lighting. By this means he was able to abolish the spatial illusion of *La Grande Jatte* and achieve the effect of a relief.

If to these facts we now add Seurat's particular love of a rhythmically constructed picture we shall have enumerated all the qualities that he shares in common with Ingres. In every other respect he is the opposite of Ingres. For he did not share the naturalistic painter's technique of representing everything in detail, and in consequence rejected the illusion of representing objects as though they were palpable. Seurat's great discovery was an expressive stylization of the human body. Seurat's figures sometimes remind one of machine-turned wooden dolls. The primitivism which characterizes the figures in Seurat's pictures is perhaps his most characteristic and most modern trait. Certainly it was familiarity with these figures which made it possible for the next generation to appreciate the art of Henri Rousseau.

Only now can we speak of Seurat's ' Neo-Impressionism,' that is to say of his colour. And one might perhaps say that in a painting by Seurat one has the feeling that the little spots of colour which the Impressionists scattered like a shower of confetti, in the space by which objects were separated, have come to rest on the objects. Space has been emptied of atmosphere. As with Ingres, light and shade are once more directly related to objects.

As for his spiritual outlook, Seurat—who painted scenes of bathers, of Sunday afternoon promenades, of music-halls and circuses—ranks, just like Degas and for the same reasons, as one of the realistic painters of modern life.

Seurat attracted to himself a number of young painters, of whom *Paul Signac* (born in 1863), who was a pointillist, was the most gifted. Signac painted landscapes exclusively. But Seurat's influence was more important in its effect on some other painters who did not belong to the pointillist group.

Pissarro, who was aged 55 in 1886, certainly did not need Seurat to teach him about the decomposition of colour. But what he did learn from Seurat was the Neo-Ingrist idea.

Three other artists who, with Cézanne, were among the most radical opponents of Impressionism—Gauguin, Van Gogh and Toulouse-Lautrec—were also influenced by Seurat during their apprentice years : Gauguin in 1886, Van Gogh in 1886-87 and Toulouse-Lautrec in 1887.

Cloisonnisme : Gauguin

Gauguin in his early years was subject to a variety of influences. He began as a *pleinairiste*, then by 1879 had advanced to an Impressionism like that of Pissarro ; at the same time, in 1881 he began to be interested in the accentuated volumes given to objects by Ingres and Cézanne. In 1884 he began to paint with a series of short parallel brush-strokes, to define objects with lines and to model plastically with violet shadows and warm lights. Then, in 1886, he learnt the use of pure colour from pointillism. His first visit to the tropics —Martinique in 1887—encouraged him in the use of elongated and flowing lines.

In August 1888, at Pont-Aven, Gauguin and Emile Bernard created *Cloisonnisme*, and this technique remained his principal means of artistic expression till the end of his life. *Cloisonnisme* consists in surrounding areas of pure colour with heavy, sinuous contours. (The technique known as *cloisonné* enamels consists in pouring melted coloured glass into compartments made with thin metal plates set on edge on a foundation plaque.)

With *Cloisonnisme* one finds the same tendency as with Degas, to do away with space by using a sharply descending angle of vision and by pushing the horizon far up the canvas. But whereas Degas presents upright standing figures seen from above so that a perspective right angle is formed between the figures and the ground, Gauguin places figures, trees and horses in a frontal perspective on a ground which rises vertically. By this means Gauguin completely did away with naturalistic perspective, whereas in the hands of Degas it was merely somewhat abused. In Gauguin's work no angle is formed between the figures and the ground on which they are supposed to be standing ; the figures are presented frontally and appear to be stuck down flat on the surface of the vertically rising ground. By comparison with Degas this represents a considerable advance in flat representation of the pictorial image. To the same end Gauguin also suppressed cast shadows —a classic means of suggesting space—although he retained the internal shading by which objects are modelled. In fact Gauguin's easel paintings are really murals. Gauguin was one of the founders of the modern style of fresco-painting. Japanese prints, of course, also contributed to this stage of the development.

However, despite Gauguin's strong feeling for preserving the flat surface of the canvas, he also had an equally strong urge to paint figures in the round. Gauguin modelled figures with strong effects of light and heavy shadows. And, as with Cézanne, the planes of light and shade are juxtaposed without any transition, somewhat as in cubist paintings. Gauguin painted still-lifes of fruit which were directly influenced by Cézanne. Gauguin was the only painter of importance who was influenced by Cézanne during his life-time.

Gauguin's feeling for plasticity is undeniably overlaid with a strong expressive tendency, such as one finds in the Neo-Ingrists generally. Gauguin had the same yearning for the elemental and natural life, the same nostalgia for the lost paradise, that one finds in the late work of Renoir.

Gauguin's painting is the most powerful expression of that mood of boredom with city life and with civilization which marked the closing years of the XIXth Century. Nothing could be further removed from the optimism of the Impressionists. And yet the two are separated by no more than twenty years—1870 to 1890.

In 1888 Gauguin had hoped to find his dreams come true among the Breton peasants and fishermen. But city life was still too close. In April 1891 he took ship to Tahiti. He came back to France once, spending time in Paris and Pont-Aven between 1893 and the spring of 1895, and then went back to the South Seas for ever.

But Gauguin never found the paradise of which he was in search, even among the primitive peoples of the South Seas. In the first place the long tentacles of European civilization—colonial administration, missionaries, traders—had already penetrated there long ago and disturbed the old native civilization. Then, too, even native life is far from being blissful and untroubled ; on the contrary, it is dominated by a fear of spirits, by slavery and by social misery.

Gauguin fled as far as he could from Europe : to Tahiti. But his search for an aesthetic paradise proved vain, and his art gained in depth by this very admission. Gauguin allowed echoes of the tragic reality of man's earthly existence to creep into his pictures of native life. A common bond of destiny was established between him and the natives.

It is, however, undeniable that Gauguin never completely renounced his nostalgia for some imaginary paradise of beauty. His handling of figures always has about it something of Ingres ; his lines have a hint of aestheticism, his colours a degree of refinement. At heart Gauguin was a realist in spite of himself.

There is no exaggerating the extent of Gauguin's influence on the development of modern painting. His broad planes of colour and his use of line reappear in the work of Bonnard and Munch, and of course with the Fauves. His habit of accentuating the cubic form of figures influenced the early work of the Cubists in about 1908.

As for his subject-matter, Gauguin is still the one painter who has most profoundly expressed the longing of the city-dweller to escape into nature. But Gauguin's most decisive contribution has been that of making us look at the art of primitive peoples not as a curiosity but as a creative art-form which has both artistic and spiritual value.

Expressionism before its time : Van Gogh

Van Gogh arrived in Paris in the Spring of 1886 and immediately the expressive dark tonalities of his early Dutch period were replaced by silvery greys. At the end of 1886 he learnt from Pointillism the use of pure colour and the principle of contrasted complementaries. Seurat was manifestly more in keeping with his rigorous theorizing than the empirical nonchalance of the Impressionists. Technically speaking, Van Gogh's *Petit Café* painted in the Autumn of 1886 is purely pointillist : the wall is dotted with red and green, the floor with blue and orange. To the last Van Gogh was to remain faithful to the principle of complementary colours. In a letter from Arles he stated expressly that he advocated " the Pointillism of Seurat." But for Van Gogh, line—expressive line—was at least as important as pure colour. Van Gogh's main problem therefore was the reconciliation of colour and line. He solved this problem at Arles in the Spring of 1888.

After repeated and pressing invitations, Gauguin finally arrived in Arles in October 1888 to stay with Van Gogh and form the advance-guard of a small group of modern artists. But in December of the same year occurred the famous and tragic rupture between two artists, whose temperaments were so utterly opposed. Van Gogh never looked just for beauty ; he always pursued truth. For him Gauguin was the aesthete whom he secretly envied and loathed. Gauguin tried to escape from suffering as much as he could ; Van Gogh tried to take suffering upon himself in the early Christian sense. Gauguin tried to forget and to enjoy life ; Van Gogh tried to know the truth and to proclaim it.

While things went well at Arles, Gauguin and Van Gogh talked of painting together a picture of a *Woman Rocking a Cradle*, an image of a nurse, of a mother to every sailor, who when they were far away from their homes and families, would sing to them a song of the green countryside and of a warm and loving presence. This is the picture in which Van Gogh came closest to Gauguin : it is pure *Cloisonnisme*. And yet, how hard and angular are its contours, how primitive and harsh its colours ! But what humanity, what faith, what truth as well ! Beside this picture by Van Gogh, so like a Gauguin in many respects, a great deal of Gauguin's

work nevertheless looks like the products of an aesthete crying out for drugs.

For Van Gogh (as for Gauguin), after he had found himself at Arles in the Spring of 1888, line and colour became the essential basis of painting. But unlike Gauguin he did not use line simply to surround forms nor colour to express a spiritual state. Van Gogh made every plane pulsate with linear vitality, the internal line was as important to him as the contour. Planes such as Gauguin used were, on the one hand, too empty to satisfy Van Gogh's insatiable desire for self-expression, and, on the other, too insubstantial for one with his craftsmanly approach. Thus Gauguin tended to use thin washes, as in frescos, whereas Van Gogh was always a true user of oil paint. Every one of Van Gogh's brush-strokes carries the imprint of his personal handwriting, so vital, so full of his own joys and sorrows. With Van Gogh every colour conveys the essence of the object precisely, whereas with Gauguin colour is no more than a pleasing note of music.

Van Gogh made use of the impressionist form of brushwork, which he pushed to the limits of its expressive possibilities ; Cézanne on the other hand stressed its rhythmic possibilities. In his use of colour Van Gogh followed Gauguin in contrasting planes of pure colour. But whereas Van Gogh remained faithful to the last to the law of contrasting complementaries, Gauguin avoided contrasts of the primary complementaries and preferred more refined harmonies of related colours : red-orange, orange-yellow, yellow-green, green-blue, blue-violet, violet-red.

Both Van Gogh and Gauguin were attracted towards simple man. However Van Gogh did not go in search of him far away, outside time and contingency ; Van Gogh found him in his immediate surroundings. The people in Van Gogh's pictures, unlike those in the pictures of Gauguin, do not look at us from a mysterious distance but reveal the secrets of their soul with naïve confidence. Van Gogh's men are active workers of our own time. His landscapes are made up of fields cultivated by man, of roads built by man and of trees planted by man. The objects in his still-lifes are objects which man uses and which he needs. There is a profound contrast between the still-lifes of Cézanne and Van Gogh : in the former everything is objectified, in the latter everything is humanized.

Both artistically and spiritually Van Gogh's influence has been no less than that of Gauguin. A great deal of Fauvism derives from Van Gogh, and his attitude to life had a profound effect on expressionist painting.

The generation of 1860-1870

Going back now to thinking in terms of generations, we find a remarkable number of important painters who were born during the decade 1860-70 : Ensor in 1860, Munch in 1863, Toulouse-Lautrec in 1864, Vallotton in 1865, Kandinsky in 1866, Bonnard and Nolde in 1867, Vuillard in 1868, Matisse in 1869. With this last painter we come to the generation of the Fauves, who were born between 1870 and 1880.

From the point of view of their art we may group the painters of the generation of 1860 as follows :

Toulouse-Lautrec and *Edvard Munch* take their place beside Gauguin, Van Gogh and Hodler as representatives of " the 1900 style " with its expressive lines. Toulouse-Lautrec influenced the young Picasso, and Munch was to some extent the father of German Expressionism.

Ensor and *Odilon Redon*, twenty years his senior, belong to the group of post-impressionist symbolists. Ensor's period was between 1890 and 1900, Redon's during the years after 1900. Both fulfilled themselves completely in their own subjective style and exercised no immediate influence on those around them.

Vuillard, *Bonnard* and *Vallotton* are directly descended from Degas, Gauguin and Toulouse-Lautrec. But with these painters, colours and planes were of more importance than line. Vuillard's most characteristic works were painted between 1890 and 1905, Bonnard's after 1900 ; while Vallotton returned after 1900 to an expressive form of *Ingrisme*.

It was in about 1897 that *Matisse* discovered the decomposition of colour, and in about 1900 began to use planes of colour surrounded by heavy outlines. In 1905 he was recognized as the leader of the Fauves, all of whom were his juniors.

It was not until about 1908 that Nolde began his expressive use of colour. He, like Rouault, Kokoschka and Soutine, belongs to the Expressionist movement, which indulged in an anarchic breaking-up of forms.

Finally, *Kandinsky*, who began by painting Fauve landscapes during the years 1908-10. In 1911 he took the supreme step, the consequences of which have been enormous, and began to paint *Improvisations* without figures or objects. These were the immediate outcome of the use of line and colour by the Fauves.

Expressive Line : Toulouse-Lautrec

After a youthful period characterized by dark brown tonalities, *Toulouse-Lautrec* adopted Impressionism in 1882 in the form in which it was practised by Manet during his last years. In 1884, Toulouse-Lautrec made the acquaintance of Degas. Primarily what interested him in Degas' work were plastic qualities rather than types of composition, but he was of course specially attracted by the subject-matter. In 1887, Toulouse-Lautrec began to combine Degas' handling of figures with a use of complementary colours, with short and deliberately controlled brush-strokes and with a form of composition based on horizontals and verticals. In 1887, the year in which Van Gogh adopted Pointillism, Toulouse-Lautrec made a drawing of him in coloured chalks in which he used this technique.

It was in 1890, two years after Van Gogh and Gauguin, that Toulouse-Lautrec, who had been profoundly impressed by Japanese prints, came to understand the expressive possibilities of pure line. But like Van Gogh he could not adopt the principle of *Cloisonnisme* because, being essentially a draughtsman, his temperament needed more to play with than mere contour lines. Even though contour lines seem predominant in Lautrec's work, and even though plastic values were reduced to the absolute minimum, the interiors of his planes are covered with a passionate network of lines. As with Gauguin, Van Gogh and Hodler, line in Lautrec's work has the sweeping, sinuous movement of " the 1900 style."

In 1884 it was the sense of volume in Degas' work which made an impression on Lautrec ; after 1890 he fell for his sense of planes, for his daring, sharply descending angle of vision focussed on a table or a floor, and for his high horizons. But whereas Degas' use of perspective was always true, Lautrec, like Cézanne and Gauguin, suppressed true perspective and began to vary the spectator's angle of vision in any one picture. Thus was the means by which he kept the whole of his pictorial image on a single plane, and in a more noticeable manner than that used by the other two artists. Toulouse-Lautrec too had a tendency towards mural painting.

From Degas he learnt yet something more : the expressive force of figures cut by the sides of the canvas and the possibilities of tension between empty and well-filled planes. However, as opposed to Degas, he followed Gauguin and Hodler in suppressing cast shadows and in placing his figures (seen from above) flat against a vertically rising ground. At this same period Hodler and Munch made use of the same high horizon line.

During the 1880's Lautrec's compositions were static and built up on a system of verticals and horizontals ; after 1890, on the contrary, his most important means of expression became the dynamic diagonal. And his compositions are frequently built up on a series of opposing diagonals. It is therefore easy to understand why Toulouse-Lautrec became the precursor of the modern poster.

It is in no sense derogatory to the genius of Toulouse-Lautrec to say that in his work colour was of far less importance than with Gauguin or of course Van Gogh. With Lautrec rhythm was everything, melody but little. Van Gogh and Gauguin were musicians ; Lautrec expressed himself in prose like some great novelist. Even with a brush in his hand he was first and foremost a great draughtsman.

To this let us add that, by comparison with the first great adversaries of Impressionism—Cézanne, Gauguin and Van Gogh—, Lautrec was more respectful of true anatomical proportions. He no doubt had no more use for the classical anatomy than he had for the classical scheme of perspective. In fact he was prepared to take any liberty with anatomy in order to increase the expressive value of his figure. But yet one cannot accuse him of distortion, as one can Cézanne, Gauguin and Van Gogh. For Lautrec was much too fascinated by the character of every individual human being. Of all these painters, Lautrec was the greatest portraitist even though he pushed expression to the extent of caricature. For him every figure was unique ; it might be comic, grotesque or tragic, but somehow he would manage to capture it.

The post-impressionist painters sum up the position of the XIXth Century, the century of cities and combustion engines. Gauguin proclaims the great illusion of being able to return to a state of nature ; Lautrec turns his back coldly on all illusions ; Van Gogh proclaims his faith in humanity ; Cézanne proclaims his confidence in the objective laws of construction.

Symbolism : Ensor and Redon

Realist art and idealist art are the two poles by which first Degas and Renoir, then Van Gogh and Gauguin were attracted respectively. The same divided attraction characterizes the work of Ensor and Redon.

James Ensor began by painting in dark colours but then in 1885 adopted the pure colours and free technique of the Impressionists. Even at that date, however, his art had an expressive quality. Ensor painted his first picture of masks in 1883 already. It was not until 1890 that he invented the personal idiom which he retained for the rest of his life.

In painting interior scenes Ensor made great play with the horizontal and vertical lines of floors, tables and walls, which he used as a sort of scaffolding on which to hang his fantastic objects. His outdoor scenes, on the other hand, were always more imaginary. Ensor made use of the decomposition of colour, but his pictures are always full of linear elements. The graphic element in his work is always strong. One might even say that his paintings are drawings coloured with a brush. Ensor's colours bear no relation to his objects, they are purely poetical.

Ensor's profoundest experiences are expressed in terms of masks ; human beings are metamorphosed into a masquerade, and the masquerade has a human appearance. Ensor's is a dream world. But his dreams are not gloomy and full of anguish ; on the contrary, they are light, clear and full of a cheerful irony. Ensor turned his back more radically on representation of the world around us than did any of those painters whom we have discussed hitherto. This does not, however, make him less of a realist, because instead of using dreams as a means of escaping from the reality of human passions, he uses them as a means of recognizing and giving expression, with a wry smile, to the deepest aspects of our existence.

In parenthesis let it be added that confusion reigns in the use of the terms 'naturalism,' which is a means of representing external reality, and 'realism,' which implies a will to know both inner and outer realities. This confusion is one of the greatest obstacles to an understanding of all non-naturalistic art, that is to say of practically all modern forms of art.

Odilon Redon began to paint before 1870, and was at that time chiefly influenced by Delacroix. Then, following a bereavement, he painted not a single picture between 1870 and 1900, but confined himself to black and white, that is to say to engraving and lithography. All the paintings on which his reputation depends to-day were painted after 1900. When he began to paint again Redon took up subjects such as one finds in the work of Delacroix—a mythological universe peopled with centaurs and winged horses. Like Delacroix, too, his world is not a pure dream-world but a pure imaginary world. Beneath the dream symbolism, which is expressed in Redon's graphic work after 1880, there is much psychological realism and repressed eroticism, but his idealistic pathos is at least as strong. Instead of proclaiming his erotic pangs, as Cézanne did in his early works, Redon conceals them under a literary symbolism.

Redon's graphic work has a psychological reality, and he does not hesitate to combine naturalistic detail with anti-naturalistic dream elements. To this extent he was a sort of forerunner of the surrealism of Max Ernst.

After 1900 Redon abandoned both the naturalistic and the realistic elements of his middle period; his late oils and watercolours are composed entirely in planes and appear to be a lively *divertissement*. The masks and shells of Ensor are replaced by Redon with flowers and butterflies. And against this delightful microcosm Redon likes to set off heads larger than nature, with stern profiles, which push into the picture from the edge and seem like sleepwalkers about to enter the imaginary pictorial space.

In 1884, Redon joined with Seurat in the foundation of the Society of Independent Artists. He learnt the use of pure colours and contrasting complementaries from Seurat.

As with Ensor, Redon's painting contains a strong element of drawing; and, again like Ensor, he pushed the use of colour to the extreme of its luminous possibilities. In Redon's watercolours one finds the same use of transparent planes of colour laid one on top of the other as in the late work of Cézanne; it was through his growing passion for watercolour that Cézanne too discovered this technique.

The Intimists: Vuillard, Bonnard, Vallotton

Although Vuillard, Bonnard and Vallotton accepted and made use of the discoveries of Post-Impressionism —especially the use of colour and the technique of composition by planes—they shrank from the ultimate consequences of this form of art. Vuillard and Bonnard, in particular, diluted the expressive element of Post-Impressionism and so, spiritually speaking, moved back again towards Impressionism.

Edouard Vuillard discovered a personal style more quickly than Bonnard. Bonnard did not find himself until about 1900, after which he pursued, till his death

in 1947, a style of remarkable flexibility and freshness; Vuillard's most important work however was done between 1890 and 1905.

Vuillard began, like most other painters of his own and subsequent generations, by using dark tonalities. Then in about 1890, like the Pointillists, he began to use pure colours. At about this time he had a decisive meeting with Toulouse-Lautrec, who taught him that in painting it is not only objects but the whole composition of a picture which has to be built up in planes.

In every other respect, for example in his choice of subjects, Vuillard's work is far removed from that of Lautrec in his maturity. Nor did Vuillard follow Lautrec in his exploitation of the possibilities of line and expressive diagonals. Vuillard also turned his back on *Cloisonnisme*, which was the principal subject of discussion in 1890. He let each plane fade vaguely into the next without using contour lines but setting them at right angles to each other. Vuillard had a definite predilection for objects which contained the fundamental directions of his composition within themselves, that is to say verticals and horizontals: a door with its panels, a window with its panes, a framed picture on a wall, a bookcase with shelves, a squared table-cloth, a carpet in parallel stripes.

Vuillard's pictures are themselves rather like a patterned carpet. As a child he had acquired a taste for fabrics, such as he saw in his mother's little dressmaking establishment. For this reason his most personal works were his large decorative panels of the 1890's—the *Public Gardens* of 1894, and the panels painted for Dr Vaquez in 1896.

We have already referred to Toulouse-Lautrec's love of empty spaces; Vuillard, on the other hand, had a horror of emptiness. As in a tapestry or an embroidery, the surface of Vuillard's picture is always covered with little passages of painting which fill in and give a feeling of movement. Every single plane is marked by a different sort of graphic sign, just like a decorative motive in tapestry or a form of stitching in embroidery. Van Gogh used a similar technique, but in his case there was an expressive justification for such signs, whereas with Vuillard they were the result of some decorative necessity.

In his use of colours, too, Vuillard was not as radical as Cézanne, Gauguin and Van Gogh. The Impressionists' discovery of pure colours was, of course, accepted by him without question. But whereas these other three painters confined themselves more or less to the primary and secondary colours of the spectrum —red, blue, yellow, green, orange and violet—Vuillard had a pronounced taste for ternary mixtures, brown and grey with their coloured refractions. Nevertheless he did not revert to painting in tonalities. He treated brown and grey as pure colours, not as elements of chiaroscuro. Compared with Cézanne, Gauguin and Van Gogh, Vuillard's use of colour was more attenuated, more built on nuances. This discretion, which has at the same time a certain dignity, is the revelation of Vuillard's own personality.

But with Vuillard this use of form and colour is made to serve a definite purpose: the description of man's sheltered existence in his own setting. After 1905 his pictures were entirely concerned with the bourgeois world. Gauguin fled to the paradise of the South Seas to escape from the problems of modern city life. Vuillard took refuge in bourgeois drawing-rooms, where he was fascinated by the objects he found— carpets, arm-chairs, mantelpieces, clocks and gilt frames. Van Gogh humanized the objects at which he looked, but Vuillard even turned man into an object. That is why, after 1905, he was constantly in danger of falling back into naturalism and using the illusions of space, of roundness and of solidity. He was, however, saved from this simply by his remarkable sense of composition, by the highly sensitive line of his brushwork and lastly by his taste for exquisitely palpable colours.

Vuillard painted almost nothing except interiors. Even his gardens and parks are shut in with houses. Impressionist interiors always have wide-open windows to allow the light to come streaming in. Vuillard covers his windows with curtains and draperies, the air is motionless, time is suspended, light settles like a silvery dust over men and objects.

Félix Vallotton began as a *plein-air* naturalist, painting with an intensity reminiscent of the old masters. After meeting Vuillard and Bonnard in 1895 he became a painter of modern life. But his interior scenes painted between 1896 and 1900 have a note of psychology and expressiveness which one does not find at all with Vuillard and Bonnard. Moreover his use of colour has a more expressive than purely pictorial function and he uses line predominantly as a medium for expression. Vuillard and Bonnard made coloured lithographs of a quite remarkable tenderness and sensibility ; Vallotton preferred the harsher blacks and whites of wood-engraving. There is something of Strindberg in Vallotton's work between 1896 and 1900 and for this reason it is not unlike that of Edvard Munch at the same date.

In 1905, however, Vallotton started on a new line, which he has pursued alone, without disciples and without any influence on his contemporaries. In his still-lifes, Vallotton has returned to a form of unconditional naturalism. His large nudes are painted in an expressive Neo-Ingrist idiom which is stubbornly bizarre. His landscapes look like wood-engravings painted in oils and sometimes have a powerfully suggestive harshness.

In his early years, between 1890 and 1900, *Pierre Bonnard* drew inspiration from many sources : Degas, Renoir, Gauguin, Van Gogh and especially Toulouse-Lautrec. Bonnard learnt from Degas and Toulouse-Lautrec his infallible sense of flat composition, his taste for sharply descending angles of vision, for figures cut at surprising angles by the edges of the canvas, and his love of creating a tension between full and empty spaces. From Gauguin he learnt to use large areas of pure colour, from Van Gogh the value of a restless brush-work, from Renoir a naïve delight in highly variegated colouring and figures with accentuated curves.

One thing, however, he did not take from Toulouse-Lautrec and Gauguin ; their use of continuous outlines. Like Vuillard, he tends to efface contours by an almost impressionistic transition from plane to plane, from colour to colour.

Like Vuillard, Bonnard invented no really new means of expression. But again like Vuillard, he did extract a very personal idiom out of the legacy of Post-Impressionism.

Although, like Vuillard, Bonnard too had a taste for inhabited interiors, he had only a limited interest in the objects they contained or in them as objects. He was primarily sensitive to objects as colour, he reacted to the music of their colours. He was the one Post-Impressionist who was nearest to the Impressionists. That therefore is why he was never as much in danger as Vuillard of falling back into naturalism. Above all Bonnard loved landscapes and still-lifes with the most varied and brilliant colouring.

Vuillard conveys the gentle melancholy of autumn, Bonnard the splendid gaiety of late summer. Bonnard is like an *allegro finale* to Impressionism at a time when this sort of liveliness was virtually out of fashion.

Just occasionally one finds in Bonnard's scenes of bourgeois life a tiny grain of irony which enables him to keep his distance. This irony is particularly visible in one of his largest and most important canvases, *Une Après-Midi bourgeoise* painted in 1903. It is Sunday afternoon and the family are in the garden : father, mother, grandmother, uncle, aunt, the good children and the naughty children, the dogs and the cats. The fact that Bonnard was able to preserve an air of freshness till the end (he died in 1947) was due to his native irony.

Bonnard's passion for colour was already a foretaste of the Fauves of 1905.

FAUVISM

BY

MAURICE RAYNAL

Matisse makes a stay in Brittany (Belle-Ile).
Periodical **Die Jugend** launched at Munich (January).
Munch frequents the circle of Mallarmé and of " Le Mercure de France."
Kandinsky and **Jawlensky** come to Munich from Russia.
Lautrec does the programme-cover for Wilde's " Salomé."

1897   Impressionist Exhibitions at London and Stockholm.
" La Revue Blanche " publishes Gauguin's manuscript : **Noa-Noa.**
In Tahiti Gauguin paints vast triptych : **Whence come we ? What are we ? Whither go we ?**
Munch makes a long stay in Paris. Lithographs, **woodcuts.** Influence of Gauguin.
Matisse paints **La Desserte.**
Le Douanier Rousseau paints **La Bohémienne Endormie.**

1898   Mellerio publishes La Lithographie originale en Couleurs.
Bonnard illustrates Peter Nansen's **Marie** ; Lautrec, Jules Renard's **Histoires Naturelles.**
Toulouse-Lautrec Exhibition. Death of Stéphane Mallarmé (September 9).
Matisse exhibits **La Desserte** at the Salon de la Nationale.
Matisse visits Corsica and Toulouse. **Marquet** works at Arcueil and in the Luxembourg Gardens.
Friesz enrols at the Ecole des Beaux-Arts in Bonnat's class. **Dufy** joins him in 1900.
Neo-Impressionist Exhibition at Keller and Reiner Gallery in Berlin.

1886-1918

FIRST PART (1886-1903)

FROM VAN GOGH'S COMING TO PARIS TO THE FOUNDING OF THE SALON D'AUTOMNE

For the convenience of the reader, we enumerate below the chief events, in France and abroad, relating to the history of painting that took place between 1886 and 1918. Elsewhere in the volume, where they seemed appropriate, we have included other summaries which will assist the reader in forming a clear idea of each particular art-period and group of artists. Part of the following table will reappear in the third volume of our History of Painting, *From Picasso to Surrealism*. Instead of terminating with 1918, however, it will there be extended up to 1940.

1886 **Vincent Van Gogh** comes to **Paris.**
Eighth and last exhibition of the Impressionist group.
The Douanier Rousseau exhibits for the first time at the Salon des Indépendants; attracts wide attention.

1888 Bonnard, Vuillard and Maurice Denis meet at the Académie Julian.
James Ensor paints his large-scale work: **Entrance of Christ into Brussels.**

1889 Gauguin paints his **Yellow ' Calvary. '**

1890 **Matisse** explores the technique of painting. Paints his " Still Life with Books."

1891 Retrospective Van Gogh Exhibition at Salon des Indépendants. Death of Seurat. Gauguin leaves for Tahiti.
Foundation of **La Revue Blanche** by the Natanson brothers. Drawings by Steinlen in the **Gil Blas** illustrated
magazine.
Gatherings of Symbolist poets at the **Café Voltaire.** Aurier's Manifesto in **Le Mercure de France.**
Bonnard shows for the first time at Salon des Indépendants. First Lautrec **poster** for the Moulin-Rouge.
Hodler exhibits **Night** at the Champ-de-Mars.

1892 Lautrec's first **colour-lithographs.** Posters for the " Divan Japonais " and " Les Ambassadeurs."
Retrospective Seurat Exhibition at the ' **Revue Blanche** ' Gallery. First Salon de la Rose-Croix at Durand-Ruel's.
Small monochrome paintings on cardboard by Bonnard, Vuillard and Vallotton.
Le Douanier Rousseau paints **Bonne Fête** and **Le Centenaire de l'Indépendance.**
Matisse comes to Paris, enrols at the Académie Julian.
Munch sends 55 pictures to the exhibition of the Berlin Artists'Association, where they are sharply criticized
and withdrawn after one week.
Foundation of the **Munich Secession** (Stuck, Trübner, Uhde).

1893 Lugné-Poë founds his **Théâtre de l'Œuvre.** Sets and programmes by Vuillard and his friends.
Matisse enrols at the Ecole des Beaux-Arts. He and **Rouault** work in Gustave Moreau's class.
Opening of the Vollard Gallery.
Gauguin returns from Tahiti. Exhibits 40 pictures at Durand-Ruel's (November).
First exhibition of the **Munich Secession**: Böcklin, Corot, Courbet, Liebermann, Millet.
Exhibition at Berlin of pictures rejected for the ' Great Exhibition.' Munch is a committee-member.

1894 Uproar regarding the Caillebotte bequest to the Musée du Luxembourg (executor of the will is Renoir).
First murals by Vuillard. Appearance of **Le Rire** and **L'Ymagier** (R. de Gourmont, A. Jarry).
Odilon Redon Exhibition at Durand-Ruel Gallery (April).
Vuillard makes sets for Ibsen's **Master Builder.**
Lautrec does an Oriental set for Barrucand's **Chariot de Terre Cuite.**
Tristan Bernard sporting editor of **La Revue Blanche.**

1895 **Cézanne** Exhibition at **Vollard Gallery** (November-December, over 100 pictures).
Lautrec visits London. Sets for La Goulue's booth at the **Foire du Trône.**
Salon de la Nationale: stained-glass windows by Tiffany after designs by Vuillard, Lautrec, Bonnard, Sérusier,
Vallotton.
Vollard publishes **Quelques aspects de la Vie de Paris.** Lithographs by Lautrec, Bonnard, Vallotton.
Second Gauguin auction sale at the Hôtel Drouot. He leaves again for Tahiti.
Publication of Rimbaud's " **Poésies complètes** " with preface by Verlaine.
Munch's first lithographs printed at A. Clot's in Paris.
Lautrec paints Oscar Wilde's portrait.
Launching at Berlin of the magazine **Pan.** Editors are Bierbaum and Meier-Graefe.

1896 At Durand-Ruel's, Bonnard's first one-man show (49 paintings, posters, lithographs).
Lautrec travels in Spain. **Ubu-Roi** performed at the Théâtre de l' Oeuvre (December 10).
Matisse's first appearance at the **Salon de la Nationale.**
Deaths of Verlaine and E. de Goncourt. Marcel Proust publishes **Les Plaisirs et les Jours.**
Libre Esthétique Exhibition at Brussels.
S. Bing opens the **Art Nouveau** Gallery in the rue de Provence. Munch Exhibition.

VINCENT VAN GOGH

FOURTEENTH OF JULY

1886-1887

Van Gogh's art is, by general consent, one of the sources of Fauvism and Expressionism. And this **Fourteenth of July** is one of the works best illustrating the

Matisse makes a stay in Brittany (Belle-Ile).
Periodical **Die Jugend** launched at Munich (January).
Munch frequents the circle of Mallarmé and of " Le Mercure de France."
Kandinsky and **Jawlensky** come to Munich from Russia.
Lautrec does the programme-cover for Wilde's " Salomé."

1897   Impressionist Exhibitions at London and Stockholm.
" La Revue Blanche " publishes Gauguin's manuscript : **Noa-Noa.**
In Tahiti Gauguin paints vast triptych : **Whence come we ? What are we ? Whither go we ?**
Munch makes a long stay in Paris. Lithographs, **woodcuts.** Influence of Gauguin.
Matisse paints **La Desserte.**
Le Douanier Rousseau paints **La Bohémienne Endormie.**

1898   Mellerio publishes **La Lithographie originale en Couleurs.**
Bonnard illustrates Peter Nansen's **Marie ;** Lautrec, Jules Renard's **Histoires Naturelles.**
Toulouse-Lautrec Exhibition. Death of Stéphane Mallarmé (September 9).
Matisse exhibits **La Desserte** at the Salon de la Nationale.
Matisse visits Corsica and Toulouse. **Marquet** works at Arcueil and in the Luxembourg Gardens.
Friesz enrols at the Ecole des Beaux-Arts in Bonnat's class. **Dufy** joins him in 1900.
Neo-Impressionist Exhibition at Keller and Reiner Gallery in Berlin.
Rodin's **Balzac** is refused by the Société des Gens de Lettres.
Paul Klee studies under Knirr in Munich.
Opening of the Cassirer Gallery in Berlin.

1899   Cézanne sells Le Jas de Bouffan and retires to Aix. Renoir ' discovers ' Cagnes.
Nabis give Group Exhibition at Durand-Ruel's as a ' Homage to Odilon Redon.'
Second Cézanne Exhibition at Vollard's. Chocquet auction-sale at the Hôtel Drouot.
Matisse, Derain, Jean Puy, Laprade meet at the **Académie Carrière.**
Signac publishes his study : " D'Eugène Delacroix au Néo-Impressionnisme."
Special issue of the Belgian review " La Plume " devoted to the Belgian painter **James Ensor.** Death of Sisley.
Derain meets Vlaminck at Chatou. **Nolde** attends the **Académie Julian.**
Cézanne finishes Vollard's portrait, begun in 1897.

1900   **World's Fair.** Exposition Centennale of French Art at the Champ-de-Mars.
Retrospective Seurat Exhibition organized at the ' **Revue Blanche** ' Gallery by Félix Fénéon.
Bonnard illustrates " Parallèlement " for Vollard (109 colour-lithographs).
Picasso's first stay in Paris.
Friesz exhibits at the **Salon des Artistes Français.**
Dufy comes to Paris. Enrols at the Ecole des Beaux-Arts in Bonnat's class.
Munich : **Kandinsky,** Klee and Marc study at the Academy. No personal contact between them as yet.
Paula Modersohn at the Académie Colarossi in Paris. Much impressed by Cézanne exhibit at Vollard's. Meeting
       with Nolde.

1901   Hodler paints " Retreat from Marignano " murals at the Swiss National Museum in Zurich.
Friesz meets Pissarro. Apollinaire comes to Paris. Redon Exhibition at Vollard's.
Van Gogh Exhibition at Bernheim-Jeune Gallery. Derain introduces Vlaminck to Matisse at the Van Gogh
       Exhibition. Matisse visits Derain and Vlaminck at Chatou.
Dresden : **Kirchner** and Bleyl study architecture at the Technical Institute.

1902   Matisse exhibits at Berthe Weill's.
Picasso returns to Spain. Picasso Exhibition at Berthe Weill's.
Lautrec Memorial Exhibition at Salon des Indépendants. Lautrec Exhibition at Durand-Ruel's.
Vollard publishes **Daphnis et Chloé** with lithographs by Bonnard.
Dresden : Impressionist Exhibition at Arnold Gallery.
Munich : Kandinsky opens his own art school, becomes chairman of the **Phalanx.**

1903   On Ivanhoë Rambosson's initiative, Desvallières, Rouault and Piot found the **Salon d'Automne,** seconded by
       Matisse, Marquet and Bonnard.
Deaths of Gauguin, Pissarro and Whistler. " La Revue Blanche " ceases publication.
Matisse, Derain, Vlaminck and Marquet exhibit at **Salon des Indépendants.**
Matisse, Derain, Vlaminck, Marquet, Friesz and Dufy exhibit at **Berthe Weill's.**
Gauguin Exhibition.
Berlin : Works by Cézanne, Gauguin, Van Gogh, Bonnard and Munch exhibited by the **Secession.** Launching
       of periodical **Kunst und Künstler** (Art and Artists), published by Cassirer.
Vienna : Secession Exhibition—Impressionists and Neo-Impressionists (Seurat : La Grande Jatte).
Kandinsky travels to Tunis and Kairouan. Klee begins his series of grotesque etchings.

VINCENT VAN GOGH

FOURTEENTH OF JULY
1886-1887

Van Gogh's art is, by general consent, one of the sources of Fauvism and Expressionism. And this **Fourteenth of July** is one of the works best illustrating the
immediate origin of the early manifestations of ' Fauve ' art. We can well understand how Vlaminck, for instance, was swept off his feet by the sheer driving force
and brilliance of this amazing canvas. It demonstrates that colour in itself can
suffice not merely to fill out surfaces but to conjure up a new world. During his
' Dutch ' period, when using very low-pitched tones, Van Gogh had already proved
that " black, too, is a colour, " as Matisse was to say ; and when, from 1886 on, he
painted his Parisian scenes—amongst them, those ' boat wash-houses ' on the
Seine, and the Chatou bridge, which Derain and Vlaminck found so attractive—, he
achieved effects of equal intensity with the purest, most vivid colours. Here,
however, we do not find that system of building exclusively with colour practised
subsequently by the Fauves. What this **Fourteenth of July** showed them was that
' shock tactics ' and impassioned handling of colour can achieve an intensity of expression undreamt of by such painters as Delacroix or Monticelli. In the **Fourteenth of
July** we detect those moods of alternating exaltation and depression characteristic
of Van Gogh. Contrasting with long, savagely slashed brushstrokes, are the shorter
ones which bespeak lulls, pauses, or (to borrow a term from music) the ' rests ' in
the symphony of colour. For this canvas has that symphonic quality which was
what the Fauves aimed at so persistently. Here instinct alone determines the artist's
record of his visual experience. There is no planning in advance, no archaism, not
a trace of Cloisonnism or Symbolism. Only the immediate, instinctual rendering of
a sensation on a surface—almost such as a child occasionally and miraculously
produces with his first box of paints.

Here, then, we have the starting-point of Fauvism, before scruples and
sophistications led it, as we shall see, to deviate from its initial path.

IT WAS ABOVE ALL VAN GOGH WHO USHERED IN THAT LIBERATION OF COLOUR FROM REPRESENTATIONAL SERVICE WHICH THE
FAUVES CARRIED TO ITS EXTREME LIMIT. WE ARE TOLD THAT VAN GOGH OWED MUCH TO HIS 'DISCOVERY' OF RUBENS,
DELACROIX AND MONTICELLI; YET THOUGH MANY ARTISTS SHARED HIS CULT OF THESE MASTERS, THIS WAS NOT ENOUGH
TO MAKE ANY OF THEM A VAN GOGH. AND THIS 'FOURTEENTH OF JULY' BESPEAKS A RAPTUROUS DELIGHT IN COLOUR WELLING
UP FROM THOSE DEEP INSTINCTIVE LEVELS WHENCE GENIUS TAKES ITS RISE.

VINCENT VAN GOGH

PORTRAIT OF AN ACTOR
1888

Van Gogh came under Gauguin's influence, and took over from Cloisonnism the technique of binding surfaces with contour-lines, of strongly emphasized brush-strokes and the use of extremely high-pitched colour. These practices led him to interpret and to stress the expression of the subject, if not so much its form as did the Fauves. And Expressionism was to turn this technique to good account.

Such were the methods employed in this **Portrait of an Actor.** When we compare the expressive art of such painters as Munch, Rouault and Soutine, we find that the passionately dramatic style of Expressionism used exactly these same methods and aimed at the same clean-cut visual effects. Thus we have angular, jagged, incisive drawing which, violently contrasted with emphatic curves, undergoes 'emotive distortions' that override all aesthetic considerations, so as to attain the maximum of psychological truth. With Van Gogh these distortions never serve merely that 'deforming for the sake of form' which we find in some contemporary artists. The same applies to his handling of expressive colour, on very personal lines. Thus, here, with the object of expressing anguish on this actor's face, he envelops it with green, and also streaks the nostrils with that colour—green being for him the colour-equivalent of 'those terrible things, men's passions.' The Expressionists, too, used colour in this way, as in itself expressive of their personal emotions. We see this in some of the colourplates reproduced hereafter : in the green streaks on the cheeks of Rouault's **Tragedian,** the red-tipped beard of Munch's 'Jealous Husband,' the red hands in Kokoschka's self-portrait ; and this indeed applies generally to the colours chosen by the Expressionists.

In Van Gogh, however, we have the most striking example of this direct express-ion of the artist's inmost self. There is indeed something specifically 'Nordic' in this will to exteriorize in his art his reactions to a world which forces on him not only disillusionment and distress but a rankling sense of guilt. His revolt against this world he 'never made' is less organized than anarchic, and he finds in his painting sometimes as it were an accomplice seconding his anguish, but sometimes a means of excusing, or a 'compensation' for, what he deems his personal responsibility.

VINCENT VAN GOGH (1853-1890). PORTRAIT OF AN ACTOR, 1888. 24¾×20½″.
RIJKSMUSEUM KROELLER-MULLER, OTTERLO.

VAN GOGH HAD AN ALMOST UNCANNY INSIGHT INTO THE SECRET PLACES OF THE HEART. INDEED IT WAS FROM HIM THAT
EXPRESSIONISM LEARNED THE SECRET OF THOSE ANODYNES WHICH DERIVE EITHER FROM A FRANK AVOWAL OF THE CAUSES
OF A PROFOUND DISTRESS OR FROM A STOIC ACCEPTANCE OF ITS PRESENCE. WITH ITS HARSH, PEREMPTORY DRAWING AND THE
POIGNANCY OF ITS COLOUR, THE FACE OF THIS 'ACTOR' TELLS OF A PROUD REJECTION OF ANY ISSUE FROM HIS SORROW
THAT OTHERS MIGHT SUGGEST; ANY ESCAPE WHICH IS NOT DUE TO HIS PERSONAL RESOLVE TO FORCE THE HAND OF FATE.

PAUL GAUGUIN

THE YELLOW 'CALVARY'
1 8 8 9

As in the case of Van Gogh, we find that Gauguin's influence on Fauvism and Expressionism took a dual form. The very title of this canvas implies that colour is moving towards that liberation from representational service in which, like Van Gogh, Gauguin played a leading part. Here we have not a ' Christ in Glory ' or a ' Christ in Majesty,' but, to render literally the French title **Le Christ Jaune**, a ' Yellow Christ.' Gauguin had the intention of calling another canvas ' The Green Christ.' All of which indicates that colour played a dominant part in his conception of this work. The Fauves were not slow to profit by the lead thus given. Indeed i iis canvas is a practical illustration of various methods taken over by them for the   y-out of the surface of a picture : thick contour-lines, the use of large tracts of flat colour, juxtaposed colours, the suppression of shadows and of coloured light, and so forth. In this connexion **The Yellow ' Calvary '** may be compared with Matisse's **Luxe, Calme et Volupté.**

It was to Gauguin, too, that Fauves and Expressionists owed that return to favour of the woodcut which, while catering for the taste for the Primitive and the simple thrills of childhood cherished by every artist in his heart of hearts, was so prolific, from Munch to Derain, of brilliant results.

Expressionism, moreover, found in Gauguin, and especially in **The Yellow ' Calvary,'** certain suggestions of an order other than purely technical. Gauguin was always talking of his " physical and moral distress," and on one occasion tried to kill himself. " I'm an utter failure," he used to say, and his disgust with so-called civilization led him to throw in his lot with " unspoilt barbarians." In fact Gauguin was a neurotic, self-tormented type of man, much like Van Gogh. Thus, naturally enough, Expressionism took him to its heart. His ' Yellow Christ,' too, is the ' man of sorrows and acquainted with grief,' yet patiently resigned, whom we see in old German woodcuts. Despite his accesses of vain revolt, Gauguin was spiritually akin to the Breton women here depicted, so forlornly, dully submissive to their lot. " There is not a heart on earth," he once said, " into which I can pour my sorrows." And thus we need not be surprised if the Expressionists found in Gauguin a kindred spirit, and in this fine picture, a stimulating precedent.

PAUL GAUGUIN (1848-1903). THE YELLOW 'CALVARY,' 1889. 36¼×28¾″. ALBRIGHT ART GALLERY, BUFFALO.

HERE WE FIND A FORETASTE OF THAT EMANCIPATION OF COLOUR WHICH FAUVISM WAS SOON TO ACHIEVE. THE EXPRESSIONISTS
SET MUCH STORE BY THIS PICTURE OF A WAYSIDE CROSS IN BRITTANY, ALL THE MORE 'LIVING' TO THEIR MIND BECAUSE ITS
CENTRAL FIGURE PASSED FOR A LIKENESS OF GAUGUIN'S FRIEND, THE PAINTER EMILE SCHUFFENECKER.

PAUL GAUGUIN (1848-1903). TE PO (WOODCUT), 1892. 8×13″. P. PROUTÉ COLLECTION, PARIS.

GAUGUIN SAID IN A LETTER TO HIS FRIEND MONFREID : " I'M SURE THAT ONE DAY MY WOODCUTS, SO DIFFERENT FROM ANYTHING THAT'S BEEN DONE BEFORE, WILL BE HIGHLY PRIZED."

THE WOODCUT

Amongst the various factors influencing Fauvism and Expressionism, the woodcut calls for special mention.

It is common knowledge that the first incunabula (printed from woodblocks) made their appearance before the invention of the printing-press. The first pack of playing-cards was presented to Charles VII in 1457. But it was not till 1476 that (almost simultaneously at Basel and Cologne) the first book entirely illustrated with woodcuts came out : *Der Spiegel menschlicher Behältnisse.* These earliest designs have a savour all their own. The draughtsmanship is a little rough and gives the impression of having been hacked out laboriously with the graving knife in the woodblock, the grain of which runs lengthwise ; but it was quite adequate not only for dramatic compositions, but also for depicting homelier scenes, conjuring up a world that, while naïvely interpreted, is rich in poetic inventions and imaginings.

We may recall Gauguin's advice to artists desirous of creating a new world ; that they should hark back to the origins of art, and have recourse to archaism of all kinds, even though its methods seemed primitive to the point of clumsiness. The technique of the woodcut had much in common with the use of the thick contour-lines whose value as constructive elements had much impressed him, evidenced no less in the stained-glass window than in the colour-prints, whether those produced for popular consumption or those of a higher artistic quality, which have always abounded in France. In Japanese art, too, and in Manet's he had found this usage of the contour-line. Gauguin indeed, like Munch, seemed to court difficulties, and, like the early woodcut artists, preferred to use wood cut ' with the grain '—that is to say planks sawn vertically in the trunk, which involve the craftsman in all sorts of difficulties, adventures and mishaps ; whereas the modern method of using woodblocks cut across the grain, *i.e.* slices of wood sawn transversely, enables him to proceed with more assurance, since the texture of the wood he works on is more uniform.

Munch, too, was attracted by the work of the old craftsmen, and he saw in their use of strongly marked line a method consonant with his desire for sharply defined forms. Moreover the ' expressionist ' quality of the themes treated in these old woodcuts appealed to him, as did the less visual than emotional lay-out, characteristic of all Primitives.

But what Fauvism and Expressionism made their aim was to exploit all the new possibilities afforded by the woodcut line for implementing their chief preoccupation—that of intercalating form in a flat surface. Also, the Fauves discovered how well line can bring out the values of the zones environing an object ; how effective it is for suggesting volume ; and how appropriate it is to that " vigorous, even exaggerated " type of drawing which Van Gogh championed, and which was to lead to the thick contour-line, the *cerne*. Also the woodcut suggested to Fauves and Expressionists alike synthetic methods appropriate to what they had at heart : thoroughly constructive composition, an almost architectural ideal.

Subsequently, when the Fauves decided to endow colour alone with that capacity for tectonic expansion which is their distinctive contribution to modern art, line became for them but one more obstacle, the last, that they must take in their stride ; and this they did by turning to account the characteristic radiation of each colour left to its own devices, since this, in itself, had an intensity sufficient to bring forms to life on the surface of the picture.

In brief, the woodcut furnished the rough outlines of an aesthetic to which adhered (in a general way) not only Kirchner, Schmidt-Rottluff, Pechstein and Nolde (of the ' Die Brücke ' group) but Matisse, Derain, Vlaminck and Dufy amongst the Fauves.

HERE MUNCH IS SYMBOLIZING THE DESTINY OF MAN AND WOMAN, SUBJECT EVEN IN DEATH TO THE DOMINION OF LOVE.
DURING 1896 AND 1897 MUNCH FREQUENTED SYMBOLIST CIRCLES IN PARIS.

EDVARD MUNCH (1863-1944). MEETING IN INFINITY, 1899. 7×9¾″.
NATIONAL GALLERY, OSLO.

1897-1903

PRELUDE TO FAUVISM

EXPERIMENTS AND ENCOUNTERS

Several notable events which contributed to the birth and rise of Fauvism took place between 1897 and 1903.

The first was the appearance of Matisse's *Desserte*. In this canvas, whose influence was immediate and decisive, Matisse, while abiding by the aesthetic of his immediate predecessors, gave expression for the first time to that conception of pure colour which was to be Fauvism's starting-point. The whole work is vibrant with touches of colour intense to the point of harshness, though still governed by the accepted notions of ' values.' But Matisse's friends made no mistake about it ; the *Desserte* opened up to them a new, rich field of possibilities.

We must not forget that, on his arrival in Paris in 1892, Matisse entered the Académie Julian, in which Bouguereau and Ferrier, members of the Institute, were teachers. Admitted to the Ecole des Beaux-Arts in 1893, he was lucky enough to escape the classes of Bonnat and Gérôme, and entered Gustave Moreau's studio, where he met Marquet, Rouault, Piot, Camoin and Manguin. Moreau gave them the excellent advice that they should follow when their inspiration led. Friesz joined the Ecole in 1898 and studied in Bonnat's class, where he was joined by Dufy in 1900. In 1898 there forgathered in Eugène Carrière's studio Matisse, Derain, Jean Puy, and Laprade, who found in this teacher a helpfully broad-minded counsellor.

The year 1896 had witnessed the death of Verlaine and the production of Jarry's *Ubu Roi*, whose first performance evoked a storm of protest. Munch was now a regular visitor at Mallarmé's ' Tuesdays,' and the *Mercure de France* receptions. 1897 was marked by events of some importance for the course of art, notable amongst them being the publication of Gauguin's famous manuscript *Noa-Noa* by the *Revue Blanche*. In 1898 the Société des Gens de Lettres which had commissioned it, refused to take delivery of Rodin's *Balzac*, the result being a sensation of the first order. Stéphane Mallarmé died in this year. Matisse exhibited his *Desserte* at the Salon de la Société Nationale. The World's Fair of 1900 and its official show, the ' *Centennale* ' of French art, met with immense success. Picasso paid his first visit to Paris and became acquainted with Montmartre. Apollinaire came only in the following year and did not meet Picasso till 1905.

The *Revue Blanche* organized a retrospective Seurat Exhibition. In 1901 the Bernheim Jeune Gallery held that famous Van Gogh Exhibition which did so much for starting the Fauve movement. Matisse and Vlaminck, introduced to each other by Derain, met on the opening day. That was the day when Vlaminck said, " I love Van Gogh better than my father."

It was now that friendships were struck up between the younger artists, some of which have lasted to the present day. Derain and Vlaminck had met at Chatou in—of all things !— a railway accident, and now they shared a studio there.

The artists travelled according to their tastes and means. Thus Matisse was in Belle-Ile in 1896 ; in Toulouse and Corsica in 1898. Thus he ' discovered ' the Mediterranean. He worked with Marquet in the Luxembourg and at Arcueil in 1899.

The year 1903 witnessed the deaths of Gauguin, Pissarro and Whistler ; also the demise of the *Revue Blanche*. The Salon des Indépendants now enjoyed a new vogue, due to the participation—which was to last—of all the ' deserters ' from the Ecole des Beaux-Arts.

From 1901 onwards Matisse, Marquet and Puy exhibited there; in 1903, Friesz, Matisse, Dufy, Marquet and Derain. Press and public followed each successive exhibition with interest, if not always with admiration.

Meanwhile in an unpretentious picture-shop in the rue Victor-Massé (Montmartre) Berthe Weill, a witty, excitable, short-sighted youngish woman, passionately devoted to the new art, had gathered round her the young men soon to be known as 'Fauves.' Far from well off, she could not pay high prices—but likewise could sell practically nothing. For picture-dealers, too, are capable of heroic ventures. In 1902 Matisse exhibited in her little

HENRI MATISSE (1869). TOULOUSE LANDSCAPE, 1900. 8½×13½".
PRIVATE COLLECTION, PARIS.

FOR THE FIRST TIME MATISSE GIVES A NEW DIRECTION TO HIS PENCHANT FOR BRIGHT COLOUR. HERE THE THEORY, ALREADY ENDORSED BY HIM, OF SUBSTITUTING IMAGINED REALITY FOR SEEN REALITY IS PUT INTO PRACTICE. HIS EARLIER CONCERN FOR DEPTH IS WAVERING. COLOUR SEEMS ON THE WAY TO BECOMING SELF-SUFFICIENT. IN SHORT, WE ARE NEARING FAUVISM.

gallery, so did Picasso. In 1903 came Manguin, Puy, Marquet and Friesz. All with outstanding names in modern art figured amongst those whom Mlle Weill called her "colts." She wrote poems, spiced with a rather caustic wit, on painters and art in general, published a periodical, gave artistic evening parties, and did her apostolic best for her young friends. She was the first woman picture-dealer to write on painting. Many years later at the age of eighty, an invalid, nearly blind, and suddenly reduced to destitution, she reaped her reward. The great painters for whom she had done so much in their young days presented her with pictures—which now, unlike the past, brought her in a small fortune.

So now the group had definitely shaped itself, a certain unity of outlook was evident in its diverse tendencies, and its golden age was near. All that was needed was an opportunity for making its impact in the public at large, and that opportunity was not long denied. October 1903 was a memorable date in the annals of the young movement, for in that month was held the first Salon d'Automne and the sensation it created left nothing to be desired.

The Salon d'Automne

Presided over by Frantz Jourdain the architect, and installed by Jansen, the Salon d'Automne opened its doors in October, 1903, in the Petit Palais (Champs-Elysées). Not however in the lofty halls of that august building, but in the basement ; for thus its conservator, H. Lapauze (who resented this intrusion of the ultra-modern) had decreed. Nevertheless the *vernissage* of the first exhibition, which took place in the evening, and at which—amazingly enough—evening dress was *de rigueur*, was quite a social event. Such prominent people as the Countess de Noailles, Robert de Montesquiou, Proust, and Arthur Meyer were present. Amongst the artists shown at it were Gauguin, Redon, Matisse, Desvallières, Guérin, Laprade, Marquet and Rouault. However, it was not very successful, and H. Lapauze made this a pretext for refusing to let his Petit Palais house the next year's Salon d'Automne. Thanks to the good offices of Henry Marcel, Directeur des Beaux-Arts, this second exhibition took place in the Grand Palais des Champs-Elysées. Largely owing to the inclusion of a one-man exhibition by Cézanne, it was a success. But now the members of the Institute banded together to have the Salon d'Automne expelled from the Grand Palais, claimed as the preserve of the Salon des Artistes Français, exclusively. However Eugène Carrière had championed to good effect the new Salon, and, despite the Press campaign and a preposterous attack on it made by a town-councillor (in private life a photographer), the Salon held its ground. The 1905 exhibition, in which Matisse, Marquet, Derain, Vlaminck, van Dongen, Manguin, Rouault, Friesz, Puy and Valtat figured, elicited protests not only from the academic reactionaries but from the Old Guard of Impressionism. Nevertheless the tide had turned, Fauvism had made good, and the Salon d'Automne become an Institution.

GEORGES ROUAULT (1871). LES FILLES, 1903.   10¼×7½".   HAHNLOSER COLLECTION WINTERTHUR.

AT THE SALON D'AUTOMNE, BREAKING FOR THE FIRST TIME WITH HIS 'BROWN' MANNER, ROUAULT SHOWED THE FAUVE PREDILECTION FOR REDS, GREENS AND BLUES.

1886-1918

SECOND PART (1904-1918)

FROM THE SALON D'AUTOMNE TO THE DEATH OF GUILLAUME APOLLINAIRE

1904   Matisse at Saint-Tropez with Signac. First exhibition at Vollard's (preface by Roger Marx).
Braque comes to Paris.
Kandinsky exhibits at the Salon d'Automne and at the **Exposition Nationale des Beaux-Arts.**
Cézanne, Gauguin, Van Gogh Exhibition at the **Munich Kunstverein.**
Cézanne Exhibition at Cassirer's in Berlin.
Foundation and first exhibition of the **Deutscher Künstlerbund,** an alliance of groups of modern artists.

1905   Seurat and Van Gogh Exhibitions at Salon des Indépendants.
Picasso meets Apollinaire. **La Plume** carries articles on Picasso by Apollinaire.
At Montmartre Vlaminck meets Van Dongen, Picasso, Max Jacob, Apollinaire. (Le Bateau-Lavoir.)
First Vlaminck Exhibition at Salon des Indépendants.
Van Gogh Exhibition at Arnold Gallery in Dresden.
Matisse exhibits **Luxe, Calme et Volupté.**
The **Fauves at Salon d'Automne** (Vlaminck, Derain, Matisse, Manguin, Rouault, Marquet, Van Dongen).
Large-scale Retrospective Manet Exhibition at the Salon d'Automne.
Derain joins Matisse at Collioure.
Formation of the group of artists, **Die Brücke,** at Dresden.

1906   Gris, Modigliani and Severini come to Paris.
Braque exhibits at the Salon des Indépendants.
Gauguin Exhibition at the Salon d'Automne. Russian Art Exhibition.
Matisse buys negro statuettes from Sauvage, curio-dealer in the rue de Rennes.
Picasso and Matisse meet at the Steins'. Matisse exhibits 55 pictures at Druet's.
Opening of **" 291 "** (Photo Secession—Albert Stieglitz) at 291 Fifth Avenue, New York.
Matisse leaves his studio at 19 quai Saint-Michel, moving first to the Couvent des Oiseaux in the rue de Sèvres,
        then to the former Couvent du Sacré-Cœur.

1907   Matisse's **Le Bonheur de Vivre** causes an uproar at the Salon des Indépendants.
The famous **Rousseau Banquet** takes place in Picasso's studio. Kahnweiler settles in Paris.
Picasso paints **Les Demoiselles d'Avignon.** Beginnings of **Cubism.**
Cézanne Exhibition at Salon d'Automne, watercolours at Bernheim-Jeune's.
Cézanne, Matisse, Munch Exhibition at Cassirer's in Berlin.

1908   Matisse publishes his **Notes d'un Peintre** in **La Grande Revue.**
Braque rejected for the Salon d'Automne. One-man show at Kahnweiler's, 23 rue Vignon.
Chagall comes to Paris.
Nolde quits **Die Brücke** and Van Dongen joins the group.
In the first Vienna 'Kunstschau' **Kokoschka's** works are violently attacked by the public.
Matisse exhibits at the Photo Secession Gallery, 291 Fifth Avenue, New York.

1909   Diaghilev puts on **Russian Ballet** at the Théâtre du Châtelet.
Milan: **Futurist Manifesto.**
Matisse makes two new versions of " La Desserte ": **a red harmony** and **a blue harmony.**
Munich: Foundation in January of **Neue Künstlervereinigung** by Jawlensky, Kandinsky, Kubin, Münter.
Derain does the woodcuts to illustrate Apollinaire's **L'Enchanteur Pourrissant.**
First Lautrec Exhibition at Photo Secession Gallery, New York.
Munich: Franz Marc's first exhibition. Hans Arp settles in Switzerland (Weggis).

1910   Gauguin Exhibition at Arnold's.
La Fresnaye, Marcel Duchamp, Marcoussis, new recruits to Cubism.
Modigliani sends in a series of etchings to Salon des Indépendants.
Exhibition of young American painters at ' Photo Secession ': Marin, Max Weber, Hartley, et al.
Exhibition of works by Cézanne, Rousseau.
Delaunay stays at Nantua, paints **La Tour Eiffel** and **La Ville de Paris.**
Cubist Show at **Salon d'Automne.** Delaunay and Metzinger at Salon des Indépendants.
Léger paints **Nus dans la Forêt** (Kroeller-Müller Museum).

1910   First Retrospective Matisse Exhibition at Bernheim-Jeune's. Matisse exhibits **La Danse** and **Musique** at Salon
          d'Automne.
        Mondrian comes to Paris. Braque's Analytical Cubism; he spends summer at l'Estaque.
        Derain stays at Cagnes; at Cadaquès, meets Picasso. Interest in architectural lay-out.
        The magazine **Der Sturm** launched on March 8.
        Munich: Meeting of Macke and Marc on January 6. Kandinsky writes "Über das Geistige in der Kunst" (The
          Art of Spiritual Harmony), published in 1911.
        Munich: Second Exhibition of the **Neue Künstlervereinigung** in September, with works by **Braque, Derain,
          Le Fauconnier, Picasso, Rouault, Van Dongen, Vlaminck** and other guest artists.

1911   Matisse travels to North Africa (Tangier).
        Chirico paints "La Nostalgie de l'Infini." **Soutine** comes to Paris, enrols in Cormon's class.
        First Picasso Exhibition in the United States (Photo Secession Gallery, New York).
        Salon d'Automne: Gleizes, Metzinger, Léger, Duchamp-Villon.
        Dufy does woodcuts for Apollinaire's **Bestiaire.**

1912   **Cubist demonstration at Salon des Indépendants.** Large-scale Cubist Exhibition in Brussels.
        Sonderbund Exhibition at Cologne.
        First exhibition of Matisse's sculpture at 'Photo Secession,' New York.
        Meeting of **Nolde** and **Ensor.**
        La Section d'Or founded at Villon's studio by Metzinger and the three Villon brothers.
        Futurist Exhibition at Bernheim's. Delaunay, Picasso, Léger, Metzinger, Le Fauconnier exhibit with the
          Futurists Boccioni, Severini, Carrà.
        Chagall paints **Hommage à la Fiancée**; Marcel Duchamp, **Le Moulin à Café.**
        Kandinsky's first **Improvisations. Collages** by Braque and Picasso.
        Macke and Marc meet Delaunay in Paris. Juan Gris exhibits at the Salon des Indépendants.
        Derain enters on his Gothic period. Gleizes and Metzinger publish **Cubism.**
        Munich: Meeting of Kandinsky, Klee, Macke and Marc. Marc joins the "Neue Künstlervereinigung." On
          December 13 at Thannhauser Gallery, Kandinsky and Marc open the first **Blaue Reiter** Exhibition with
          works by Arp, Delaunay, Kandinsky, Klee, Macke, Marc and Münter.

1913   Paul Klee translates part of Delaunay's **La Lumière Colorée.**
        Léger exhibits **Nus dans un Paysage** at Salon des Indépendants. His article "The Origins of Contemporary
          Painting" is published in **Der Sturm.**
        Guillaume Apollinaire's **The Cubist Painters.**

1914   Apollinaire heralds Chagall's Berlin exhibition with an article in **Der Sturm.**
        The magazine **Blast** is launched. Kandinsky returns to Russia. Death of Macke.
        Braque-Picasso Exhibition at 'Photo Secession,' New York.

1915   New York: **Stieglitz Group,** 291 Fifth Avenue. Publication of the magazine **" 291 "** (Picabia, Picasso, Apollinaire).
        Duchamp arrives in New York. The American painter Demuth meets Duchamp.
        Italy: First metaphysical painting (Chirico, Carrà).
        Arp exhibits at the Tanner Gallery in Zurich.

1916   Ozenfant founds the magazine **Elan.**
        Matisse paints **Les Marocains, La Leçon de Piano** and **Jeunes Filles au Bain.**
        Zurich: First issue of the Dada review **Cabaret Voltaire** (Apollinaire, Picasso, Modigliani, Arp, Tzara,
          Kandinsky, Marinetti, Ball, Cendrars).

1917   Picasso travels in Italy. Russian Ballet: Stravinsky, Cocteau, Satie. Picasso does sets for "Parade."
        Tzara publishes Dada I and Dada II.
        Matisse settles at Nice, meets Renoir.
        Mondrian, Van Doesburg and a small group of artists found **De Stijl** (Style).
        Duchamp edits two reviews: **The Blind Man** and **Wrong-Wrong.** Picabia and Arensberg publish the first
          issue of **" 391."**
        Nord-Sud magazine, on which **Apollinaire, Reverdy, Max Jacob, Breton, Soupault** and **Aragon** collaborate.

1918   Léonce Rosenberg: **L'Effort Moderne.**
        Switzerland: **L'Histoire du Soldat**: sets by Auberjonois, libretto by Ramuz, music by Stravinsky.
        Death of **Guillaume Apollinaire.**
        Ozenfant publishes the first Purist manifesto: **" After Cubism."**
        Picasso does the sets for the ballet **Le Tricorne.**
        Derain does the sets for **La Boutique Fantasque.**

FAUVISM

We may regard Fauvism as a transitional movement in the course of Modern Painting. A movement of extreme importance, nevertheless, in that it enthusiastically carried on that young tradition of individualism which Cézanne, Gauguin, Van Gogh, Lautrec and Seurat had inaugurated, and which had been forgotten by the neo-Impressionists, then by the ' Nabis,' and still more noticeably by the long, tedious succession of pseudo-moderns— *pompiers qui avaient pris feu*, as Degas ironically called them—practitioners of an Impressionism diluted with rose-water and a mild dash of classicism.

The originality of the incipient movement manifested itself from the very outset in no uncertain manner. Among its salient characteristics were a vigorous rejection of the delicate sophistications of the impressionist palette, a cult of pure colour straight from the tube, a taste for pictorial architecture on the grand scale, a repudiation of nature in favour of imaginative visions of green skies, vermilion rivers, lemon-coloured trees, and emerald-green, Veronese-green or chrome-yellow faces. And the Fauves brought to this refashioning of the traditional, harmonious language of the art preceding them, a young enthusiasm no less sincere than daring, that expressed itself in rapturous and often highly complex colour symphonies.

It is unquestionably Henri Matisse who, with his intense physical delight in colour and the *matière* of painting, ushered in this movement—of which indeed he had given premonitions in those early days when his teacher Carrière warned him against what he called " dyer's work." Yet, inventor though he was of Fauvism, Matisse strikes us as—theoretically anyhow—the least Fauve of the Fauves ; much as Picasso who ' created ' Cubism was the least Cubist of his group. It was, however, Matisse who applied himself the longest to exploring certain possibilities of Fauvism, whilst his earliest associates tended to revert to more traditionalist views. Also, Matisse's influence in France and abroad, on his own generation and the next, owed less to his position as leader of a school than to the universal appeal of a new, amazing type of art, which went even beyond the premisses of what was known as Fauvism.

The circumstances under which the artists dubbed " Fauves " (literally, wild beasts !) acquired this sobriquet are common knowledge. At the 1905 Salon d'Automne a gallery was reserved for the works of the new group, and these provoked an outburst of indignation recalling that which greeted the advent of Impressionism. The hostility voiced by the press critics was even more pronounced than that of the public (which usually in such cases shows itself more cautious). Such epithets as " crazy," " sensation-mongering," " preposterous," were applied to the brilliant, utterly sincere, if greatly daring work of these young men. Louis Vauxcelles, noticing a small child's head, of Florentine inspiration, in a corner of the room (it was a work by Marque, the sculptor) exclaimed, " Look ! There's a Donatello cowering in this den of wild beasts *(fauves)* ! " The term caught on, and even gave birth to a new -ism, " Fauvism." And this room at the exhibition came to be called the " Wild Beasts' Cage." Thus, as has often happened, a casual, scornful jest furnished a great art movement with the name under which it has taken its place in history.

Always indeed there lurks something of the *fauve* in every young man who tries to earn his livelihood on lines which have not yet won general approval. And young painters, of every period, have never balked at the dictum : " We must start by killing off what went before us." Thus our Fauves, then in their early twenties, whetted their teeth on the pundits of the older generation. And in 1893, as the result of a series of coincidences, which might almost seem purposive, were it not that such encounters are so frequent in the annals of art, the Académie Julian and the Ecole des Beaux-Arts—in which the teachers were Bouguereau, Gérôme, Ferrier, Bonnat and Gustave Moreau—received successively within their precincts Marquet, Matisse, Camoin, Manguin, Friesz and Dufy. Others to meet at Julian's or at Carrière's studio were Matisse (who worked there nearly a year), Puy, Derain, Laprade, Chabaud and Braque—to mention only the outstanding figures of the group.

Our young Fauves did not hesitate to " kill off " more illustrious predecessors. For one thing—this was one of their common traits—they were united in a passionate cult of the dynamic possibilities of colour. But they were well aware of its fragility and material impermanence, and, though determined to body forth the sensuous and poetic visions colour inspired in them, they proceeded, after a brief alliance, vigorously to attack Impressionism. For they were not slow in detecting its shortcomings ; above all, its lack of solidity, and its rejection of that notion of permanence to whose virtues, despite their revolutionary ardour, they, half unconsciously perhaps, paid homage. Thus they were drawn instinctively to such elements in the art of their great predecessors as seemed best to sanction their desire to establish the ' divine right ' of colour. Their attention was necessarily drawn to the (for their time) novel essays of structural organization made by Manet, Cézanne, Gauguin and Van Gogh. Had not the cult of colour been restored in all its plenitude when these masters lifted the impressionist ban on black and ' earthen ' hues ? And it was in the light of the discoveries made by these artists that the Fauve aesthetic gradually took form, and, in turn, enounced its private and particular way of viewing the world. The Fauves aspired to body forth a reality other than that of mere appearance, a reality apprehended by their imaginative vision alone, if conditioned by such contact as was indispensable with aspects of the ' objective ' world around them. But, above all, they must *build with colour*.

What the Fauves were aiming at was a new poetry in visual form, and, rejecting the classical notions of idealistic realism, while equally hostile, in the last analysis, to the theatrical evocations of Impressionism, they offered the spectator those egocentric visions which their sensibility conjured up in its responses to things seen. As Matisse said, it was a matter of " shocks," the personal sensations provoked by sudden epiphanic experiences, flashes of ecstatic apprehension—like the pictures that well up almost incoherently before the mind's eye of a poet.

We can see easily enough the technique and the newness of this kind of inspiration and we even glimpse certain still hesitant approaches towards the notion of a total re-creation. For what these new factors pointed the way to was practically a re-invention of the art of painting. Thus in putting up its opposition to the new tendencies, embattled Academicism knew what it was about. For the Fauves were specially set on the abolition of all technical methods which sponsored formulas of art obsolete to their mind. They would have nothing to do with perspective and all its works—e.g. the rendering of volumes, illusionist chiaroscuro, modelling and the like. The flat art of the Primitives of all periods won their favour, and they were drawn to the ' Gothics ' and their tendency to replace purely plastic by expressive art.

It was thus that, in opposition to impressionist realism and, by the same token, to the purely imitative decoration of the ' Nabis,' the Fauves took to painting in flat colour, as they found it in the work of the above-mentioned Primitives and the makers of popular colour-sheets, in stained-glass windows and in Japanese prints. That old opprobrium of " playing-card art " (with which Courbet once had taunted Manet) cropped up again, and it was not surprising that the young generation fell back on Manet, Cézanne, Gauguin and Van Gogh, when they sought to shore up the new aesthetic of which these masters had had but glimpses, and whose ideal could be now defined in good, set terms : the insertion of Space into a surface.

Thus Fauvism, it seemed, was preconizing an aesthetic wholly instinctual, in accordance with Friesz's saying that the better part of art pertains to the instinct. Also, it must be admitted, a certain conscious ruthlessness, which the young German school of painting was deliberately to foster, inspired in these artists their addiction to raw colours ' as they came out of the tubes '—which tubes Derain likened to dynamite cartridges. There was now no question of reconstituting life's emotions in the manner of representational art ; the artist's aim was, like Matisse, to render the sensation of life itself ; not to imitate nature, but to act as nature does. The artist produced his picture as an apple-tree its apple, and the Fauve was, so to speak, a sensation-bearing tree.

Yet, almost unawares, certain doubts and hesitations began to infiltrate. True, the Fauves lost none of their early zest for freedom. But like the true Frenchmen that they were, permeated with the famous 'Cartesian' spirit (if we may assume that the Frenchman, since Descartes' day, has the monopoly of shrewd mistrust or, academically speaking, discretion), they suddenly took thought for 'order' and that moderation which is the apanage of thinking man. For the perils involved in headlong freedom—the blunders and excesses which may ensue—had dawned on them, and, when, as now, they cast a backward look on Cézanne, it was on Cézanne the great architect. Thus they conceived the notion of remaking (so to speak) Cézanne, not 'after' nature, but 'after' Cézanne himself. Aware of the self-contradiction implicit in this project, the Fauves took heroic measures and tried to give colour the task of imposing its own discipline. Henceforth the degree of a tone's intensity, the relative dimensions of the painted surfaces, the distribution of the 'whites' and expressive contour-lines, the course taken by intuitively patterned arabesques—all these furnished the cohesion and the equilibrium the painter sought for. And under cover of a happy flow of metaphors, allusions, elisions, reticences and the like, that immemorial problem of depth and make-believe Space was solved by the relative intensity and distribution of the tones. Light was no longer a source of illumination, but one of intensity ; all accidental data were ruled out, leaving only the essentials, and simplification warranted the multiplicity of tones. In short, a new grammar was devised, formulated in terms of each artist's personal logic.

Thereafter this epoch-making movement lasted but long enough to give the world, in the space of a mere five years, some splendid works of a lofty lyrical inspiration and couched in terms of dynamic colour, but suffering from the defect of being merely attempts and not fulfilments. The emotional drive in Fauve art lacks the authenticity of that in a Van Gogh. One of the most eminent Fauves twitted another member of the group for being " a lion who fed on grass." But we might well ask what the others ate. At bottom Fauvism was more an 'artistic' than a deeply human movement, despite its professedly total allegiance to the instinct. The rapid disruption of Fauvism and of the theories it began with shows that the venture was never pressed to its logical conclusion. We have already raised the question whether this was due to prudence or to lack of conviction. There is certainly a considerable gulf between what the Fauves set out to be and what they became. Towards 1911 Matisse foresaw where Fauvism would lead if carried to its limits ; and he preferred to go no farther, for fear of breaking with that traditional reality of nature which he could not forgo. In his heart of hearts Matisse felt himself nearer Delacroix than Cézanne. Of the Fauves Braque alone dared, in the early days of Cubism, to try his hand at that new rendering of forms in space of which his companions once had dreamed. The influence Fauvism had on German painting (which adapted it to its expressionist programme) is well known. Which may go to show that, fundamentally, Fauvism was a technique which never quite succeeded in becoming an aesthetic. The reason was that, great though they were, the Fauve artists cannot be looked on as thorough-going innovators ; rather they resemble the Masters of the past, irrevocably anchored to traditional conceptions.

Between the art of the past and that of the Fauves there was never that *essential* difference existing between (for example) the art of the Primitives and that of the Renaissance ; there was only a difference of degree.

Some twenty artists, all told, played a more or less active part in the Fauve movement. At one extreme there were those who took over the principles of Fauvism lock, stock and barrel, and applied them uncompromisingly ; at the other, those who, while drawing inspiration from it, attuned their procedure to academic concepts, and thus developed an eclectic art.

We shall describe hereafter how Matisse, Derain and Vlaminck 'pooled' as it were their early discoveries ; not merely when they first met in the art schools, but at Chatou and then at Collioure. Those three became the protagonists of the Fauve movement, each contributing his personal quota, while on one point they were in complete agreement : their determination to build the picture with bricks of colour and of colour only. And in their friendly intercourse, this trio of young artists put their ideas into the common stock without reserve. Hence the kinship we see between their works of this period ; a kinship always apparent in the early stage of a great art movement.

What Albert Marquet, whose art underwent a rapid evolution, brought as his contribution to the little group was a thorough knowledge of the *métier* and a fine sense of balance : qualities which tended to counteract the extravagances, and even to give a direction to the ventures of his friends. But already in his earliest works, the persistent quest of ' atmosphere ' suggests that, in his association with the Fauves-to-be, what drew him to them was really no more than a fellow-feeling for young men who were bent on erecting a ' system,' even if that system were not his.

Friesz, too (who had met the others either at the Ecole des Beaux-Arts or at the *Vernissage* of the 1903 Salon des Indépendants), while taking part in their experimental work, was mindful of his friendship with Pissarro and his devotion to Cézanne, and, from his earliest work onwards, evidenced a preoccupation with modelling and depth.

Raoul Dufy, when at the Ecole des Beaux-Arts, as early as 1901, was interested in the experiments of Matisse, whose influence was already making itself felt. Impressionism, which was his first love, sponsored his taste for objects calling for luminosity and bright colour in their treatment : flags, parasols, the sails of yachts, floral decorations, colourful dresses—pending the day when he was to subject these to a highly personal calligraphy and his vision of an imaginary world, with which the strictly realistic outlook of the Impressionists had nothing in common.

Four other notable artists, Louis Valtat, Manguin, Puy and Van Dongen also figured at the 1905 Salon d'Automne.

Louis Valtat shared the ' honours ' of the special number of *L'Illustration* in which all the exhibitors at the Salon d'Automne were soundly trounced. With his exuberant colour-effects he, too, served the cause of Fauvism ; likewise his vivid ceramics lacked nothing of the fierceness which gave the Fauves their name.

Henri Manguin, another outstanding figure at the 1905 Salon d'Automne, displayed a neophyte zest for warm, emphatic colour. But, loving Nature in her most realistic aspects, he was led to serve her rather than bend her to his will, as did the Fauves. And in the end he repudiated the ' misdeeds ' of his youth.

Jean Puy met Matisse at Carrière's studio and, like the others named above, exhibited in the Salon d'Automne of 1905. He, too, did not wholly endorse the theories of Vlaminck, Matisse and Derain. He had a well-balanced mind, a desire for simplification of both form and colour—and thus had little relish for the exuberance, however inventive, of his friends.

Though he, too, figured in this Salon d'Automne, Van Dongen was relatively a late-comer to Fauvism, having spent much of his youth in a struggle to earn his living. (At one time he worked as a market-porter.) His contribution was an unbridled enthusiasm for contrasts of colours. And he tended more towards purely ornamental than architectural decoration. Chiefly interested in the human figure, he soon became immensely popular with that section of fashionable society which always patronizes ' ultra-modern ' art, not so much for its creativeness, as for its seeming eccentricity. He did many portraits of actresses and dancers ; also of such eminent statesmen as Barthou and Painlevé, and of such great men of letters as Anatole France. He deliberately adapted some of the doctrines of Fauvism to a style of portraiture whose aim was much more that of rendering likeness than that of a constructive metamorphosis.

We conclude by naming some artists of the Fauve generation who, while admirably gifted, tended to ' academicize ' the methods used by their more venturesome contemporaries, by introducing elements of traditional chiaroscuro and perspective. They were Jacques Laprade (1875-1931), Henri Lebasque (1865-1937), Jacqueline Marval (1866-1932)—not to mention others whose dreams of ' tectonic ' art were haunted by memories of the ' Nabis.'

HENRI MATISSE (1869). INTERIOR AT COLLIOURE, 1905. 23½×28¾″. PRIVATE COLLECTION, ASCONA.

HERE WE SEE COLOUR TAKING ITS REVENGE ON TRADITIONALISM WITH THE ZEST, THE BRIO AND BRAVURA OF A GAY ICONO-
CLAST. THE OBJECTS ARE PLACED WITH A FINE DISREGARD FOR ANY FUNCTION THEY MAY SERVE ; IN FACT THE ARTIST SEEMS
UNAWARE OF THE SERIOUS SIDE OF THE ADVENTURE AND THE 'TRANSMUTATION' WHICH, AN ALCHEMIST OF COLOUR, HE IS
UNDERTAKING. THIS 'INTERIOR' MARKS THE BIRTH OF FAUVISM.

HENRI MATISSE

Almost every writer on aesthetics who has dealt with Matisse's work admits that no
great master's art is harder to analyse and expound. Yet actually, few painters have had
so much written about them—which suggests that writers on art have a predilection for the
practically inexplicable. The truth is that a mystery lies at the heart of the matter ; that of
the origin of the tremendous power of light and colour present in all Matisse's work. And
here a disturbing memory well may cross our minds—of those great colour magicians who,
after having given proof of an almost incredibly keen eyesight, became all but blind : Pissarro,
Degas, Monet. Matisse has, one might say, forestalled this danger ; he has been short-
sighted from his earliest days. And perhaps the secret of that amazing alchemy of colour
peculiarly his lies as it were midway between his spectacles and his imagination. The credibi-
lity of the incredible finds a striking confirmation in the fact that, handicapped as he seems to
be, Matisse has the keenest, most penetrating, most ruthlessly acute vision of all painters,

A SKETCH: THE FIRST CREATIVE UPRUSH OF THE ARTIST'S IMAGINATION. DESPITE THE GREAT FREEDOM COLOUR IS
ALLOWED, MATISSE IS BENT ON GIVING THE HUMAN BODY ITS FULL PLASTIC DIGNITY. HERE WE SEE THE PLAY OF FANCY
DEVELOPING PROGRESSIVELY; THE ARABESQUES SET IN CONTOUR-LINES ARE FRETTED WITH RECTIFICATIONS, AND AMEND-
MENTS ARE NECESSITATED BY THE EXPANSION OF THE COLOURING (CF. THE FIGURE ON THE LEFT). WHEREAS, IN THE
FIGURE ON THE RIGHT, PROFFERING FLOWERS, THE IDEAL FORM IS GLIMPSED FROM THE VERY FIRST MOMENT, AND BUILT
UP WITH COLOUR ALONE, AND FROM THIS VERY CONFLICT ARISES THAT UNITY, SO HARDLY COME BY, OF THE COMPOSITION;
THE UNITY THAT MATISSE RELISHED SO MUCH IN COURBET.

HENRI MATISSE (1869). LUXE, CALME ET VOLUPTÉ. COLLIOURE, 1905. 82¾ × 54¼".
MUSÉE D'ART MODERNE, PARIS.

HERE WE HAVE THE FINAL, CONSUMMATE VERSION. THE PRELIMINARY HESITATIONS HAVE VANISHED, THE ARABESQUE IS CLEARLY DEFINED, ITS DRAWING FULLER, MORE ASSURED. MATISSE'S AESTHETIC HAS COME INTO ITS OWN. EACH TRACT OF COLOUR IS REINFORCED BY THE LINE, VOLUMES ARE BROUGHT OUT BY SWEEPING ANTITHESES OF PLANES. THE COMPOSITION IS NOTICEABLY COMPACT. WHILE FORESHADOWING THAT OF 'LA DANSE' (THE VERSION AT THE MOSCOW MUSEUM), IT HAS NEITHER ITS DYNAMISM NOR ITS POETIC APPEAL. IN THIS WORK SOMETHING OF THE SLIGHTLY DISCONCERTING TANG OF THE SKETCH STILL LINGERS. HERE MATISSE ALREADY WISHES HIS PAINTING TO GIVE A RESTFUL EFFECT; NOT TO RAISE PROBLEMS. HENCE ITS FINE SERENITY, EVOKING THE ATMOSPHERE OF REPOSE DEAR TO THE ARTIST'S SENSIBILITY.

HENRI MATISSE (1869). LUXE, CALME ET VOLUPTÉ. COLLIOURE, 1905. 82¾×54¼".
J. RUMP COLLECTION, ROYAL MUSEUM OF FINE ART, COPENHAGEN.

HENRI MATISSE (1869). LANDSCAPE: STUDY FOR 'LE BONHEUR DE VIVRE.' COLLIOURE, 1905. 18×21¾".
J. RUMP COLLECTION, ROYAL MUSEUM OF FINE ART, COPENHAGEN.

THE FINAL COMPOSITION FOR *LE BONHEUR DE VIVRE* IS NOW IN THE BARNES COLLECTION, MERION (U.S.A.).

and has even invented some new colours. Have we here a physiological reaction, and is the natural weakness of sight so vigorously counteracted by a massive effort of the will to see as to force upon the artist a competence for seeing better than the most clear-sighted ? A hazardous conjecture ! Indeed the problem seems insoluble unless we fall back on one of those long abstract words dear to the psychologist which, seeming to explain away a difficulty, merely camouflage it ; or unless, carried away by the dazzling splendour of Matisse's art, we are content simply to account for it by the action of that ' queer thing Genius.'

Those who expect a painter's life to be appropriately colourful may well be disappointed by the life-story of Matisse. It is perhaps more than a coincidence that, in much the same way as throughout his career the artist has ruled out from his work all that in the terminology of aesthetics is named the ' accidental,' thus, up to his eightieth year (which he has just triumphantly inaugurated), no unusual or dramatic incident has ruffled the even tenor of Matisse's life. Indeed it may seem surprising that one who has been so bold an innovator and opened up so many new approaches to art's high places, should have led such a calm existence, seconded by a happily robust constitution. Which obviously is far from tallying with the romantic portrait one might hope to give of a ' revolutionary ' artist, when we call to mind the lives of such men as Delacroix, Courbet, Jongkind, Gauguin or Van Gogh.

Nor must we forget that in his youth Matisse dutifully copied such works as Chardin's *The Ray*, Philippe de Champaigne's *Dead Christ*, and Carrache's *Chasse*. The truth may be that the anxieties and uncertainties which inevitably beset a genius so daring as his always operated far below the surface, and thus have left no mark on his appearance.

One of the 'human' interests of art-criticism lies in discovering just what it was that gave great artists in their early years their love of painting and the impulse to paint. In Matisse's case, the fact that his mother had a charming talent for painting flowers on china seems inadequate as an explanation. Nor have we much to go on in the circumstances of the artist's early youth—such as the fact that Matisse, who was born at Le Cateau in the north of France, was originally intended by his father to enter the magistracy and duly studied law (without, as we are told of some other budding artists, making sketches in his exercise-books when his teacher was not looking).

We may, perhaps, begin by recalling what Matisse himself has told us: " The work of art should be, for the tired business man no less than for the artist in literature, a cerebral sedative, rather like a comfortable armchair." Now (this is a well-established fact) it was in the course of a slow recovery from an attack of appendicitis that Matisse, then in his twentieth year, was advised by a friend to try his hand at painting, as being " a nice, restful

MATISSE SEEMS TO HAVE BEEN INSPIRED BY THE THEME OF THIS *PASTORAL* IN PAINTING HIS *BONHEUR DE VIVRE*. GENERALLY SPEAKING, THE COMPOSITION FOLLOWS THE SAME CADENCES; THIS IS PARTICULARLY TRUE OF THE CENTRAL FIGURES. ON THE RIGHT WE FIND AGAIN THE YOUNG FLUTE-PLAYER. THE RHYTHM OF THE TREE ON THE LEFT MATCHES THAT OF THE TWO NUDES IN *LUXE, CALME ET VOLUPTÉ*. HERE THE EASY FLOW OF THE ARABESQUES, THE GENTLENESS OF THE COLOURS CONJURE UP AN 'ARCADIAN BLISS,' CLASSICAL BOTH IN OUTLOOK AND IN COMPOSITION.

HENRI MATISSE (1869). PASTORAL, 1905. 18×21¾". PRIVATE COLLECTION, PARIS.

HENRI MATISSE (1869). PORTRAIT WITH THE GREEN STRIPE, 1905. 15¾×12½".
J. RUMP COLLECTION, ROYAL MUSEUM OF FINE ART, COPENHAGEN.

MATISSE HAS CONFESSED THAT WHAT INTERESTS HIM MOST IS NOT LANDSCAPE OR THE STILL LIFE, BUT THE FACE. WITH A
SELF-RESTRAINT CONTRASTING WITH THE UNABASHED ENTHUSIASM OF FAUVISM FOR THE SHRILLEST TONES, THE ARTIST, WHEN
EVOKING Mᵐᵉ MATISSE'S FACE, SHOWS A SUDDEN TENDENCY TOWARDS A SORT OF ABSTRACTIONISM. HE DISINCARNATES OR
SPIRITUALIZES IT, SO AS TO DISTIL THE SECRETS OF ITS PLASTIC QUALITIES. PUT ON IN BROAD TRACTS OF FAINTLY SUB-ACID
COLOUR, THE TONES YIELD AN EQUIVALENT OF DEPTH. ONCE MORE, WITHOUT AIMING AT VIRTUOSITY, MATISSE CONTRIVES
TO JUXTAPOSE THE MOST STRIDENT TONALITIES WITHOUT LESSENING THE INTENSITY OF ANY.

HERE WE SEE A FIXITY OF GAZE THAT IS PERHAPS DIFFICULT TO JUSTIFY ; THE FACE LOOKS LIKE A MASK, A TRAGIC MASK, OR THE MASK WORN IN A '*NO*' PLAY. EVERYTHING THAT SOUNDS A CASUAL OR PERSONAL NOTE IS OMITTED ; THE SPECTACLES AND THAT GENTLENESS OF HIS EYES WHICH STRIKES ALL WHO MEET MATISSE HAVE BEEN RELEGATED TO THE PROPERTY-ROOM. THE PLANES AND VOLUMES ALONE CONFER, BY RICOCHET, A SEMBLANCE OF LIFE ON THE IMPASSIBILITY OF THE MASK, MUCH AS THE GESTURES OF A GREEK ACTOR MAY HAVE GIVEN VICARIOUS LIFE TO HIS. SUCH STABILITY AND SERENITY SHOW THAT MATISSE, GOING BEYOND FAUVISM, IS NOW INCLINING TO A CLASSICISM WHICH HIS HIGHLY PERSONAL IMAGINATION ENABLES HIM TO PRACTISE WITHOUT THE RISK OF LAPSING INTO ACADEMICISM. IN FACT IT IS A WHOLLY CLASSICAL EFFECT THAT HE HAS HERE ACHIEVED AND WHICH HAS ENABLED HIM—TO USE A PHRASE COINED SUBSEQUENTLY AND EAGERLY ADOPTED BY OUR ACADEMICIANS—TO "MAKE A HEAD" OF HIS PORTRAIT.

HENRI MATISSE (1869). PORTRAIT OF HENRI MATISSE, 1906. 21¾×18″.
ROYAL MUSEUM OF FINE ART, COPENHAGEN.

—   —

II. 14

occupation which would help to while away the time." Accordingly his mother supplied him with a box of paints, a gift which was frowned on by Matisse *senior*, who would rather have seen his son engaged in serious work. And the combined effect of copying some colour-prints and reading Goupil's *How to Paint* was enough, not merely to take his mind off his physical discomfort, but to give him a feeling of contentment, almost one of bliss, such as he had never known before. " I felt transported," he writes, " into a sort of paradise in which I felt gloriously free, at ease and ' on my own,' whereas in my everyday life I was usually bored and rather worried by the various things that people were always telling me I must do."

We need not linger on the opposition put up by Matisse's father to the young man's abrupt decision to be an artist ; the encouragement, on the other hand, that he got from his mother ; and the consent finally wrung from Matisse *senior*, who had the practical good sense of the French countryman and was bitterly disappointed by his son's rejection of the material and social advantages accruing from a legal career.

Thus the origins of Matisse's vocation may probably be attributed to that burning desire for freedom which so often goes with the ' artistic temperament,' and to the yearning for ' escape ' which never left him. His predilection for being left at peace and to himself bore witness to an individualism already strongly marked, though, owing to his youth, it could not yet make headway against the pressure of the outside world. Indeed it is clear that he already suffered from the feeling that a social order, in which he had never felt at home, was trying to foist on him its habits and conventions, and it was for him to resist it.

Even at this very early stage Matisse showed himself amazingly gifted for art ; but, as we all know, the same things might be said about a great many adolescents. Picasso knew what he was talking about when he said, " At bottom, it depends entirely on oneself. It's like a sun in the belly, a sun that's inextinguishable. Nothing else matters, really. That's the sole reason why, for instance, Matisse is ... Matisse. It's because he has a sun in his belly." Often as not such gifts lie fallow ; those possessing them do not necessarily feel the need to make them fructify, and thus they do not get beyond the stage of amateurism. The period of Matisse's early youth was one in which people did not so much appreciate the cleverness of youngsters as they do now, nor was so much attention paid to their naïve (and often still-born) attempts at ' making pictures.' True, as a school-boy Matisse won drawing-prizes, but that proves little ; the Master-to-be was a good pupil in all branches and always did well at his examinations. Indeed we can detect nothing in his boyhood that throws any light on that precocious gift for colour which Matisse was to develop to a perfection unexcelled by any other artist. Let us content ourselves with saying he was born a colourist (as others are born singers) and that he painted—to use Monet's phrase—" as a bird sings " ; also that, though we cannot trace the cause of this, colour was for him like a tree's sap, something in his blood conditioning already the evolution of his physical being. It was a faculty, if not (in Braque's phrase) of " thinking in forms and, still more so, in colours," of at least *living* in colours. Still the mere definition of a phenomenon whose causes we have failed to ascertain takes us, admittedly, little farther. However, there is one fact well worth considering here, a fact of a physical order, and not purely psychological, like the innate imaginative powers we attribute to many highly gifted persons. It goes far to explain why Matisse fostered this unique gift and developed it to the utmost, as being something he felt, half unconsciously perhaps, as, more than a mere source of pleasure, a vital necessity to him. The fact to which we are referring relates to Matisse's eyesight, which from birth has been very weak. This may well have stimulated him to the cultivation of visualizations ever richer and more grandiose ; much as nature's weaklings are, as we so often see, drawn towards dreams of power and glory. Had Matisse been temperamentally less strong-willed, less diligent, or inclined to disperse his interests, this faculty might, perhaps, have led him in some other direction. But not only was he endowed with a feeling for colour so intense that it amounted to a ruling passion ; he was also an extremely level-headed man. All his life long he has had his feet solidly planted on the earth ; indeed his cautiousness is proverbial. Nevertheless from his earliest days he has been endowed with tremendous energy, which has never failed him,

HENRI MATISSE (1869). STILL LIFE WITH PINK ONIONS, 1906. 18×21¾".
J. RUMP COLLECTION, ROYAL MUSEUM OF FINE ART, COPENHAGEN.

AS THOUGH TO TEST THE RANGE OF HIS SENSATIONS, THE PAINTER'S INSTINCT LEADS HIM HERE TO ABANDON RAW COLOUR
'STRAIGHT FROM THE TUBE' AND TO TRY HIS HAND AT MUTED TONES. ULTRAMARINE, EMERALD GREEN AND WHITE ARE BROUGHT
INTO CONTACT WITH BLACK AND OCHRES, CREATING AS IT WERE A SYMPHONY IN A MINOR KEY IN WHICH THE COUNTERPOINT OF
TONES SEEMS TO CONVEY THE CONFLICT BETWEEN THE LIVING THING, VULNERABLE BY TIME, AND THE PERMANENT.

even in circumstances which would have discouraged any ordinary man. Moreover he has
always had not only a feeling for balance and proportion but a habit of introspection somewhat rare in artists, who are generally inclined to accept the promptings of their 'inspiration'
wholesale and without more ado—indeed they would judge it almost sacrilegious to subject
these to any intellectual control. So we need not be surprised if he has always mistrusted
following the guidance of his instinct. It is indeed quite likely that he was the first to be
astonished by that gift of his for colour, whose origin he could not trace. Hence his set
purpose never to play the 'self-taught' artist, that is to say the ignoramus who thinks he can
do everything by the light of nature. This explains why he so assiduously, and over such long
periods, frequented schools, academies and museums, and likewise studied so painstakingly
the works of his talented contemporaries. Also his tendency to ponder over his own aptitudes
and the masterpieces of the past—and to draw enlightening comparisons.

It is seldom profitable to linger over the earliest works of a great master. Inevitably
they are a mixture of borrowings, hesitations, precocious skill, bold yet pregnant clumsinesses.
Only the early influences are significant. Thus in 1890 Matisse drew his inspiration from
Chardin *(Les Livres)*, and in 1894 he interpreted in his manner Ruysdael's *Tempest*. Logic
and intuition skilfully and sensitively blended—all Matisse is in these works.

29

ALBERT MARQUET (1875-1947). CIBOURE, 1907. 16¼×13½". PRIVATE COLLECTION, GENEVA.

has been given its run, in turn. His art is that of an intelligent man, with a highly refined
sensibility, who has the gift of carrying the lyrical, not to say caricatural, bravura of his
brushstrokes and his drawing to just that danger-point where the accuracy he always aims at
is imperilled—but no further. Nevertheless Marquet was certainly a Fauve, but one who
sometimes flung himself against the bars of the *Cage des Fauves* described by Vauxcelles, in a
frantic effort towards freedom, yet sometimes retired to a corner of it, to dream serenely of
his native forest.

MARQUET

Born at Bordeaux on March 27, 1875, Marquet came to Paris in 1890 where, while still in his 'teens, he struck up a friendship with Matisse, whom he met in Gustave Moreau's studio. The two young men shared hard times together, as when, for instance, they were employed by Jambon the decorator, and for a pittance spent their days painting hideous scenery for the Paris theatres. This period of privation undergone in common saw the beginning of that deep affection, strengthened no doubt by the friendly give-and-take of two very different but complementary temperaments, which lasted unbroken until Marquet's death in 1947.

The contrast between the two men's outlook was evident from the start. While Matisse had little relish for the much-talked-of " movement that displaces lines," Marquet, in the heyday of Fauvism, was, so to speak, dynamism incarnate. Nothing could have been more to his liking than the clash of strident tones and the mobile volumes characteristic of Fauvism. At the same time he had a lively wit, involuntarily bitter on occasion, and was obsessed with a passionate desire to remedy the defects of nature, to redress things and people. A superb draughtsman, he had Lautrec's gift of bringing out in one significant line all the essentials of a face, but he was no less capable of transforming a decrepit cabhorse into a prancing Pegasus, though he was the first to smile at the animal's capers—and his own. We find in Marquet a constant tug-of-war between the promptings of his fiery Southern temperament and his distaste for all irrelevant exuberance. Often, indeed, what fascinates us in a Marquet canvas is not that he has reconciled thees two conflicting tendencies, but that each

MARQUET'S ' FAUVISM ' LIES MORE IN AN INTENSITY OF MOVEMENT THAN IN THAT OF COLOUR. LOOKING DOWN FROM HIS BALCONY THE ARTIST HAS TRANSFORMED A RATHER DRAB PEASANT MASQUERADE INTO A WONDERFULLY ANIMATED SCENE. SOMEWHAT IN THE MANNER OF THE ' NABIS.'

ALBERT MARQUET (1875-1947). BEACH CARNIVAL, 1906. 19¾×24".
PRIVATE COLLECTION, PARIS.

II. 17

VLAMINCK AND DERAIN

On April 4, 1876, Vlaminck was born in the busy heart of Paris, the district including Les Halles (Central Market). On his father's side he came of Flemish stock ; his mother was a Lorrainese protestant. Both parents were musicians, and are said to have led a Bohemian life, giving little thought to the education of their son. From his early childhood up to the present day Vlaminck has always lived in the country, working the land. In fact he regards himself as primarily a farmer, and has always disliked being described as an artist. Moreover, he persisted in teaching himself. This may explain why he has always had a fondness for the types of art that appeal to the peasantry, such as the gaudy colourprints dear to rustic eyes. From them he got his taste for bright pigment, extremely violent clashes of tones, and indulging the spontaneous flow of a fancy of the same order as that of the pleasant little poems he has given us—for nothing if not versatile, Vlaminck is a poet also, besides being a talented violonist. His feeling for nature, too, is quite in the country-dweller's vein ; he loves to evoke the joys of Sunday outings in the countryside, even if sometimes a passing storm throws the obvious contrast of its shadows on the colourful group of merrymakers. Nature, in his art, wears romantic trappings, like those of the colourprints he copied, as a boy ; it has something of the quality of those sentimental ballads which always end up " with a whimper " ; also of the " soft-hearted ' tough ' " that Vlaminck claims to be.

Though he has ended up by transmuting his conception of the visible world, purely pictorial in his early days, into a dramatic, emotional interpretation, Vlaminck was the ' Fauve ' who, of all the group, best deserved that appellation. If indeed it had depended

MAURICE VLAMINCK (1876). THE CIRCUS, 1906. 23½×18¾″. PRIVATE COLLECTION, BERN.

MAURICE VLAMINCK (1876). BOATS, 1905. 18×20¾". PRIVATE COLLECTION, PARIS.

NOTABLE HERE IS THE PLAY OF CURVES—OF SAILS AND OUTLINES OF THE TREES; NOT TO MENTION THE FLICKERING
RED STREAKS, OF AN ALMOST ABSTRACT NATURE, WHICH THE ARTIST OBVIOUSLY PUT IN SOLELY FOR THEIR PICTORIAL EFFECT.
THIS WORK IS LESS SCHEMATIC, LESS TRUCULENT, AND MORE POWERFUL THAN ITS PREDECESSOR.

on him alone to keep the flag flying, Fauvism would not have beaten its premature retreat.
In his art the use of strong tonalities is not determined solely by their associations or
contrasts ; it acts as a demonstration of the power of colour in itself, regarded as an architectural element rather than a surface coating. If, when little more than a boy, Vlaminck
amused himself going round his village with his friend Derain, and smearing red-lead on the
railings of premises owned by the more prosperous members of the community, this was not
so much for the pleasure he got out of putting on that aggressive colour, as because he wanted
to stress, as it were, the incarceration of these 'bourgeois' behind their prison bars. " The
most authentically 'painter' of us all," Derain once said of him. The truth was that, far
more than the novel-writing he practised for a while, more even than music (by teaching
which he earned his living), painting both appealed to his deepest instincts, and satisfied his
craving to express in concrete form the sensuality ever present in his strong, athletic body.
Hence his aversion for abstractions, for subtlety, and even for scientific theory—indeed, as
already mentioned, science " set his teeth on edge."

Vlaminck was, above all, a rebel ; or, rather, naturally undisciplined. At school he
was noted for his unruliness, and three years' military service failed to fulfil his father's hope :
that it would " drub some commonsense into the lad." Hence the headlong violence of his
early work, saved, however, from catastrophe by the sureness of his eye, the resourcefulness
of his drawing, and the charm of his thick, fluent brushstrokes. The truth is that though he
affected ruthlessness, and was in fact self-willed, he was always ready to be disarmed by a
child's smile or a penny bunch of flowers.

ANDRÉ DERAIN (1880). LE FAUBOURG, COLLIOURE, 1905. 23½ × 28¾". PRIVATE COLLECTION, PARIS.

MATISSE AND DERAIN MET AT COLLIOURE IN 1905, AND UNDER THE RADIANT SOUTHERN SUN THE FAUVIST PROGRAMME TOOK
FORM, THOUGH NOT WITHOUT SETBACKS. DERAIN SAID, " SOMETIMES I FELT QUITE DESPONDENT, BUT MATISSE ALWAYS HEART-
ENED ME UP." THIS WORK, SO RICH IN HAPPILY INSPIRED PASSAGES, AND AS SPARKLING AS A BYZANTINE MOSAIC, SPLENDIDLY
BELIES HIS APPREHENSIONS.

André Derain was born at Chatou, near Paris, on June 10, 1880. His father, a prosperous merchant, wanted him to enter the Ecole Polytechnique, but young Derain was far
less interested in engineering than in painting, sport, music and the less obvious by-ways of
knowledge. In 1899 at Chatou, he made the acquaintance of Maurice Vlaminck, a young man
of abounding energy, who had amazingly combined the *métiers* of professional racing cyclist,
violonist and popular novelist, but now, following Derain's lead, turned painter. In 1900
Derain got into the habit of dropping in at the Académie Carrière, when visiting Paris, and
made the acquaintance of Matisse, his senior by eleven years, who proved a friend in need.
For it was thanks to Matisse's good offices that the young man's parents were persuaded to let
him take up painting as a career. And the rosy picture drawn by Matisse at the interview, of
his prospects in art, was fully justified by the event. Derain was no less captivated by
Vlaminck's undisciplined enthusiasm than he had been by the sager personality of Matisse.
And his first contribution to Fauve art bespoke his full acceptance of the method (whose
legitimacy and ' modernity ' Matisse had championed) of creating a sort of super-space
conditioned solely by the surface of the canvas.

From his earliest days Derain betrayed a sort of indecision, due to two antagonistic
elements in his temperament, his instinct and his culture. And this conflict was intensified

ANDRÉ DERAIN (1880). FIGURES IN A MEADOW, 1906. 15×21¾". PRIVATE COLLECTION, PARIS.

EVEN WHEN FAUVISM WAS AT ITS TEMPESTUOUS HEIGHT (1905) DERAIN FELT THAT 'BUILDING WITH COLOUR' NEEDED MORE THAN THE 'DYNAMITE' OF CRUDE TONES; THAT OCHRES AND BROWNS AS WELL WERE CALLED FOR, IF HE WAS TO GET THE FULL EFFECT HE WAS AIMING AT.

by the circumstance that in Matisse with his erudite circumspection, and Vlaminck with his uncontrolled instincts, he found personifications of the tendencies at war within him.

Derain's superb ability was apparent in his very first works; indeed, as often happens with highly gifted artists, he displayed qualities that he was never to surpass in after-years. He may tell us that, at the dawn of Fauvism, he often felt terribly despondent and needed Matisse to " hearten him up," but his work belied this. He had already a forceful, pregnant brushstroke, put on with consummate ease, a gift of ranging from delicate nuances to the most emphatic colour with amazing virtuosity, and, moreover, a gift for drawing at once bold, confident and charged with feeling; in short he gave superb expression to a sensual tempera- ment sponsoring a genuine passion for art. This passion was revealed in an exuberance of colour carried to a point that startled even Vlaminck. It was Derain who likened paint to " dynamite," projected straight on to the canvas from the tubes; but he never indulged in this for the mere sensation's sake, as sometimes his friend Vlaminck did. He was always guided by a desire, fundamentally opposed to all Fauve theory : a desire to create harmonies rather than those ' symphonic ' tonal clashes which Matisse and Vlaminck had in mind.

True, Derain used the shrillest, warmest colours, but we can see he made a point of modulating them with softer tones, and even sought to contain their violence by the restraints of classical composition. The three works here reproduced show traces of this intention, especially if we compare them with Vlaminck's *Circus*.

Thus Derain was actuated by a very personal ideal, which Fauvism, despite its emphasis on architectural build-up, could not wholly satisfy. Possessed of a wide and varied culture, he was even in his early days eager to explore the less-known hinterlands of art, and spent much time in those museums which Vlaminck so heartily detested. He made

HENRI MATISSE (1869). STILL LIFE WITH PINK ONIONS, 1906. 18×21¾".
J. RUMP COLLECTION, ROYAL MUSEUM OF FINE ART, COPENHAGEN.

AS THOUGH TO TEST THE RANGE OF HIS SENSATIONS, THE PAINTER'S INSTINCT LEADS HIM HERE TO ABANDON RAW COLOUR
'STRAIGHT FROM THE TUBE' AND TO TRY HIS HAND AT MUTED TONES. ULTRAMARINE, EMERALD GREEN AND WHITE ARE BROUGHT
INTO CONTACT WITH BLACK AND OCHRES, CREATING AS IT WERE A SYMPHONY IN A MINOR KEY IN WHICH THE COUNTERPOINT OF
TONES SEEMS TO CONVEY THE CONFLICT BETWEEN THE LIVING THING, VULNERABLE BY TIME, AND THE PERMANENT.

even in circumstances which would have discouraged any ordinary man. Moreover he has always had not only a feeling for balance and proportion but a habit of introspection somewhat rare in artists, who are generally inclined to accept the promptings of their 'inspiration' wholesale and without more ado—indeed they would judge it almost sacrilegious to subject these to any intellectual control. So we need not be surprised if he has always mistrusted following the guidance of his instinct. It is indeed quite likely that he was the first to be astonished by that gift of his for colour, whose origin he could not trace. Hence his set purpose never to play the 'self-taught' artist, that is to say the ignoramus who thinks he can do everything by the light of nature. This explains why he so assiduously, and over such long periods, frequented schools, academies and museums, and likewise studied so painstakingly the works of his talented contemporaries. Also his tendency to ponder over his own aptitudes and the masterpieces of the past—and to draw enlightening comparisons.

It is seldom profitable to linger over the earliest works of a great master. Inevitably they are a mixture of borrowings, hesitations, precocious skill, bold yet pregnant clumsinesses. Only the early influences are significant. Thus in 1890 Matisse drew his inspiration from Chardin *(Les Livres)*, and in 1894 he interpreted in his manner Ruysdael's *Tempest*. Logic and intuition skilfully and sensitively blended—all Matisse is in these works.

HENRI MATISSE (1869). THE YOUNG SAILOR, 1906. 39½×31½″. HANS SELIGMANN COLLECTION, BASEL.

"THE YOUNG SAILOR" WAS PAINTED IN 1906, A YEAR MEMORABLE FOR THAT 'HIGHLIGHT' OF MATISSE'S ART, "LE BONHEUR DE
VIVRE." HERE MATISSE PRODUCES AN EQUIVALENT OF DEPTH—WHOSE EFFECTIVENESS IS INDISPUTABLE—BY CLASHES OF DISCORDANT
TONES. SIMILARLY HE REPLACES THE CLASSICAL MODELLING BY AN EQUIVALENT, EFFECTED BY ANALOGIES (SUCH AS INTERIOR
'CONTOUR' LINES AND THICKENINGS OF CERTAIN BRUSHSTROKES) WHICH BY NEW METHODS, GIVE MUCH THE SAME RESULTS.

ALBERT MARQUET (1875-1947). CIBOURE, 1907. 16¼×13½". PRIVATE COLLECTION, GENEVA.

has been given its run, in turn. His art is that of an intelligent man, with a highly refined sensibility, who has the gift of carrying the lyrical, not to say caricatural, bravura of his brushstrokes and his drawing to just that danger-point where the accuracy he always aims at is imperilled—but no further. Nevertheless Marquet was certainly a Fauve, but one who sometimes flung himself against the bars of the *Cage des Fauves* described by Vauxcelles, in a frantic effort towards freedom, yet sometimes retired to a corner of it, to dream serenely of his native forest.

MAURICE VLAMINCK (1876). LES BATEAUX-LAVOIRS, 1906. 19¾×28¾″. PRIVATE COLLECTION, PARIS.

WHAT FASCINATED VLAMINCK IN THE BOAT WASH-HOUSES ON THE SEINE WAS THE INTERPLAY OF PARALLELS, THEIRS AND THOSE
OF THE RIVER AND THE BANKS.

CHATOU - A SECOND ARGENTEUIL

*This charming little village on the outskirts of Paris is perhaps destined to go down to history as the
"Argenteuil" of Cubism, having given its name to what is known as the Ecole de Chatou. A curious " School"
consisting as it did of only two " pupils"; but in this case eminence can well replace mere numbers, the two in
question being Maurice Vlaminck and André Derain, who, around 1905, were painting at Chatou.*

*The rolling plains and woodlands all around, the skiffs on the river and those queer contraptions peculiar
to the Seine, the* bateaux-lavoirs *(boat wash-houses) seem to have inspired these young men with the ambition
of rebuilding and consolidating the forms Impressionism had pulled to pieces. And in these building operations
they laid on the shrillest tones of the colour-gamut, with a wilful, indeed aggressive disregard for every local tone;
behaving, in short, as if they were mischievously cultivating a deliberate, self-induced colour-blindness.*

*Meanwhile the two young artists alternated their excursions in the realm of colour at its wildest, most
dynamic, with philosophical and aesthetic debates, in which they indulged when boating on the river or exploring
on their bicycles the countryside; and records of these have been preserved. In fact the School of Chatou can be
said to vie in its small way with the famous Schools of Athens and Alexandria. One of the problems threshed out
related to the eternal conflict between instinct and knowledge. " I never set foot inside a museum," Vlaminck
boasted. " The very smell of such places makes me sick, no less than their pedantry and boredom. I loathe the
word ' classical.' And ' science' sets my teeth on edge." To which Derain sagely retorted : " What's
gained by lacking culture ?" Together they were trying to strike a balance between over-sophistication
on the one hand and the surrender to uncultured instinct on the other. A compromise might seem to lie in aiming
at a cultured instinct—but only at the risk and peril of eclecticism. Actually Degas and Seurat, Courbet and
the Douanier Rousseau had found the true solution—that of letting both the cultivated intelligence and crude
instinct have their say, but overruling both by genius.*

Only in 1897 with his famous *Desserte* did Matisse draw his inspiration from Impressionism. He now became intimate with Pissarro, 'discovered' Turner in London, stayed in Brittany. He had broken loose from the Ecole des Beaux-Arts and, temporarily, from the thrall of Classicism (with which his teachers had somewhat sickened him). In his *Still Life with a Stone Jug* (1897) we see Matisse fired with enthusiasm for tones of a violence that shocks and startles. The doctrines of Fauvism are, in fact, taking form. In 1898 and 1899 Matisse painted monumental nude figures of men in aggressively bold blues and greens. From 1900 on, his freely ranging imagination induced visions of an intensity such as even the absolute purity of the tones he used could hardly cope with, and now Matisse did his best to *organize* his sensory responses (which, we suspect, amazed and perhaps even startled him a little). Thus he applied himself to rendering them within the framework of classical composition. Examples are his *Académie Bleue* (1900) and *La Coiffeuse* (1901). He also reverted to 'museum' tonalities, and tried to discover the secrets of a composition that he desired to be, while solidly built, both untrammelled and inspired. Now that he felt surer of his craftsmanship, he harked back to colour (1904). The use of flat, unmodelled tones, thick impasto, the Pointillist discoveries—all these were tested by him in the course of his research-work.

It was not till 1905 that the Fauve aesthetic came definitely to the fore. Matisse and Derain had met at Collioure. Colour now reigned supreme and imposed its will on form. From his experimental period Matisse retained only the usage of flat colours, but he renovated it in terms of a technique whose resources he reveals to us not only by his use of judiciously placed 'whites' which (like the 'rests' in music) sometimes indicate tactfully suggestive hesitations, but also in the use of deliberate retractions, of arabesques begun, then rectified or recommenced or duplicated—all of which betray the artist's qualms of doubt, but likewise his determination to press technique to the utmost limit of its possibilities.

Nevertheless, Matisse's wish to control his emotions was not due solely to his feeling for order and proportion. He had under his eyes a salutary warning, in the aftermath of Impressionism, of the fragility of an art that depends overmuch on the artist's sensibility. Matisse, moreover, throughout his life, has (to use his own words) made a point of " organizing his brain." Nor must we forget that, having studied law (and ' on the side ' philosophy), Matisse may well have made his own the maxim that " the senses deform, the mind forms." But it was above all in studying the works of the Great Masters that Matisse perceived the virtues of equilibrium, just proportion and an economical use of the materials at the artist's disposal. And such was his admiration for Cézanne's architecture that, poor though he then was, he bought that famous *Baigneuses* which he kept for thirty-seven years before presenting it to the City of Paris.

It may seem almost paradoxical that an artist whose watchword was 'prudence' should by creating 'Fauvism' have revolutionized the art of his day. While claiming, as a very young man, his right to freedom, and making (as we have seen) no secret of his distaste for the tasks imposed on him, Matisse gave proof of a temperament all the more exceptional in that, rebel though he was, he made a point of subjecting his art to strict control. Fully aware of the risks he courts, Matisse makes no secret of his inconsistencies and, if he is sometimes skating on thin ice, acknowledges this quite candidly. Thus, when creating visual effects that have been planned out wholly in his " organized brain," and at the same time falling back (ostensibly) on the authority of nature, he brings off victories that are doubtless of a Pyrrhic order—but none the less effective.

In conclusion, we may point out that Matisse's art is never static, but continually evolving through a series of actions and reactions ; sometimes brutally direct, sometimes all grace and charm ; now dynamic, now smoothly flowing ; now good-humoured, now imperious ; now crystal-clear and now hermetic ; now sensual and now cerebral. Likewise, according to the artist's mood, his art is now the mistress and now the servant of colour (or, perhaps, both at once). And the result is that, though his avowed aim is merely to help us to relax, we have a series of visual adventures, startling and inexplicable, which compel our wonder and delight.

MARQUET

Born at Bordeaux on March 27, 1875, Marquet came to Paris in 1890 where, while still in his 'teens, he struck up a friendship with Matisse, whom he met in Gustave Moreau's studio. The two young men shared hard times together, as when, for instance, they were employed by Jambon the decorator, and for a pittance spent their days painting hideous scenery for the Paris theatres. This period of privation undergone in common saw the beginning of that deep affection, strengthened no doubt by the friendly give-and-take of two very different but complementary temperaments, which lasted unbroken until Marquet's death in 1947.

The contrast between the two men's outlook was evident from the start. While Matisse had little relish for the much-talked-of " movement that displaces lines," Marquet, in the heyday of Fauvism, was, so to speak, dynamism incarnate. Nothing could have been more to his liking than the clash of strident tones and the mobile volumes characteristic of Fauvism. At the same time he had a lively wit, involuntarily bitter on occasion, and was obsessed with a passionate desire to remedy the defects of nature, to redress things and people. A superb draughtsman, he had Lautrec's gift of bringing out in one significant line all the essentials of a face, but he was no less capable of transforming a decrepit cabhorse into a prancing Pegasus, though he was the first to smile at the animal's capers—and his own. We find in Marquet a constant tug-of-war between the promptings of his fiery Southern temperament and his distaste for all irrelevant exuberance. Often, indeed, what fascinates us in a Marquet canvas is not that he has reconciled thees two conflicting tendencies, but that each

MARQUET'S ' FAUVISM ' LIES MORE IN AN INTENSITY OF MOVEMENT THAN IN THAT OF COLOUR. LOOKING DOWN FROM HIS BALCONY THE ARTIST HAS TRANSFORMED A RATHER DRAB PEASANT MASQUERADE INTO A WONDERFULLY ANIMATED SCENE, SOMEWHAT IN THE MANNER OF THE ' NABIS.'

ALBERT MARQUET (1875-1947). BEACH CARNIVAL, 1906. 19¾×24".
PRIVATE COLLECTION, PARIS.

VLAMINCK AND DERAIN

On April 4, 1876, Vlaminck was born in the busy heart of Paris, the district including Les Halles (Central Market). On his father's side he came of Flemish stock; his mother was a Lorrainese protestant. Both parents were musicians, and are said to have led a Bohemian life, giving little thought to the education of their son. From his early childhood up to the present day Vlaminck has always lived in the country, working the land. In fact he regards himself as primarily a farmer, and has always disliked being described as an artist. Moreover, he persisted in teaching himself. This may explain why he has always had a fondness for the types of art that appeal to the peasantry, such as the gaudy colourprints dear to rustic eyes. From them he got his taste for bright pigment, extremely violent clashes of tones, and indulging the spontaneous flow of a fancy of the same order as that of the pleasant little poems he has given us—for nothing if not versatile, Vlaminck is a poet also, besides being a talented violonist. His feeling for nature, too, is quite in the country-dweller's vein; he loves to evoke the joys of Sunday outings in the countryside, even if sometimes a passing storm throws the obvious contrast of its shadows on the colourful group of merrymakers. Nature, in his art, wears romantic trappings, like those of the colourprints he copied, as a boy; it has something of the quality of those sentimental ballads which always end up " with a whimper "; also of the " soft-hearted ' tough ' " that Vlaminck claims to be.

Though he has ended up by transmuting his conception of the visible world, purely pictorial in his early days, into a dramatic, emotional interpretation, Vlaminck was the ' Fauve ' who, of all the group, best deserved that appellation. If indeed it had depended

MAURICE VLAMINCK (1876). THE CIRCUS, 1906. 23½×18¾". PRIVATE COLLECTION, BERN.

MAURICE VLAMINCK (1876). BOATS, 1905. 18×20¾". PRIVATE COLLECTION, PARIS.

on him alone to keep the flag flying, Fauvism would not have beaten its premature retreat.
In his art the use of strong tonalities is not determined solely by their associations or
contrasts; it acts as a demonstration of the power of colour in itself, regarded as an architectural element rather than a surface coating. If, when little more than a boy, Vlaminck
amused himself going round his village with his friend Derain, and smearing red-lead on the
railings of premises owned by the more prosperous members of the community, this was not
so much for the pleasure he got out of putting on that aggressive colour, as because he wanted
to stress, as it were, the incarceration of these 'bourgeois' behind their prison bars. "The
most authentically 'painter' of us all," Derain once said of him. The truth was that, far
more than the novel-writing he practised for a while, more even than music (by teaching
which he earned his living), painting both appealed to his deepest instincts, and satisfied his
craving to express in concrete form the sensuality ever present in his strong, athletic body.
Hence his aversion for abstractions, for subtlety, and even for scientific theory—indeed, as
already mentioned, science "set his teeth on edge."

Vlaminck was, above all, a rebel; or, rather, naturally undisciplined. At school he
was noted for his unruliness, and three years' military service failed to fulfil his father's hope:
that it would "drub some commonsense into the lad." Hence the headlong violence of his
early work, saved, however, from catastrophe by the sureness of his eye, the resourcefulness
of his drawing, and the charm of his thick, fluent brushstrokes. The truth is that though he
affected ruthlessness, and was in fact self-willed, he was always ready to be disarmed by a
child's smile or a penny bunch of flowers.

copies of, or rather interpreted, works by the old masters ; for example that *Descent from the Cross*, after Ghirlandaio, which, legend has it, led to Derain's being expelled by the museum-attendants, so outrageous were the liberties he had taken. Even in Fauvism's most revolutionary phase, he could never rid himself of his desire for colouristic unity and classical harmony. He was perhaps the first to observe that though Fauve technique could ' put together,' it could not *build* a picture in the architectural sense.

Moreover, without awaiting his friend Vlaminck's verdict on the matter, he soon discovered for himself that the interplay of pure colours was often no better (as he put it) than a sort of " orchestration run amok." Also, we may be sure, he too, was painfully conscious of having reached the limit of intensity obtainable by the colourman's reds and blues straight from the tube. So it was that Derain resolved to speak his own language only, that which his culture bade him speak and, refusing to yield to the lure of idle prattle, so to speak, however brilliant, to turn his natural gifts to serious account.

In Derain's work, from the very start, there are intimations of a dramatic struggle of divided aims. Great as was his curiosity, he was not, perhaps, greatly daring. Thus it was when, at a later phase, Cubism, seconded doubtless by his instinct, invited him to overstep the limits that his calmer, intellectual self enjoined him to observe. After having said in his youth, " What's gained by lacking culture ? " he went so far as to say (much later in life) : " Art's greatest danger is an excess of culture ! " Doubtless he realized that there are two kinds of culture : one well assimilated and constructive, the other a mere perfection of the mind. It was his awareness of this dilemma that brought him to that state of indecision, from which there was no escape, since his passionate devotion to painting exactly balanced his conscious craftsmanship. And yet, though his art may lack that single-mindedness to which he certainly aspired, this very indecision accounts for some of its most brilliant triumphs.

DERAIN IS ALL FOR RENDERING DIRECT EMOTION ; HIS LOVE OF NATURE DETERS HIM FROM 'INTERPRETATIONS' DERIVING FROM THE MIND ALONE. WHILE HERE CONFORMING TO THE NEW PRACTICE OF BUILDING FORM WITH COLOUR, HE NONE THE LESS ABIDES BY THE EXPRESSION OF HIS IMMEDIATE RESPONSES, IN THIS CASE TO THE ATMOSPHERE OF LONDON.

ANDRÉ DERAIN (1880). A LONDON STREET, 1906. 26×39¾". PRIVATE COLLECTION, PARIS.

LE HAVRE—CRADLE OF PAINTERS

Birthplace of Boudin and Monet and always a favoured resort of the Impressionists, this great Channel port was also the hometown of Friesz and Dufy, and Braque, too, spent his childhood and adolescence here. The art of these three Fauves, with its bright colours and clean-cut effects, certainly owes something to the brilliance of the sea-mirrored light and the dynamism of the surroundings of their early days.

DUFY Born at Le Havre on June 3, 1877, Dufy had eight brothers and sisters. It was a family of workers, none too well off, and Raoul had to set to earning money at the age of fourteen. Naturally he had little formal education but, being happily gifted with brains, he turned it to good account. Le Havre, a city of cool, limpid light, the cradle of marine Impressionism, inspired in Dufy, at a very early age, a keen appreciation of light and movement. He never tired of feasting his eyes on the changeful aspects of the sea, the colourful activities of the harbour, the ocean liners, busy little tugs and sailing-ships ; and the sights of the great seaport quickened his imagination. Thus in later days, in the maturity of his vocation, he said : " The great thing is to create the world of the things we do not see." Even in his earliest essays he was less concerned with transcribing the actual scene before him than in discerning the secret processes that made it what it was. And with this in mind he did not so much try (like Matisse and Derain) to discover the ' type '—the Platonic ' form,' so to speak—of the object he was contemplating as to create a new configuration, glimpsed in a flash of insight and deriving far more from imagination than from direct observation.

It was in this spirit that he became a student at the Ecole des Beaux-Arts at Le Havre, where he daily spent his few, much prized hours of leisure. Othon Friesz was a fellow-pupil and the two youths took their lessons from a good local painter, Lhullier (" *Le Père Lhullier* " as they irreverently called him). Sometime a pupil of Cabanel, Lhullier stood for tradition and loathed " slapdash " painting.

Coming to Paris in 1901 he entered the Ecole des Beaux-Arts, studying under Bonnat. Like most of his fellow-students he did not stay long with this teacher ; just long enough to meet the Fauves-to-be, and to make the acquaintance—invaluable to him—of Matisse.

Admittedly the Louvre " scared " him ; he felt much more at home with the Impressionists (at Durand-Ruel's), with Cézanne and with Van Gogh. Also he found in the naïvely colourful fantasies of folklore a confirmation of his natural bent.

The Fauves were pleased to find in Dufy a whole-hearted supporter of their technique of ' building ' the picture by means of sheer intensity, and pitch of tone. Indeed Dufy has proved, in the event, most faithful of them all to the brilliant effects produced by unmixed pigments—as may be seen in his recent works, where blues and reds predominate at their purest. Also he brought off some brilliant successes in the technique of raising tones to their highest pitch and juxtaposing them without a hint of a neutral zone between.

Moreover Dufy handles colour contrasts with boldness and dexterity ; when a dark tone touches a bright one, he has no qualms about binding the latter with a darker contour-line so as to step-up its affective value. Noteworthy, too, is the way in which his passion for colour overrides every consideration of lifelikeness. Art, for him, is an unqualified expression of the delight of the eye, a joy essentially dynamic. More than in any other Fauve we find in Dufy that brevity which is the soul of wit, and a quickness in the uptake enabling him to record the briefest flicker of imagined beauty. And his fondness for cool tones does much to enhance that impression of amazing lightness which so much charms us in his work.

Matisse's *Luxe, Calme et Volupté* came as a revelation to Dufy—but a revelation of his own temperament. Referring to it, he said (in 1925) : " I grasped at once the new *raison d'être* of painting, and impressionist realism lost all its charms for me when I saw this miracle of the imagination at play, in drawing and in colour."

RAOUL DUFY (1877). FOURTEENTH OF JULY, 1907. 32×19¾″. PRIVATE COLLECTION, PARIS.

COMPARING THIS WITH DERAIN'S "LONDON," WE FEEL THAT DUFY HAS LITTLE USE FOR 'DIRECT EMOTION,' NOR IS HE OUT
TO CAPTURE THE ATMOSPHERE OF A PUBLIC HOLIDAY. IT MERELY SERVES HIM AS A PRETEXT FOR A GAY SYMPHONY OF
WAVING FLAGS.

OTHON FRIESZ (1879-1949). LA CIOTAT, 1905. 14½ × 14½". PRIVATE COLLECTION, PARIS.

FOR FRIESZ FAUVISM MEANT ABOVE ALL A FIELD FOR BRILLIANT RESEARCH-WORK, WHOSE DISCOVERIES HE ADROITLY PUT TO THE SERVICE OF HIS MÉTIER.

FRIESZ

FRIESZ was born on February 6, 1879, at Le Havre ; his forbears (of Dutch origin) were sailors and shipwrights. Like most of the Fauves, Friesz had a robust physique. When quite young, he took painting lessons—with Dufy, who also hailed from Le Havre—from that excellent if very traditionalist painter, Lhullier. And in the facts above enumerated we may find clues to his subsequent development.

Thus, having, so to speak, the sea in his blood, young Friesz was no stay-at-home ; though in his case his *wanderlust* took him no farther afield, at first, than Paris, whither he went in 1898. To his great physical strength and his need for activity may be attributed that ' dynamism of form ' in which he now indulged. But Lhullier's influence persisted ; not only did he spend much time in art-museums, but he never quite lost sight of the need for discipline.

For Friesz, Fauvism was little more than a passing phase. He had never had a blind faith in the efficacy of colour and painting in flat tones as sufficient in themselves for building form. Thus he soon reverted to the classical method of rendering depth by perspective and, contenting himself with the Master's practice, never tried to ' go one better ' than Cézanne, as did most of his Fauve friends. From now on Friesz gave proof of an unrivalled technical ability, while excelling as a teacher. In other words, without doing violence to his temperament, he sought to obtain from it whatever might be turned to good account under the control of the disciplines by which he stood.

Thus all his work has a delightful, full-blooded vigour, which, however, he never allows to break out in Baroque extravagance. His world is an Arcadia in which the vegetation is lush, nymphs are buxom. There are many curves (signs of quiet power) as against very few angles (signs of impatience or excitability). Noteworthy, too, is Friesz's handling of volumes, whose dynamism he so dexterously controls. It was he who said in later years : " We, the creators of Fauvism, were the first to immolate it."

BRAQUE

Though Braque's dalliance with Fauvism was brief (no more than ten of his works are definitely 'Fauve'), he made his mark on the movement in a somewhat personal manner. While sometimes indulging in very high-pitched colour, he subjected it to a constructive discipline that anticipated a famous remark he was to make in later years : " I like the rule that corrects emotion." In this *Collioure* landscape, we may note how the arabesque is wedded to the colour, on equal terms, so as both to contain and to exalt the form. Braque, too, employs those contrasts in the Cézanne manner, which counteract the aggressive crudity of bright, unmixed pigments put on without any attempt at neutralization—those contrasts which Matisse alone has succeeded in endowing with a supreme emotive power.

From his early days Braque showed a quite exceptional aptitude for art. Something of this he owed to his father, manager of a big house-painting business (also a clever amateur painter), who initiated him as a boy into all the mysteries of colour-blending.

Amongst his works of Fauve inspiration, Braque, greatly daring, actually brought off some compositions in *a single colour*. In accomplishing this feat he was obviously going beyond the premisses of the movement, and anticipating the monochrome of his earliest Cubist canvases. It is not unlikely that these works, though few in number, speeded up the evolution of Fauvism and, by exploring possibilities other than those of the merely technical research-work on which it laid such stress, pointed the way—parallel to the development of Matisse's art—towards the principles of a new aesthetic.

IT WAS AT LA CIOTAT THAT BRAQUE, LIKE FRIESZ, HEARD THE CALL OF THE MEDITERRANEAN. HERE HE STILL COMPLIES WITH SOME OF CÉZANNE'S PRECEPTS. HE IS AGAINST ANY EXCESSIVE USE OF STRIDENT TONES, AIMING AT HARMONIES RATHER THAN 'SYMPHONIC' COLOUR-EFFECTS.

GEORGES BRAQUE (1882). LA CIOTAT, 1906. 21¼×26¼". PRIVATE COLLECTION, PARIS.

THE AFTERMATH OF FAUVISM

EVOLUTION OF THE ART OF
MATISSE, MARQUET, DERAIN, VLAMINCK, FRIESZ, DUFY, BRAQUE
AFTER 1907

We may ascribe to the years 1907-1908, or thereabouts, the period when Fauvism, having reached its peak, by dint of following certain principles to their extreme limit, began to lose its hold, the artists who had gone to school with it beginning to play truant, each following the lead of his own temperament. Near, moreover, was the advent of Cubism, which, too, contributed to the dissolution of the Fauve movement—while, however, taking over from it some valuable discoveries as regards the functions of colour, and also pressing still farther its propensities for stiffening tectonic form. And now Picasso's *Les Demoiselles d'Avignon* was to open new horizons to the analytic mind.

HENRI MATISSE, no longer contented with the technical research-work which meant so much to Fauvism, was about to move beyond this theoretical phase of system-building. His so to say ' local ' period was to give place to one of the ' expansion ' which his far-ranging genius called for. His work was now to acquire a universality, uninhibited by *a priori* theorems, and to body forth the changing modes of his creative impulse. If any form of control was to be exercised, it would now be one freely chosen by him.

ALBERT MARQUET, too, breaking with the high-keyed colour patches preconized by Fauvism for its tonal symphonies, returned to the classical principles of harmony, and now we find him, oftener than not, employing a precisely determined range of colours, and, like so many Great Masters of the past, limiting himself to these.

ANDRÉ DERAIN, who had met Picasso, now came under the influence of *Les Demoiselles d'Avignon*, and took advantage of this opportunity for falling into line with a tradition that Academicism had imperilled by foolishly preconizing its letter rather than its spirit. His knowledge of, and affection for, archaic art inculcated in him notions of synthetic sobriety, which inspired him to creations in which style, in the highest meaning of the word, was allied with sincere emotion.

MAURICE VLAMINCK, too, renouncing the violent effects made by bright, unmixed pigments straight from the tubes, toned down his palette, using now mixed pigments, ochres and browns, and adjusted his composition to geometrical rhythms inspired, it would seem, by those used by Cézanne.

OTHON FRIESZ, abandoning the technique of painting in flat colours, applied himself to rendering volume—likewise in the Cézanne tradition ; and also practised a composition sometimes classical and sometimes Baroque.

RAOUL DUFY, no longer obsessed by the architectural canons of Fauvism, now let himself indulge in the quest of purely fanciful rhythms, and disclosed a poetic imagination of no mean order. For a number of years he acted as a sort of ' arbiter of elegance,' and his highly original ideas on the subject of decoration met with general acceptance. Also he excelled in the *genre* watercolour, an admirable vehicle for his delicacy and wit.

GEORGES BRAQUE, too, had come under the thrall of *Les Demoiselles d'Avignon*, and foresaw the possibility of transposing Cézanne's lessons into a modern key. His 1908 exhibition at the Kahnweiler Gallery marked an end of the Fauve adventure, which had run its course, but not in vain ; for, as always happens and will always happen with art movements of a major order, Fauvism had pointed the way to new developments (as set forth above) and handed on the torch.

HENRI MATISSE (1869). GOLDFISH AND TERRACOTTA STATUETTE, 1909. 39¼×45½".
J. RUMP COLLECTION, ROYAL MUSEUM OF FINE ART, COPENHAGEN.

HENRI MATISSE

GOLDFISH AND TERRACOTTA STATUETTE

1 9 0 9

Proper names sometimes win the distinction of an adjective designating the microcosm for which they stand. Thus it was in 1910 that the art now known as ' Matissean' came into being; from now on the artist gave free rein to his personal way of seeing the world, with a superb indifference for all classical or scientific rules determining the interplay of ' complementary colours.'

Thus when he shows us a glass jar in which goldfish are swimming, Matisse makes play with the radiations diffused by patches of vivid red throughout a tract of water, whose transparency is boldly and totally obliterated by the dark background. Matisse's creations are never hampered by any a priori *considerations. Thus he also projects upon the surface of his canvas a blue vase with vermilion flowers and some green leaves, flanking a pink terracotta statuette. The development of the whole symphony flows from the theme of the cadmium-red fish. Like the Primitives, Matisse places the various objects without reference to any ' plastic' lay-out thought up in advance. The radiation binds all together, and we see as it were a progressive disintegration of tones springing forth, one from the other, in cataracts of colour.*

At no other period was Matisse more himself, not to say more ' Fauve.' In other words he has yielded himself to the initial ' shock' of a visual sensation, without attempting to tinker with, or to improve on, that first fine rapture; still less to impose logic on it. We might invert, in this connexion, a famous remark by Juan Gris (whose ideas, however, were utterly different from those of Matisse) : " With a cylinder I make a bottle." With these goldfish Matisse has made an amazing harmony of rare tones and a subtlety of matière *peculiarly his.*

THE MANILLA SHAWL

1911

In The Manilla Shawl *we have a* résumé *of the artist's aesthetic practice. The figure is the form of expression most favoured by Matisse. But he makes no secret of the fact that he never sets out to render all the features of a face, or to portray them with anatomical precision. To his mind the human body stands for the highest manifestation of the life force, yet it is only one branch of nature's universal tree. This is why the artist aims at expressing only the sensation of a vital force that the human body imparts to him. We might indeed say that in Matisse's work there is a sort of transcendental expressionism, awareness of which he shows when he speaks of " the religious significance of life." Thus, reduced to bare essentials, the outward forms of his figures are devoid of all ' accidental ' psychological implications, while wonderfully alive. And this life of theirs has as it were an hieratic quality and something of the compelling majesty of primitive, Chaldean, Egyptian, even negro effigies. We are sometimes reminded of that unseeing gaze, mirror of eternity, in the eyes of a Greek statue ; often, too, of the sheer gorgeousness of some chryselephantine god.*

To that concept of the religious significance of life may also be due the artist's rejection of all, so to speak, ' rationalistic ' considerations, which is plain to see in The Manilla Shawl. *Here the solution of that problem, ever-present to the painter, of depth, has taken the form of a magical interplay of colour harmonies, alternately contracting and dilated, whose origin obviously owes nothing to any preconceived theory or plan, but is to be found in the purely physical responses of the artist's sensibility ; impulses akin to those attending the creation of life itself.*

The Manilla Shawl *throws new light on the ' organization ' dear to Matisse. He had seen in Spain the flowered shawls of the ' Manolas.' But gorgeous as were their patterns and the gay counterpoint of colours within the framework of their fringes, Matisse regarded these as no more than ornamental motifs. As for the floral element, he incorporated it in the surface of the picture as a constructive factor, and not a merely decorative adjunct. Elsewhere this method was frequently applied by him to costumes, walls and carpets, as well. It is easy to see that in so doing Matisse is putting into practice a concept of decoration, other than that of mere ' decor ' ; and that his chief concern is to* organize *the surface of the canvas. Nor do these flowers give rise to direct emotions ; as in the* Moroccan Landscape, *they are treated as a conceptual element subserving the tectonic structure of the composition.*

TRIPS TO MOROCCO

1911-1913

Though Matisse has travelled round the world, or almost so, he persists in regarding himself as a stay-at-home. As we shall see, however, the first trip abroad, for a really great artist like Matisse, is a major experience ; whereas subsequent journeys tend to become mere variations on a familiar theme, set by the time-tables. Actually this self-styled stay-at-home has plied the lens of his observant eye on very various scenes, from Moscow to Tahiti, by way of New York and San Francisco ; throughout Europe, America and the South Seas. " One day I fell to looking for myself," Guillaume Apollinaire says in one of his poems, and this is what Matisse was always doing ; under ever-changing skies, always he came on—his own face. In fact the most authentic landscape is the one which the artist sees with his mind's eye. He promptly relegates the picturesque surprises of his travels to the lumber-room of the ' accidental,' and once more sets up his easel before that small but permanent world of his inner vision. Thus Matisse was never much impressed by the exotic sights that came his way—none had anything new to give him—and if he aspired to discovering a ' new world ' it was in vain ; everything brought him back to that private world which supplied all the visual excitements he needed.

The story of this Moroccan Landscape *is a case in point. Matisse has told us how, after having worked for some time on painting this canvas ' from the life,' he returned from Tangier to Paris, somewhat dissatisfied with what he had done and intending to improve on it when he made his next trip to Morocco. When some friends to whom he showed the picture in Paris began to voice their admiration, Matisse cut them short. " There's far, far more to it than that ! When I've worked over it again next year you'll see the difference." So Matisse took his canvas back to Tangier—and the end of the story is as you have guessed. He was studying his canvas with the idea of overhauling it when suddenly this Moroccan scene struck him as being much smaller, triter, more obviously a ' subject ' for the landscape-painter than when he saw it first. " So that's how it is," he told himself. " What I thought was missing on my canvas was there all the time—and it isn't in the subject ! " And returned to Paris without having inflicted any ' reformation ' on the picture.*

For Matisse a landscape, whether familiar or exotic, is much like those country auberges *you sometimes come across in France, where there is no food to be had except what one has brought oneself.*

HENRI MATISSE (1869). THE MANILLA SHAWL, 1911. 46½×29½″. PRIVATE COLLECTION, BASEL.

HENRI MATISSE (1869).   MOROCCAN LANDSCAPE, 1911.   46½×31½″.   NATIONAL MUSEUM, STOCKHOLM.

Speaking of this superb work Matisse once said : " The ground was covered with acanthus-plants. I'd never come across an acanthus before except in the drawings of Corinthian capitals we made in the Ecole.' And I was thrilled as much by the tall trees as by the luxuriance of the acanthus-plants below, no less impressive than the trees."

MOROCCANS AT PRAYER
1915-1916

Matisse's work between the years 1913 and 1918 is generally reputed to have undergone the influence of Cubism. Obviously such an artist as Matisse could hardly fail to be affected by the new aesthetic; still it is going much too far to say that he was " influenced " by it.

From his earliest days, even in his most ' Fauve ' compositions, Matisse always brought his intellect to bear on all he did. Thus he was wont to advise younger men to follow nature closely up to a point, but always to hold themselves in readiness to retrace their steps. (He had not, however, Cubism in mind when speaking thus.) In short, Matisse in quite early days had intimations of that marriage of the intellect and instinct, whose consummation was to crown his life's work. The Moroccans at Prayer is a case in point. In Morocco Matisse encountered scenes which provided him with more or less vigorous ' shocks ' in respect of their movement and colour ; and, doubtless, his coloristic imagination did not fail to make the most of these. But, as he said, " The work of art contains within itself its absolute significance, and impresses this on the spectator before he is able to identify the subject." What this implies is not any such purely decorative consideration as might, on occasion, justify the emphasis laid on a given motif : e.g. a woman's hat or a carpet. The conception of the Moroccans at Prayer derives primarily from the artist's contact with a sight abounding in ' accidental ' features, and his aim was to transmute a genre scene of the oriental type into a very personal architectural ensemble. And architecture involves geometry. Thus we need not be surprised that the first impression given him of these Moroccans at prayer was built up into a massive structure—whose rhythms and syntax are of a classical order— and in the making of which the artist may have had at the back of his mind Cézanne's injunction regarding " cylinders and spheres." In this picture Matisse has restrained his natural bent for strong colour, and achieved an ordered distribution of somewhat muted tones, the build-up of a work entirely on architectural lines, in which the arabesques find their directives in the quasi-geometrical patterns of the lay-out, the result being a composition in which this great artist has carried his tendency toward the abstract to its highest pitch.

HENRI MATISSE (1869). MOROCCANS AT PRAYER, 1916. 71¼×109¾". OWNED BY THE ARTIST.

THE LORRAINESE CHAIR
1 9 1 6

There are as many chairs, whether easy or erect, among the accessories of Matisse's visual world as there are guitars in Picasso's. No figure in a picture by Matisse but has a seat available, from the humble model's stool to the Odalisque's voluptuous divan.

In this connexion we may recall the function which Matisse himself assigned to painting : " to provide for the tired business man, no less than the intellectual, a cerebral sedative, rather like a comfortable arm-chair." For in that programme of Luxe, Calme et Volupté *implicit in his aesthetic, comfort plays an obvious part. But this, so to speak, sentimental value of the chair is merely a side-issue, and we shall now regard it from the purely plastic angle. Obviously pride of place in the hierarchy must be given to the arm-chair—always richly upholstered in Matisse's pictures. There are several reasons for this. For one thing, it generally provides a background, a support, or a response—like the ' answer ' in a fugue ; a contrast to the surface of a curtain or a body's arabesque. " Eternel conflit d'une guirlande avec la même," as Mallarmé put it. The swelling curve of the back of an easy-chair conditions and carries on, as it were, the bare back of the girl who is sitting in it, while the seat of the chair does the same for the lower part of her back. For the curve is a necessary constituent of the world of* Luxe, Calme et Volupté.

But the upright chair, and especially this Lorrainese chair, serves none of these purposes ; it is merely something to sit on, faute de mieux. *As lean as the easy-chair is plump, all in ridges and angles, it seems an effigy of the austere. And here its pictorial function is to reprimand the baroque ebullitions of the arabesques running wild behind it. It is like the skeleton at the feast, a grim reminder of the transience of all fleshly beauty. While the arm-chair bespeaks prodigality, this straight-backed chair preaches economy and its spare form provides the minimum of comfort. But, without this " Lorrainese chair " and its geometrical rigidity, its dessiccated, disapproving air, the blue wall-paper would never have achieved that monumental splendour which holds our gaze. And thus, manipulated by a great artist, austerity can serve the ends of pleasure.*

INTERIOR AT NICE
1 9 1 7

The Moroccans at Prayer *has all the glamour of a new, strikingly original venture and, as such, enjoys high esteem with professional artists and connoisseurs. This* Interior with a Violin *starts out from the same premises, but here the artist associates them with his amazing gift for wedding tones seemingly the least likely to come to terms between themselves. Here we no longer have compromises or adjustments between diaphanous and* per se *enchanting—though vigorously opposed—tones, or those rainbow-glints shining through a soft, translucent scumble whose discovery was Matisse's own ; nor selected fragments, so to speak, of arabesques several times begun and broken off. Here, too, we no longer have Matisse the charmer, weaving lures of evanescent grace to hold us spell-bound ; instead we have another Matisse, an artist bent on making good his work by the qualities that lie deepest and are most durable in art. Thus he has no qualms about using as the major themes in his composition those umbers and dark pigments traditionally of such ill repute, and those blacks which " eat up " everything, not only adjoining hues but even colours lightly tinctured with them so as to tone down their native harshness. Power takes the place of grace ; but a power all the more effective for not having wholly broken with charm, as in the case of the* Moroccans at Prayer. *Here the geometrical precision of the last-named work is replaced by a more flexible composition, which gives the work we are now considering its compellingness, that calm audacity of a masterpiece " brought off." Indeed, here we not only see Matisse at his splendidly impressive best, but as being wholly and unmistakably himself.*

It may also be pointed out that from now on ' Interiors ' come to play an ever greater part in Matisse's work. And his conception of the build-up of the picture leads him to mingle interiors with exteriors more and more. Here again we see, and in a striking form, the essential difference between modern painting and the old notions of almost photographic imitation. Matisse succeeds in employing exactly the same kind of lighting for his interiors as that employed for his exteriors. That is to say, light is not used to ' illuminate ' in the classical sense of the word, but chiefly to intensify the tone, if need be ; and, similarly, its absence does imply the presence of a shadow. In the modern way of seeing, black is just a colour like any other. Thus the Odalisque *here reproduced, though located in an interior, is painted in full light as if it were an open-air scene ; and this* Interior at Nice, *like the* Moroccan Landscape, *is painted without any precise regard to the incidence of light.*

This outstanding work is one of Matisse's greatest achievements. The conception of black as a colour in its own right has rarely been applied so boldly and successfully. In its juvenile enthusiasm Fauvism had taken it for granted that, for building up with colour, the most vivid tonalities were indispensable. Here we

HENRI MATISSE (1869).   THE LORRAINESE CHAIR, 1916.   51½×35″.   PRIVATE COLLECTION, SOLOTHURN.

might almost see a wilfully paradoxical adventure, were it not that paradox implies precarious equilibrium. Whereas here Matisse brings off his Salto mortale with happy ease and superb success.

THE WHITE PLUMES
1919

When Matisse was working under Carrière, that staunch upholder of low-toned decorum was shocked by the ebullition of vivid colours in the work of the young student who was soon to be the leader of the Fauve school. " But," he politely enquired, " suppose you had to paint a parrot, how would you set about it ? " To which Matisse replied with equal politeness, " But I haven't got a parrot ! " However, in this connexion we may note that whereas Delacroix, for whom Matisse had such admiration, when painting animals, almost always shows us rearing horses, lions and tigers leaping on their prey, Matisse, following his tranquil bent, paints only birds and fishes. It is not surprising that he was so much drawn to the motif *of the plume, whose ripples illustrate to perfection the characteristic Matissean rhythm. This picture is a case in point; in the delicate tones he uses here he shows himself a master of the* nuance; *as, in other works, of pure, unmodulated colour.*

HENRI MATISSE (1869). THE WHITE PLUMES, 1919. 30¾×23½". MUSEUM OF FINE ART, GÖTEBORG.

HENRI MATISSE (1869). INTERIOR AT NICE, 1917. 45¾×35″.
ROYAL MUSEUM OF FINE ART, COPENHAGEN.

DECORATIVE FIGURE ON AN ORNAMENTAL BACKGROUND
1 9 2 7

The very title suggests some of the directive ideas of Fauvism and, a fortiori, certain aspects of Matisse's programme. " Decorative Figure " likewise recalls one of Gauguin's cherished projects, that of bringing modern art into line with decoration on the grand scale (or anyhow at its purest), in other words with the frescos of the Primitives. Thus here we find it easy to imagine the Figure, in its rigorous parallelism with the uprights of the stretcher (and, of course, the frame), complying with the lay-out imposed on it by a wall, and thus conditioned by an architectural function. This fresco-like technique is also visible in the uniform tonality of the ochre, which represents the mean, or common denominator, of all the neighbouring tones and is thus linked up with them. Also the " Floral Background " with its brightly variegated counterpoint of hues recalls the backgrounds of the Primitives, always done in luminous colours, reminiscences of which certainly encouraged the Fauves in their practice of " building with bricks of colour."

THE ODALISQUE
1 9 2 8

The second canvas of this ' foursome,' The Odalisque, shows us another phase in the evolution of Matisse's art; one in which he seems to let himself be guided by his subject. This period covers approximately the years 1918-1930. Some have thought to see in it Renoir's influence. But Matisse's sensuality was more directly and exclusively inspired by colour than was Renoir's. Unlike Renoir, Matisse was not inditing, as it were, a more or less impassioned ode to woman's beauty, and it is chiefly through the medium of colour and in terms of colour that he bodies forth the impression made on him by the model. This picture of a languorously reclining Odalisque evokes the atmosphere of some of Baudelaire's poems—the bed with its " languid wafts of perfume," the " oriental splendour " and " sonorous jewels " of the sleeping woman, the " divan deep as a tomb " and the " strange flowers " all around. But Matisse never shared in Baudelaire's goût du néant; he has always hymned the Bonheur de vivre.

Elegance of line, sensuous grace of form, bold luxuriance of colour; we are invited to feast our eyes on these, but no more to appraise the ' plastic value ' of the fleeting thrill they quicken, than, in this picture, Matisse had recourse to the counsels of his intellectual self.

HENRI MATISSE (1869). RED ODALISQUE, 1928. 21¾×15". PRIVATE COLLECTION, PARIS.

HENRI MATISSE (1869). DECORATIVE FIGURE ON AN ORNAMENTAL BACKGROUND, 1927. 51¼×38½″.
MUSÉE D'ART MODERNE. PARIS.

THE LAWS OF DECORATION...

A feature of the quarrel between purely ' plastic ' art and realistic or representational painting was the constant hostility of the latter to what it regarded as ' the decorative.' Thus, as we may remember, Courbet ridiculed that " playing-card " technique in which he accused Manet of indulging. It was Gauguin who, half unwittingly, inaugurated the movement for the rehabilitation of the decorative, which had so much influence on the future course of art. Actually Gauguin, when ornamenting wooden clogs or carving walking-sticks in his Pont-Aven days, would not hear of the term " decorative " being applied to what he did. The truth was that Gauguin never had any clear idea of the laws governing decoration, for which, however, he had natural gifts—as when he painted the lid of a cigar-box with a breadth of execution reminiscent of a fresco.

The " Nabis " on the other hand, gifted with a delicate wit and a whimsical good taste somewhat in the ' ninetyish ' manner, tended more towards ornamentation than decoration proper, which they relegated to tapestry and posters. And the Neo-Classicism sponsored by Maurice Denis and practised under the auspices of Father Didier Lenz and Dom Verkade, was more concerned with the " Holy Measure " and in particular, a revival of religious art, than with aesthetic considerations or painting pure and simple.

In 1933 Matisse made for the Barnes Foundation, Merion, a huge decorative composition, La Danse, in which dynamic figures in pearl-grey monochrome move on a background alternately pink and black. (The first sketch for this work, made in 1932, is in the Paris Museum of Modern Art.) This is one of our great artist's noblest works; in it he combines his Dionysian inspiration and his Hellenic sense of rhythm, raising both to their highest pitch. He himself has explained how he set about this gigantic work. " Perhaps I should mention that the composition of this panel was the outcome of a strenuous tussle between the artist and the fifty-two square yards' surface of which his mind had somehow to take possession, and it did not derive from the modern procedure of ' projecting ' a composition on to a surface x times greater than itself, ' as per schedule submitted ' in business parlance, and superimposed like a tracing."

We can see what Matisse was aiming at; he began by visualizing his composition in terms of the architectural setting in which it was to figure. For obviously the coved ceiling extending above the glazed doors and against the light determines the lay-out of La Danse.

Thus Matisse ascribes more importance to the background of the composition than to what is, strictly speaking, the subject, and conforms to the directives of the flat surface to be painted, by the use of equivalent planes. Then, too, he imposes on all outlines an extreme sharpness of definition; indeed, contour plays a leading part in the composition. We are familiar with sculptors' drawings, but there is also the painter's drawing : the drawing which is painting, as is the case with Matisse. Here it is the distribution of the coloured surfaces that governs outline, and Matisse draws in terms of colour, even (and indeed, above all) in his most clean-cut drawings in pencil or Indian ink. Thus, even so, the form is still expressed by colour, though that colour is in the latent state. The relations between form and colour are conceived in terms of decoration.

In Matisse's work decoration has regained the purity of the Quattrocentists. And in this connexion it is interesting to note that Matisse is now engaged in building a Dominican chapel at Vence, in whose architecture and decoration he is synthesizing his decorative theories.

...AND THOSE OF BOOK-ILLUSTRATION

The first book illustrated by Matisse was the Poems of Mallarmé, *published by Albert Skira in 1932, the same year as that of* La Danse *(Barnes Foundation, Merion, Pa.), and this book is in effect an* exposé *of the artist's views on typographical lay-out.*

In handling the book Matisse puts into practice methods that implement his decorative theory. Thus, as in his mural paintings he defers to the autonomy of the wall, so in the book he respects that of the paper. Indeed he himself has told us that what is wanted is " etchings with an even, very thin line, without hatchings, which thus leave the printed page as white as it was before. The problem is to balance the two pages, one white (that which has the etching), and the other, which has the letterpress (relatively speaking) black. I might compare the two pages to two objects handled by a juggler; let us picture a white ball and a black ball—and, similarly, my two pages, one light, the other dark, so different, yet face to face. Despite the differences between the two objects, the juggler's art makes of them, as seen by the spectator, an harmonious whole."

Again in Jazz *Matisse has devised a method of illustration by employing cut-out bits of coloured paper. Here, too, the autonomy of the white page and its participation in the coloured* ensemble *bears out the artist's theory of decoration. Thus we see that Matisse's conception of the illustrated book, as well, is in accord with his tectonic programme.*

HENRI MATISSE (1869). GIRL ON RED BACKGROUND, 1936. 24×19¾″. OWNED BY THE ARTIST.

IT WAS MORE AS A DRAUGHTSMAN THAN AS A PAINTER THAT MATISSE SAW HIS MODEL IN THIS WORK, AND ITS BEAUTY DERIVES
FROM THE CALLIGRAPHIC RHYTHMS HE BRINGS INTO PLAY. LINE, FOR MATISSE, IS MORE THAN A FRAMEWORK, AND NOT EMPLOYED
MERELY TO BIND THE COLOUR. IT HAS ITS SPECIFIC FUNCTIONS, EXISTS IN ITS OWN RIGHT. AND IN THIS ADMIRABLE COMPO-
SITION COLOUR PLAYS CHIEFLY THE PART OF AN ACCOMPANIMENT.

STILL LIFE WITH OYSTERS

1940

This was painted in 1940, the year of the invasion of France. Matisse had just attained his seventieth year. He had been intending to travel but, under the tragic circumstances, decided to remain in Provence. It seems that from this time Matisse set himself to recapitulating memories of his life's work; much as at the end of the play all the actors come forward to 'take the curtain.' We see recalls of Fauvism emerging on the canvas: thick contour-lines, flat, unmodelled colour, broad surfaces. Likewise the colour is, once more, intense. And again we see pure tones juxtaposed, without the intervention of neutral zones, and producing extremely brilliant effects. We even find 'echoes,' so to speak, of his geometrical period (1913-1918) in the concern he shows for architectural structure, while, however, attempting to blend with it the emotional drive of Fauvism.

In the Still Life with Oysters *we see Matisse wedding the intensity of the purest possible tones to the most subtle colour modulations, while subjecting both to the control of a severely architectural rhythm. We find combined in it both the flat tones and graphic methods of* Le Bonheur de Vivre *(1905) and the geometrical build-up of* La Desserte *(1909). While the composition follows the pentagonal lay-out known as the Section d'Or—the proportions of the ideal pyramid, and while Matisse increases its effectiveness by boldly clothing it in the three primary colours, the dish of oysters between the green serviette and the mauve jug presents us with a quite classical interplay of complementary colours, which Matisse by no means invariably practised. The famous definition of a picture which we owe to Maurice Denis as " a flat surface to be covered with colours arranged in a certain order," is strikingly borne out by this* Still Life, *which is also an excellent example of that " pure painting " or " painting for its own sake " for which Denis himself blamed Matisse—though actually this was one of our great artist's most significant contributions to the advancement of painting.*

It appears that round about 1940 Matisse achieved what he had always dreamt of, a happy union between the disciplines of wholly classical-minded composition and the fervours of his genius for colour. But attempts to reconcile instinct and the intellect are bound to be precarious, tending to give rise to works that, neither logical nor instinctual, have chiefly the nature of ornamental decoration. This, in fact, is the crux of Matisse's art, a formidable problem, next to impossible to solve—unless one happens to be a Matisse.

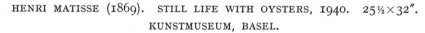

HENRI MATISSE (1869). STILL LIFE WITH OYSTERS, 1940. 25½×32″.
KUNSTMUSEUM, BASEL.

HENRI MATISSE (1869). THE GIRL WITH THE PELISSE, 1946. 36¼×28¾". OWNED BY THE ARTIST.

ONE OF MATISSE'S RECENT WORKS, THIS ILLUSTRATES THE TREND HIS ART IS TAKING AT THE PRESENT TIME. THE ARTIST HAS TOLD US THAT HE NOW IS DRAWING CONCLUSIONS, AS IT WERE, FROM THE WORK WHICH OCCUPIED HIM DURING THE LAST TWENTY YEARS. IF WE COMPARE THIS PICTURE WITH THE *FIGURE ON AN ORNAMENTAL BACKGROUND* (1927) AND THE *GIRL ON A RED BACKGROUND* (1936), WE FIND THAT MATISSE WHILE KEEPING TO HIS DECORATIVE CONCEPTIONS, ADAPTS THEM TO A LAY-OUT IN WHICH LARGE PLANES ARE DEMARCATED BY ARABESQUES. THERE IS PERHAPS A HINT OF FAUVISM IN THE PURE TONES AND THEIR JUXTAPOSITION WITHOUT TRANSITION, BUT THE GENERAL EFFECT IS ONE OF CALM AND RELAXATION. BRILLIANT AS ARE THE COLOURS HERE EMPLOYED, WE HAVE NO FEELING OF CLASH OR STRAIN; QUITE OTHERWISE, THE UNRUFFLED SMOOTH-NESS OF THE SURFACES AND THE EVEN FLOW OF LANGUID, SUPPLE RHYTHMS BEAR OUT MATISSE'S DESCRIPTION OF THE ART HE AIMED AT: "I WANT PEOPLE WHO FEEL WORRIED, EXHAUSTED, OVER-WORKED, TO GET A FEELING OF REPOSE, WHEN LOOKING AT MY PAINTING."

ALBERT MARQUET

THE EASEL

1942

For a relatively short time, following Matisse's lead, Marquet did homage to the vehemence of Fauvism; no doubt his natural loyalty to a friend for whom he had so much affection precluded him from acting otherwise. But at the back of his mind were memories not only of the rebellious young man he had been at the Ecole des Beaux-Arts, but also of the art-student who at the Louvre (almost on the sly) copied Chardin, Claude Lorrain and Poussin—or, rather, interpreted them in his own manner. Thus his definitely classical temperament led him to break away, almost effortlessly, from the doctrines of the Fauves, whose structural innovations seemed to him somewhat foolhardy.

Marquet was no addict of rash adventures. A shrewd observer, he found in almost everything that met his eye enough to stimulate his zest for analysis of every order, and to incite him to all such variations on the theme as would bring out new aspects of its significance.

Though in this sense unadventurous, Marquet was a great traveller. But we have not the impression that the chief object of these journeys was to discover new ' motifs.' In this respect a remark he once made may be illuminating. " When drawing, I have exactly the same problems in mind, whether I'm looking at a man or at a lamp-post." A whole theory of aesthetics lies behind this remark. It explains why his landscapes, whether they hail from Fécamp, Hamburg, Naples, Rotterdam, Algiers, Norway, The Piraeus or the Quai aux Fleurs at Paris, are, so to speak, cut to the same pattern, follow the same dynamic rhythm and are painted in the same tonalities.

Thus for Marquet all lamp-posts are alike; his aim is simply to portray them in the conditions under which he sees them (or, anyhow, believes he sees them). His friend Georges Besson has told us that one of Marquet's pictures, which began as a veritable orgy of the shrillest tones imaginable, came, after a certain number of sittings, to look almost like a monochrome in shades of grey. Thus Marquet, after being greatly taken by the Fauvist programme, chose to follow, rather, his own bent.

Once the golden age of Fauvism was over—and golden ages have a way of being short-lived—Marquet came to terms with his natural impulsiveness, without, however, abating his habit of ironical self-criticism. Though no Isaak Walton, he had a liking for water, preferably calm. Intelligent artists are seldom romantic; they are too much concerned to voice their truth with an extreme exactitude, by way of forms. Marquet always preferred seaports to the open sea, and, like Seurat, had a predilection for quays, jetties, clean-cut horizons. Again, like Baudelaire, he liked the water he was painting (whose flow, too, " displaces lines ") to be confined within the precincts of canals and river-banks, where parallel frontiers, so to speak, controlled the natural turbulence of the water, which he wanted deep, translucent, iridescent—silent and tranquil like himself. However, this did not prevent his dappling its smooth surface with broken gleams, whose values are brought out with an accuracy and intensity that holds us spellbound. The tranquillity of his seascapes is the only allusion Marquet makes to his ' Ego '; for a sense of dignity forbids his ever being one of those self-pitying artists of whom Matisse ironically spoke, " who are always telling you their life-stories."

In any case that ' Ego '—a term which seems stilted and pretentious when applied to one so simple and forthright as Marquet—reveals itself more modestly in various small but characteristic habits. Thus in The Easel *we see him experimenting with a technique that always appealed to him, a ' come-as-it-may perspective ' so to speak. One day when an art-expert visited Marquet, he found him on the balcony of his fifth-floor apartment quietly engaged in painting the busy scene on the Quai aux Fleurs below. " I see," the visitor remarked, " that you are interested in the problems of ' downward perspective.' " " Not a bit of it," Marquet answered. " But like this I can paint at home without bothering to go out."*

In this admirable composition Marquet seems to have been caught in his own trap. When, following his usual practice, he was about to paint what he saw from his balcony, he was suddenly struck by the effect produced by the window itself, and the technician, the craftsman, within him got the upper hand, shouldering aside the poet of light and water. The half-glimpsed scene below became a mere background, playing a minor part, and the artist indulged in a sort of grammatical analysis in which verticals and horizontals are the data for quite the most brilliant demonstration of style and syntax that Marquet has ever given us; thus showing—not without a touch of coquetry perhaps—what he was capable of making even of such seemingly unpromising material, and atoning for the bleakness of the essential lines by the use of the most exquisite tones on his palette.

ALBERT MARQUET (1875-1947). THE EASEL, ALGIERS, 1942. 10¼×8¼″. PRIVATE COLLECTION, PARIS.

MAURICE VLAMINCK (1876). THE FLOOD, IVRY, 1910. 28¾×36¼″. C. H. COLLECTION, PARIS.

MAURICE VLAMINCK

THE FLOOD

1910

Round about 1908 Vlaminck's art took a new turn. " Those effects I got by pure colours, like an orchestra playing full blast all the time, and on which I'd been so keen, were ceasing to satisfy me. For, limited as I was by the colourman's reds and blues, I'd reached the maximum of intensity; and this was upsetting."

Also, a deeper understanding of the principles of Cézanne, not to mention the influences of incipient Cubism and tendencies suggested by negro art, were leading Vlaminck towards more classical conceptions. He now revived the notion of depth, which as a Fauve he had rejected, by using those famous planes laid parallel to the sides of the frame, which Cubism was to adopt as one of its favourite devices. As regards colour, Vlaminck no longer mistook mere crudity for intensity. And his high-pitched tones now became more substantial, more solid and sustained.

After this change of heart Vlaminck began by painting his famous Baigneuses, *in which, employing a spherical calligraphy, he produces some highly effective rhythms. Then came landscapes in which, as in* The Flood, *depth is conveyed by the linear structure; after these, Still Lifes of an almost ' classical ' lay-out, despite Vlaminck's aversion for that epithet; and, finally, that fine, solidly constructed self-portrait, which evidences a gift of assimilation startling in one who set out to be so independent.*

During this phase Vlaminck kept in touch with the Cubists, but soon broke away, realizing no doubt that they were leading him towards notions of creation in the artist's mind, quite incompatible with his deference to direct visual responses. He accused the Cubists of being theory-mongers, and, after having painted the most durable works of his career, repudiated Cézanne, too. So now he swung vigorously back to what was to be his final manner, a form of art in which the delightful spontaneity of the born colourist he was, is drastically sub-jected to conceptions of nature more as a decorative than as a living entity.

MAURICE VLAMINCK (1876). SELF-PORTRAIT, 1912. 28¾×23½". PRIVATE COLLECTION, PARIS.

THIS STRIKING, SOLIDLY CONSTRUCTED LIKENESS, A 'SPEAKING' ONE INDEED, ECHOES THE ARTIST'S WORDS, "I'M A SOFT-
HEARTED TOUGH. I PAINT SO AS TO SET ORDER IN MY THOUGHTS, CALM MY DESIRES AND LET A LITTLE PURITY INTO MYSELF."
ONE MIGHT ALMOST FANCY IT WAS MATISSE SPEAKING. IN ANY CASE THE STRUCTURAL PERFECTION OF THIS WORK RANKS IT
AMONG THE ARTIST'S GREATEST ACHIEVEMENTS.

ANDRÉ DERAIN (1880). STILL LIFE WITH A JUG, 1910. 36¼×25½″. PRIVATE COLLECTION, PARIS.

64

ANDRÉ DERAIN (1880). CAGNES, 1910. 23½×32¼". PRIVATE COLLECTION, BERN.

ANDRÉ DERAIN

CAGNES

1910

French art always favours structural solidity. The Fauve technique, after a promising start, soon worked itself out, as all art movements have a way of doing. Classicist that at heart he was, Derain more than the others felt the necessity of getting to the heart of the problem. Obviously there was far too much 'jerry-building' in the Fauve edifice, and the burning question for these artists was how to promote it to the rank of real architecture. We see different ways in which they tackled the problem when we compare Derain's Cagnes and Vlaminck's Flood. To both alike geometry was tempered by an almost sentimental feeling for colour, Derain's was of a sterner mould. And yet its very starkness, achieving a new solidity, has a charm of its own. Here, while the left-hand portion of the picture is taken up by the graceful undulations of mountains, clouds and branches, the part on the extreme right massively shores up the composition as a whole, much as the buttresses of a cathedral shore up the soaring beauty of its vaults.

STILL LIFE WITH A JUG

1910

This admirable Still Life is one of Derain's greatest works. Here, as Gauguin had advised, he goes back to the fountainhead, and draws his inspiration from the Primitives. Had not Ingres himself declared that " the beginnings of certain arts are sometimes more perfect than their later, so-called 'perfected' phase ? " Here Derain has recourse to that system of building-up by superimposed planes that Cubism was to carry a stage further, and which, while disregarding the laws of perspective, unknown to (or deliberately ignored by)

65

the old fresco-painters and wood-engravers, sponsored new structural methods whose effectiveness the artist stresses here by his sober use of colour. " Provided it's solid," Corot, stealing a march upon the Fauves, once said, " I needn't trouble over-much about the colour."

In this Still Life, one of his earliest, Derain already shows leanings towards abstraction; he is feeling for the constructive, essential form of the object, " its virtue in the old use of the word," as he put it; and this is one of the aims he followed most whole-heartedly, and with such notable success.

THE TWO SISTERS

1914

Derain is aiming at the creation of a ' new classicism,' amenable to equally new methods of procedure. Whether we study The Salterns at Martigues, in which the influence of geometry implements a return to classical composition, or The Two Sisters, whose austerity, despite its overtones of Gothic expressionism, so poignantly affects us, we find that Derain is as much against mere ' experimentalism ' in art, as he is against that romantic self-exhibitionism which Matisse had in mind when he described the painter as " a man with a grievance, always wanting to talk about himself."

In The Two Sisters the technical methods are adjusted to a greater flexibility of ' syntax.' True, this syntax is no novelty in itself, but the methods, especially the way in which some forms are treated, are often quite original. Here we once more note the artist's leanings towards an archaic type of art, combined with lyrical effects from which, however, he is careful to exclude any suggestion of psychology. Thus its reserve and studied unemotionalism ensure the dignity and distinction of this work.

Yet, unwillingly we may be sure, Derain betrays a disillusioned scepticism and the realist detachment implied by his outspoken refusal to have any truck with ' absolutes.' During this period, his gifts, which comprise grace and elegance no less than forcefulness, are deliberately kept in hand. In The Two Sisters, we may compare the flat treatment of one sister's dress with the modelling of the other's; and note the almost ' Mallarméan' effect of the hand of one sister resting on the back of the chair. The truth is that, in his ironical indifference to emotional commonplaces, Derain is less interested in what he might have to say than in his way of saying it. It is, perhaps, an ingrained pessimism that leads him to observe life's human side with such aloofness. In any case, only concrete objects really interest him; faces are to him mere Still Lifes, and to try to penetrate their secrets seems mere waste of time. Perhaps because metaphysics is not his forte; feeling so much at home within it, he never rises above the natural world. Thus art for him is largely a matter of overcoming difficulties, almost a game of skill—and what attitude could be more ' classical ?'

THE SALTERNS AT MARTIGUES

1912-1913

In The Salterns at Martigues Derain is moving towards an alliance of form and feeling. The actual framework here is solid, not to say severe; but between the buttress of the wall on the right and the massive immobility of the tree, the landscape is enabled to unfold itself in smiling beauty, nature comes into her own. Indeed, did the artist continue in this direction, he would link up with Corot. From now on he is all for bold simplifications, brevity and balance, and, though the sureness of his touch is quite exempt from stiffness, he shows a very classical regard for style and synthetic precision of form. What makes this somewhat remarkable is that Derain has always been drawn to the least classical by-ways of knowledge : magic, astrology, divining, the Kabbala and occultism in general—doctrines sponsoring the secret powers of man; though in Man he has no more faith than in the ramshackle social order of to-day, with which he has no links.

In Derain's originality we may detect the secret of his unresolved inner conflicts. In his perhaps almost too deliberate quest of classicism, he is really in quest of a remedy, and to this is due, no doubt, the somewhat ' artificial ' side of his personality. For a man is born classical, he cannot become classical at will. Here we have, if not an explanation, at least a clue to the perplexing quality of his art.

ANDRÉ DERAIN (1880). THE TWO SISTERS, 1914. 76¾×51¼″. ROYAL MUSEUM OF FINE ART, COPENHAGEN.

ANDRÉ DERAIN (1880).   THE SALTERNS AT MARTIGUES, 1912-1913.   27½×23¼″.
PRIVATE COLLECTION, BERN.

FOLLOWING CÉZANNE'S ADVICE, DERAIN TRIED TO " VIVIFY POUSSIN IN CONTACT WITH NATURE."   HERE WE FIND THE TREE
FROM POUSSIN'S " ECHO AND NARCISSUS," AND THE RIGHT-HAND WALL OF CÉZANNE'S " FARM AT AUVERS."

RAOUL DUFY
L'ESTAQUE
1 9 0 8

It was in 1908 that Dufy, turning his back on the Fauve aesthetic, elected for Cézanne's constructivism.
He broke up a landscape into its geometrical constituents, and, having no blind cult of nature, thought above all
of the picture to be made. " We must create the world of things that no one sees," he said. At l'Estaque where

RAOUL DUFY (1877).   L'ESTAQUE, 1908.   22×18″.   OWNED BY THE ARTIST.

RAOUL DUFY (1877). LES BAIGNEUSES (WATERCOLOUR), 1918-1920. 31½×22″. PRIVATE COLLECTION, PARIS.

he met Braque, he had the idea of a synthetic way of seeing the world, by grace of which a new ' reality,' wholly the work of his imagination, would emerge, and make the picture's unity. When a friend accused him of playing fast and loose with nature, he replied : " But nature, my dear Sir, is only an hypothesis."

LES BAIGNEUSES
1918-1920

Les Baigneuses *shows that Dufy's art, while always a delight of the eye, does not aim at a delight that is merely static. Even when, as in this gouache, Dufy abandons scenes in which movement plays a specific part, and paints motionless figures, he lends them buoyancy, making them seem to float in the air. They are like ' snapshots ' whose dynamism is ensured by breaks or syncopations in the arabesque, or by the overlapping of tones. But here, too, the dynamism does not stem from nature but from the artist's imagination " echoing," as he once said, " on colour."*

Here the interplay of colour contrasts is admirably managed. When a dark tone touches a light one Dufy binds the latter with a rim that steps up its affective value. The way in which both by the drawing and the colours the figures are merged into the background brings to mind a tapestry—or, rather, an imaginary Space, a sort of fabulous infinite, in some respects not unlike that which Tiepolo invented for his skies.

THE RACECOURSE
1933

One afternoon in 1925 Bianchini took Dufy to the races so that he might judge how the materials they were turning out looked in the women's dresses. Dufy, however, spent his time gazing at the jockeys and horses. On his return to his studio he painted his first Racecourse. What he had seen had opened new horizons; here was a heaven-sent pretext for the most exciting fantasies, juxtapositions of the most audacious colours.

In such works as his racecourse scenes, his sea-pieces and his Jazz, Dufy's art makes us think of rippling laughter, the tinkle of wineglasses, sparkling waters, bouquets that the florist has not spoilt by formalizing. And though their dazzle is more than the eye can bear for very long, we always come back to them with undiminished pleasure.

RAOUL DUFY (1877).   THE RACECOURSE, 1933.   18½×14½″.   PRIVATE COLLECTION, PARIS.

RAOUL DUFY (1877). THE STUDIO, 1949. 18×21¾". LOUIS CARRÉ GALLERY, NEW YORK.

DUFY AND DECORATIVE ART

Between 1908 and 1911 Dufy gave a new direction to his art, in which he steadily reduced the part played by colour, the result being that those who had shown so much admiration for the brilliant effects of which he had the secret, were frankly disappointed. And his popularity underwent an eclipse.

It was now that he made the acquaintance of Poiret, the famous couturier, in collaboration with whom Dufy became keenly interested in printing textiles of all sorts, from the finest silk to the most sumptuous brocades. And now Dufy became the outstanding figure of a period famous in the history of decorative art. With Poiret he set up a small plant for printing fabrics in the Avenue de Clichy in Paris. They had very little capital, but boundless enthusiasm. " We were always dreaming," Poiret tells us, " of supremely gorgeous curtains and women's dresses decorated in the Botticelli style." The venture was a success, and the names of Poiret and Dufy were always coupled together. Dufy was amused to notice that the society ladies who, on opening days, scoffed at his pictures were wearing scarves and dresses designed by him.

Soon the big Bianchini textile company, with Poiret's consent, took Dufy on their staff, and now he had, instead of the makeshift plant with which he and Poiret had made do, all the best modern machinery at his disposal. The fabrics he designed were much sought after by the great Paris dressmakers, and for many years the influence of Dufy made itself strongly felt in textile production, not in France only but abroad as well.

THE STUDIO
1 9 4 9

Dufy has not confined himself to ' exteriors '; he has often given us glimpses of his studio, but always in a very characteristic manner. Thus in painting this interior he does not try to get its atmosphere or to inter- pret the sensations that the various objects in it give him. He treats these as an ensemble of elements building up a sort of ' show ' he is putting on, viewing them almost with the eye of a theatrical producer. Also, he plots out his interiors like an architect drawing up a plan.

Dufy was, as already said, friendly with several poets—Apollinaire, Fernand Fleuret, Vincent Muselli and Roger Allard—and illustrated their works with charming etchings and woodcuts. And it is in his interiors that Dufy shows best his affinities with a certain period of French poetry; a period when the poets aimed at an exquisite precision, whimsically old-fashioned and, above all, ' precious ' ; a bright façade of wit and daintiness and tiny thrills, making no pretensions to profundity.

THE RED VIOLIN
1 9 4 8

Of recent years Dufy has been engaged in a technical experiment as novel as it is audacious. Can it be that he, the champion of colour at its most diversified, has remembered how once the Fauves called in question the efficacy of colour by itself ? In any case he has now taken to using what he calls " tonal colour," and aims at devising harmonies in a single tone. Thus he directs his efforts to creating variations of pitch in the colour thus chosen, which is set off only by a few touches of white.

This must not be confused with monochrome painting (in which the rendering of depth is a sine qua non), nor with grisaille sketches in which chiaroscuro plays a leading part. It is always with the intention of conjuring up a new world in which his imagination can disport itself that Dufy sets out to discover a new syntax, a vocabulary, indeed an alphabet, and neologisms peculiar to himself. The fantasy with which the artist's emotion is enveloped might seem arbitrary, indeed uncalled for, were it not for the genuinely human impulse behind it, however superficial it appears.

Here Dufy seems to be toying with a discipline somewhat akin to that of plainsong; but there is something in the artist's touch which palliates its rigour, much as the beauty of a singer's voice will sometimes temper the severity of the Gregorian mode. It stands for a sort of melodious recitative, as against the Fauve polyphony.

RAOUL DUFY (1877). THE RED VIOLIN, 1948. 15×21". OWNED BY THE ARTIST.

Our study of Fauvism and the evolution of the outstanding figures of the movement would be incomplete if we left out of account the activities and achievements of a movement which had its rise round about 1905 in Germany. This movement, named " Die Brücke " (The Bridge), brought together artists who, though their aims were not wholly identical with those of the Fauves, endorsed their programme of rendering form by means of colour.

DIE BRÜCKE
(THE BRIDGE)

NEUE MÜNCHNER KÜNSTLERVEREINIGUNG
THE MUNICH "NEW ASSOCIATION OF ARTISTS"
BY
ARNOLD RÜDLINGER

1891-1911

Here follows a chronological summary of events which, taking place chiefly in Germany and Austria, are landmarks in the general history of modern art.

1891   **Paris.** Hodler's **Night** in the Champ-de-Mars. Hodler becomes a member of the Salon du Champ-de-Mars.

1892   **Berlin.** Founding of the group of artists known as the ' XI ' (L. v. Hoffmann, Leistikow, Liebermann, et al.). Munch shows 55 works in the exhibition of the Berlin Artists' Association. The pictures are sharply criticized by the majority of members and withdrawn after a week. Founding of the ' New Free Association of Artists.'
Munich. Founding of the ' Munich Secession ' (Stuck, Trübner, Uhde, et al.).

1893   **Berlin.** Exhibition of the pictures rejected for the Great Berlin Exhibition. Munch is a committee member and exhibits. At the reception on April 27, Kaiser Wilhelm II declares : '' With me open-air painters don't have an easy time of it ; I keep them under my thumb.'' Munch frequents the literary circle of Bierbaum, Meier-Graefe, Przybyszewski, Scheerbart, Strindberg, in the ' Black Pig ' Café.
Munich. First exhibition by the Munich Secession (Böcklin, Corot, Courbet, Liebermann, Millet, and others).

1894   **Berlin.** The first book on Munch appears : **The Work of Edvard Munch,** by Przybyszewsky, Meier-Graefe, Pastor and Servaes.

1895   **Berlin.** First issue of the periodical **Pan.** First editors are Bierbaum and Meier-Graefe, and the writers from the ' Black Pig ' are chief collaborators.
Paris. A. Clot prints Munch's first lithographs.

1896   **Berlin.** Hugo von Tschudi appointed Keeper of the National Gallery.
Munich. The periodical **Die Jugend** launched in January. Jawlensky and Kandinsky arrive from Russia.
Paris. S. Bing opens the ' Art Nouveau ' Gallery in the rue de Provence. Munch Exhibition at Bing's. Munch frequents the circle of Mallarmé and **Le Mercure de France.**

1897   **Munich.** Jawlensky and Kandinsky study under Anton Azbé. At the Seventh International Art Exhibition, Hodler receives the gold medal for **Night** and **Eurhythmy.**
Paris. Munch shows his **Frieze of Life** at Salon des Indépendants.
Vienna. Founding of the ' Secession,' with Gustav Klimt as chairman.

1898   **Berlin.** Max Liebermann admitted to the Academy. Opening of the Bruno and Paul Cassirer Gallery. Neo-Impressionist Exhibition in the Keller and Reiner Gallery, introduced by an article by Paul Signac : **Neo-Impressionism,** with original lithographs by Cross, Luce, Rysselberghe and Signac, in **Pan,** 1898.
Munich. Paul Klee studies at Knirr's. Emil Nolde enrols at the Friedrich Fehr Art School.
Vienna. First issue of the Secession periodical **Ver Sacrum** in January. First Secession exhibition is a great success. On November 12, opening of the second exhibition and dedication of the House of the Secession, built by Josef M. Olbrich.

1899   **Berlin.** Founding of the Berlin Secession, with Max Liebermann as chairman. First exhibition opens on May 20. Launching of the periodical **Die Insel.**
Dachau. Nolde studies under Adolf Hölzel. Hölzel has been in Dachau since 1888, Dill since 1894 ; A. Langhammer comes in 1900. Together they form the ' New Dachau ' group.
Darmstadt. Founding of the ' artist colony ' (Peter Behrens, Josef M. Olbrich, and others).
Munich. Formation of ' Die Scholle ' (Erler, Jank, Putz).
Paris. Nolde attends the Académie Julian.
Vienna. First issue of the periodical **Die Fackel,** edited by Karl Kraus.

1900   **Dresden.** Max Pechstein studies at the School of Applied Art.
Munich. Kandinsky, Klee and Marc enter the Academy ; no personal contact between them as yet. The ' Phalanx ' group of artists is formed.
Paris. Paula Modersohn studies at the Académie Colarossi. Much impressed by a showing of Cézanne's works at Vollard's ; meeting with Emil Nolde.
Weimar. Max Beckmann attends the Art School.
Zurich. Hodler paints the **Marignano Murals** in the Swiss National Museum.

1901   **Dresden.** Ernst Ludwig Kirchner studies architecture at the Technical Institute, does art work on the side.

1902   **Berlin.** Shown in the Secession Exhibition are 28 pictures by Munch (22 of them from the **Frieze of Life**), 3 pictures by Kandinsky and Hodler's **Tell.**
Dresden. Pechstein enters the Academy. Exhibition of Impressionists and Neo-Impressionists at Arnold Gallery.
Hagen. Folkwang Museum founded by Karl Ernst Osthaus.
Munich. Kandinsky opens an art school and becomes chairman of the ' Phalanx.'
Vienna. Klinger's **Beethoven** and murals by Klimt shown in the Secession Exhibition.
Weimar. Appointment of Henry Van de Veldes to the staff of the Art School.

1903   **Berlin.** Works by Bonnard, Cézanne, Gauguin, Van Gogh and Munch exhibited by the Secession. First issue of the periodical **Kunst und Künstler (Art and Artists),** published by Cassirer.
Munich. Kirchner studies two semesters (1903-1904) under Debschitz and Obrist.
Vienna. Secession Exhibition : **Impressionists and Neo-Impressionists** (including Seurat's **La Grande Jatte**). Founding of the **Wiener Werkstätte** (Vienna Workshop). **Kandinsky** travels to Tunis and Kairouan ; **Klee** begins his series of grotesque etchings ; **Marc** visits Paris for the first time.

1904 **Berlin.** Cézanne Exhibition at Cassirer's.
Dresden. Erich Heckel studies architecture at the Technical Institute. Meeting and collaboration with Kirchner and Bleyl. At the Museum of Ethnography Kirchner discovers the wood-carvings of the Palau islanders and negro art.
Düsseldorf. August Macke enters the School of Applied Art and the Academy.
Lübeck. Munch completes the second **Frieze of Life** for Linde.
Munich. Neo-Impressionist Exhibition of the ' Phalanx.' Cézanne, Gauguin and Van Gogh Exhibition at the Munich Art Association. Foundation and first exhibition of the **Deutscher Künstlerbund,** an alliance of artists and groups with modern tendencies.
Paris. Kandinsky exhibits at Salon d'Automne and at the Exposition Nationale des Beaux-Arts.
Vienna. Kokoschka studies in the School of Arts and Crafts. Hodler has great success in Vienna.

1905 **Berlin.** Nolde does his **Phantasien** etchings.
Dresden. Through Heckel, the architecture student Karl Schmidt-Rottluff meets Kirchner and Bleyl and begins collaboration with them. Formation of the group of artists known as ' **Die Brücke** ' (The Bridge). Van Gogh Exhibition at Arnold Gallery.
Vienna. The ' Stylists ' grouped around Klimt leave the Secession. **Jawlensky** paints in Brittany and Provence.

1906 **Berlin.** Sets by Munch used in Max Reinhardt's production of Ibsen's **Ghosts.** Munch paints the third **Frieze of Life** for the foyer of the Berlin Kammerspiele. With **Free Spirit** Nolde begins his series of grotesque and religious works.
Dresden. Nolde, Pechstein, and later Cuno Amiet and Axel Galén, become members of ' Die Brücke.' First ' Die Brücke ' album with original engravings comes out. In the autumn ' Die Brücke ' stages its first exhibition at Dresden-Löbtau ; in the winter, a second exhibition includes works of graphic art. Neo-Impressionist Exhibition at Arnold Gallery, including works by Seurat, Signac, Gauguin and Van Gogh.
Paris. Paula Modersohn much impressed by the Gauguin Memorial Exhibition at Salon d'Automne.

1907 **Berlin.** Cézanne, Matisse and Munch Exhibition at Cassirer Gallery.
Frankfort. Kandinsky Exhibition at Katharinenhof Gallery.
Dresden. ' Die Brücke ' Exhibition at Richter Gallery. Second album of ' Die Brücke ' comes out. Nolde leaves ' Die Brücke.'
Munich. Founding of the **Deutscher Werkbund** (German Applied Art Guild), October 5-6.
Worpswede. Death of Paula Modersohn.

1908 **Bremen.** Posthumous exhibition of Paula Modersohn's work at the Kunsthalle.
Dresden. Kees van Dongen becomes a member of ' Die Brücke.'
Jena. Hodler paints **Departure of the Jena Volunteers** for the university.
Copenhagen. Munch writes and prepares lithographs for his **Alpha and Omega.**
Vienna. Meeting of Kokoschka and Adolf Loos. Kokoschka's **The Dreaming Children,** poems and lithographs by himself, is issued by the Vienna Workshop. In the first Vienna Art Show, Kokoschka's work is violently attacked by public and critics alike, which leads to his expulsion from the School of Arts and Crafts. He paints the first Expressionist portraits **(Karl Kraus, The Trance Player). Pechstein** travels in Italy and France, stops in Paris.

1909 **Berlin.** Ludwig Justi appointed Keeper of the National Gallery.
Dresden. Third album of ' Die Brücke.'
Munich. Hugo von Tschudi appointed director of the Bavarian State Galleries. Founding of the ' New Association of Artists ' in January, by a group including Jawlensky, Kandinsky, Kubin, G. Münter, Werefkin. First exhibition in the Thannhauser Gallery, December-January, 1910. Van Gogh Exhibition at Brackl Gallery.
Vienna. Kokoschka's works and the performance of his stage-plays, **Sphinx and Straw Man** and **Woman's Hope,** excite new outbursts. Heckel travels in Italy. Munch works on his murals for the University of Oslo. **Nolde** paints his first great religious pictures : **The Last Supper** and **Pentecost.**

1910 **Berlin.** The jury of the Berlin Secession rejects the work of 27 artists, including Nolde's **Pentecost.** ' Exhibition of Artists Rejected by the Berlin Secession ' organized at Macht Gallery, resulting in the ' New Secession ' whose most significant members come from ' Die Brücke ' and from the ' New Association of Artists ' in Munich. The periodical **Der Sturm** launched on March 3. Kokoschka's first one-man show at Cassirer Gallery.
Dresden. Fourth album of ' Die Brücke ' appears. ' Die Brücke ' Exhibition at Arnold Gallery. Otto Müller becomes member of ' Die Brücke.' Gauguin Exhibition at Arnold Gallery.
Düsseldorf. First exhibition of the ' Sonderbund.'
Munich. Meeting of Macke and Marc on January 6. First exhibition of Kandinsky's abstract drawings and water-colours. Kandinsky writes **The Art of Spiritual Harmony** (published in 1911). Second exhibition of the New Association of Artists in September, with participation of Braque, Derain, Le Fauconnier, Picasso, Rouault, Van Dongen, Vlaminck and other guest artists. Girieud and Le Fauconnier became members of the group.

1911 The painter Carl Vinnen publishes **A Protest by German Artists** (against the excessive importation of French art wares). The counterblast—**The Struggle for Art : Reply to the Protest by German Artists**—contains contributions by Amiet, Beckmann, Cassirer, Corinth, Flechtheim, Kandinsky, Klimt, Liebermann, Macke, Marc, Osthaus, Pascin, Pechstein, Wilhelm Uhde and others. (Munich, Piper Verlag.)
Berlin. Heckel, Kirchner and Schmidt-Rottluff move from Dresden to Berlin. Expelled from the Secession, Nolde travels in Belgium and Holland, where he meets Ensor. The periodical **Die Aktion** is launched in February.
Munich. Meeting of Kandinsky, Klee, Macke and Marc. Marc joins the New Association of Artists. Following a clash of opinion in the selection of works for the third exhibition, Kandinsky, Kubin, Marc and Gabriele Münter leave the group. On December 13 Kandinsky and Marc open the first ' Blaue Reiter ' Exhibition at the Thannhauser Gallery, with works by Burljuk, Delaunay, Kandinsky, Macke, Marc, Münter, Henri Rousseau, Arnold Schönberg, and others. Kandinsky and Marc work on the book **Der Blaue Reiter** (The Blue Rider), published in 1912 by Piper, in Munich.

P. MODERSOHN-BECKER (1876-
1907). PORTRAIT OF THE PAINTER,
1906. 24×19¾". ÖFFENTLICHE
KUNSTSAMMLUNG, BASEL.

MODERSOHN

"My paintings here look dark and treacly. I must aim at a much purer colour. I must work and work, and then perhaps I shall become something." Thus Paula Modersohn wrote from Paris on March 19, 1906. In a letter of May, 1906, to her sister she says : " I *am* becoming something— I am living the most intensely happy time of my life." Between the two dates, between the " perhaps I shall become something " and the jubilant " I *am* becoming something," lay the meeting with the sculptor Hœtger, who recognized the importance of Paula Modersohn's work and gave her the encouragement she needed to believe in herself.

Born in Dresden in 1876, Paula Becker spent her youth partly in Dresden, partly in Bremen. After passing a schoolteachers' examination, she obtained her parents' permission to study art. At twenty she entered an art school in Berlin. In the summer of 1897 she met some members of the Worpswede artists' colony, the leading figure of which was the painter Mackensen. After a second winter semester in Berlin, Paula Becker settled in Worpswede in the autumn of 1898 and started taking lessons with Mackensen. Here began her friendship with Clara Westhoff, who later became the wife of Rainer Maria Rilke. In 1901 she married the Worpswede painter Otto Modersohn.

The naturalistic genre painting cultivated by her circle of friends, set off with decorative elements from ' Jugendstil,' could not satisfy her for long. In 1902 she wrote in her Journal : " The manner in which Mackensen paints people is not big enough for me, there is too much ' genre ' about it. To be brought off, it should be writ large, in runic characters." Her lett- ers and journals mirror a lofty, forceful personality. In them, however, painting is hardly ever mentioned and few of her works can be identified with any of the entries. She writes much that is general and human, and tries to describe what she is aiming at, but not what she is doing or has already done. There is lacking that precision of statement which makes Van Gogh's letters the basis for a catalogue of his works, and furnishes a revealing commentary on his artistic development. With Paula Modersohn, it is far less a matter of any particular work than of her painting as a whole, of the clarification and realization of her creative vision, which, after 1900, was ever taking clearer and clearer form. In depicting the human figures she found around her, she tried to express the most elemental of human moods and feelings ; she shared this striving with Van Gogh, Gauguin, Munch, without knowing them. A comparison with the work of these three giants brings out the substance and character of her art. She was a woman and dispensed with the Messianic ardour of Van Gogh. Her instinct never failed her and she had no need to make adventurous journeys to distant islands to discover the underlying truths of human emotion. Simple, strong, naïve, she herself experienced all the basic human feelings, untouched by the sophistications of city life.

Her intuition was stimulated by the lonely grandeur of the Worpswede moorland, and by her friendly relations with the lean, gawky peasant children and the old people at the poorhouse. The peace and innocence of such subjects ensured the simplicity and grandeur of the painting. Paula Modersohn often went to Paris, to harvest new impressions and relax her mind. She attended the Académie Colarossi and the anatomy courses at the Ecole des

THIS NUDE STUDY OF A GIRL IS ONE OF PAULA MODERSOHN'S MATUREST AND MOST COLOURFUL CREATIONS. AS IN THE *OLD WOMAN WITH A BOTTLE*, GAUGUIN'S LIBERATING INFLUENCES ARE HERE PERCEPTIBLE.

P. MODERSOHN-BECKER (1876-1907). NUDE STUDY OF A GIRL WITH FLOWERS, 1907. 35½×43¼".
VON DER HEYDT LOAN, WUPPERTAL.

Beaux-Arts. It speaks for her lack of false self-esteem that as late as 1906, during her last visit to Paris and after she had painted several of her best pictures, she still attended courses in anatomy and drawing from plaster casts. She visited the galleries and jotted down pertinent comments on Courbet, Manet, Renoir, Bonnard and Vuillard—remaining all the while herself. Instinct and her amazing independence always enabled her to absorb just what was needed for the development of her own insight. In Cézanne she recognized the greatest of modern masters, and yet his direct influence is perceptible in only a few still lifes, at most. She admired in him the creator of a new order in painting and revered his absolute devotion to his art. Gauguin, temperamentally so remote from her, helped her more in externals. The Gauguin Memorial Exhibition in the Salon d'Automne confirmed and clarified her own method of composition : by surface arrangement and form at its most expressive. The most valuable thing she got from Gauguin was the courage to use colour—a godsend to her—paving the way to the big portraits and compositions upon which her fame is founded.

One year of intensely creative work, heightened by the sense of coming motherhood, was yet granted her. Hardly three weeks after the birth of her daughter, when she got up from bed for the first time and was sitting with those dear to her, a heart-attack ended her life. "What a pity !" were her last words. Her death inspired Rainer Maria Rilke to write his *Requiem for a Friend*.

DIE BRÜCKE

After taking his degree at Chemnitz, in 1901, Ernst Ludwig Kirchner pursued his studies at the Technical College, Dresden. In 1904 young Erich Heckel came to study at Dresden, followed in 1905 by his friend Karl Schmidt (who came from Rottluff). All three took a course in architecture, but this was no more than a pretext for getting regular allowances from their families ; their true interest lay in painting, and this common bond ensured a firm friendship between them. In 1905, with Fritz Bleyl, they founded the group known as *Die Brücke* (the Bridge). In 1906 the Swiss artist Cuno Amiet and the Frisian Emil Nolde exhibited at the Arnold Gallery at Dresden, and, seeing in them kindred spirits with like ideals, the Die Brücke artists invited them to join their group. In the same year they had two new recruits : Max Pechstein and the Finn, Axel Galén. In 1908, Van Dongen, regarded at Paris as an *avant-garde* artist, was likewise invited to membership of the group, with which he professed himself in sympathy. The last painter to join was Otto Müller ; this was in 1910, shortly before the move to Berlin. Nolde had fallen out in 1907, Bleyl in 1909 ; Pechstein was excluded from the group in 1912. When Kirchner proposed in 1913 to publish a *Chronik KG (Künstlergruppe) Brücke*, his colleagues refused to co-operate. This led to the final break-up of the group, whose members in any case, having followed different trends of evolution both as to art and their general outlook on life, had been steadily drifting apart.

Art in Germany, as in other European countries, had been working out its problems in its own way. There were occasional contacts with French art ; Leibl, for instance, was influenced by Courbet, and Liebermann took up Impressionism. But, apart from such rare exceptions, German art had followed, with the ' Nazarites ' and the Romantics, with Schwind, Böcklin and Marées, a curious course, distinctively its own.

Now, however, the Die Brücke artists were led to apply their minds to the same problems as the Fauves in France, and from a similar angle, with the result that thus they gave the evolution of French art the magnitude of a European movement. In the North, Munch had already come into contact with France ; while Amiet, who had studied with the

Pont-Aven school, had done the same for Switzerland. And such foreign artists did not merely benefit themselves by rubbing shoulders with their French contemporaries ; they also contributed something of their own to the international development of art. If we would form a just estimate of the truly ' revolutionary ' nature of the action of the Die Brücke group, we must remember that at the beginning of the century Liebermann was only just beginning to gain support for his impressionist handling of tones, and that painting in Germany had never had such pioneers as Seurat, Gauguin and Van Gogh.

Some art-lovers and writers who thought and felt on European lines helped to pave the way for these German artists. Thus *Pan*, a review edited by Otto Julius Bierbaum and Meier-Graefe from 1895 to 1900, reproduced woodcuts by Vallotton, Beardsley drawings, etchings by Munch and lithographs by Toulouse-Lautrec. Another review, *Die Insel*, published in Berlin by Alfred Walter Heymel, Rudolf Alexander Schröder and Otto Julius Bierbaum, reproduced works by the same artists, and in 1902 gathered together in an art-book original colour lithographs by Bonnard, Vuillard and Denis. In 1898 Kirchner had already lit on the single-copy woodcuts of the XVth Century, and the cuts by Beham and Dürer. In 1904, he visited a Neo-Impressionist Exhibition at Munich where he saw works by Seurat, Signac and Luce. At the Zwinger Museum of Ethnology at Dresden, in the same year, he ' discovered ' negro art and the art of the Palau Islands. Also he copied the illustrations in a book on Indian mural painting. In fact the young men of the Brücke group were almost bewildered by the host of new impulses and impressions, often rich in suggestion, crowding in upon them. Working in common, they discussed these, tested them, and put them into practice, when they proved their worth. Their activities now ranged over almost every form and technique of creative art : painting, woodcuts, lithography, etching, wood-carving, printing on textiles. The result was that in 1907, after two years of feverish experiments, there emerged the first style of Die Brücke, showing a remarkable similarity of outlook, technique and graphic methods between all these artists. They had discovered the possibilities of pure colours, and they let these flow freely at the bidding of their creative emotion. The theme presented was handled in broad surfaces, bounded by contour-lines moving in lively rhythms. Rejoicing in his liberation from any sort of representational service, the artist set up against the object his personal constructive will. The mild, 'bourgeois' romanticism that had lingered on from the last century was dust before the wind of this new freedom ; instead of looking for ' soulful ' subjects, the painters fixed on scenes of everyday life, culled from the cafés, the music-hall, the circus, the studio, the countryside or the streets. Freed from the static chiaroscuro of the studio, their mistresses posed in the open countryside. It was their enthusiasm that gave the group the driving force and self-confidence that led them to build " bridges " giving young talents access to the new painting. Thus in the letter of invitation sent to Nolde we find : " One of the aims of Die Brücke is, as its name implies, to conduct towards it all the revolutionary elements now in gestation."

The social problems of the day were for them not merely a source of inspiration ; they lay at the heart of the problem, at once practical and human, whose solution these artists sought for and found in their collective manner. Working in cheerful *camaraderie*, they did away with narrow individualism, sharing their studios, models and mistresses. Their physical privations and their passion for art combined to make them scorn all bourgeois morals and conventions and replace these by a rebelliously Bohemian way of living.

After the group moved to Berlin, the bond between them slackened ; it is also possible that they came under Otto Müller's influence. Their lively contours, the free, impulsive handling of surfaces, brilliant colour, all the first fine rapture of their contacts with nature, died away. The restless atmosphere of a great capital city worked on the nerves of Kirchner and Heckel. " Gothic " pointed forms and fan-shaped patterns were now worked into a complicated lay-out of the painted surface. Dark, livid, or broken lines invaded the composition, to which reckless discords added a wanton stridency. Rifts began to show, and gradually, its unity shattered by the tension of their nerves and senses, the group broke up, each artist going his own way.

E. L. KIRCHNER (1880-1938). THE STREET, 1907. 58¼×78¾″. KIRCHNER ESTATE, BASEL.

THIS STREET SCENE ILLUSTRATES THE FIRST ' DIE BRÜCKE ' STYLE. ITS FLOWING OUTLINES JUSTIFY US IN LINKING UP THIS PICTURE WITH 1900 ' JUGENDSTIL '; THE FRONTAL VIEW AND THE DISTRIBUTION OF THE FIGURES INDICATE A PENCHANT FOR BUILDING IN PLANES, RHYTHMICAL LAY-OUT, AND PURE COLOURS.

KIRCHNER

It is hard to distinguish, and precisely to delimit, the characteristics of the various artists who took part in creating the first style of ' Die Brücke.' During this period (1905-1913) Heckel, Kirchner, Pechstein and Schmidt-Rottluff worked in such close co-operation that we cannot draw any clean-cut lines of demarcation. Kirchner tells us in his *Chronik* that he was the pioneer in respect of woodcuts, while the group as a whole studied lithography with Schmidt-Rottluff, and etching with Nolde. When we compare the output of these men, we are forced to recognize that Kirchner's personality was at once the most sensitive, most vigorous and most amenable to transformations. To make good his status, dominant from the outset, he had no need to resort to any artifice or mannerism. The fact that in later life he wilfully antedated some early works he had in his possession (from a wish to make it appear that they synchronized with Fauve art, and to establish his priority as regards his friends) can be attributed only to a foolish vanity.

Kirchner had a never-failing interest in all the aspects of the visible world. Rembrandt's example had taught him to draw, above all, from nature and to record the fleeting moment with a few distinctive strokes, based on a personal system of abridgements. His method of ' transposition ' (for which he was always inventing new hieroglyphics, and which he never allowed to stiffen into a ' manner ') is illustrated most clearly by his engraved work, which comprises nearly two thousand woodcuts, lithographs and etchings. This, not only for its copiousness, but for its artistic value, is the most noteworthy contribution in this field of art that the XXth Century has given us.

After the break-up of ' Die Brücke ' Kirchner went on working at Berlin without joining any group. Active service in the 1914 War left him with a nervous breakdown attended by partial paralysis and necessitating stays at sanatoria in the Taunus, by the Lake of Constance and at Davos, where in 1917 he settled down. He found life amongst the peasantfolk and the Alpine scenery to his liking, and treated these subjects with his customary verve during the years that followed. Beginning in 1926, he applied himself to the problem, already tackled by Picasso and the Cubists, of expressing simultaneously the various aspects of an object as seen from different angles, putting his theories into practice in a series of woodcuts, and the pictures named *The Lovers, Colour Dance, The Trotters.* In 1929 Kirchner was commissioned to do the murals for the concert-hall of the Folkwang Museum at Essen. But the government of the Third Reich put a stop to this. The combined effect of his distress at the turn political affairs were taking in Germany, and at the discovery that the path he had been following since 1926 was unsuited to his natural gifts, had disastrous effects on Kirchner's morale. To make things worse, he now fell victim to an incurable intestinal disease. And thus at last he decided that suicide was the only way out.

KIRCHNER'S GRAPHIC ART HAD MUCH INFLUENCE ON PAINTING. THE TRANSPOSITION OF THREE-DIMENSIONAL FORMS INTO PLANES AND THE RESTRICTION OF COLOUR TO A FEW LOCAL APPLICATIONS ARE BORROWED FROM THE TECHNIQUE OF THE COLOUR WOODCUT. THE CHARACTERISTICS OF WOODCUT ART ARE PARTICULARLY EVIDENT IN THE DRAWING OF THE HEAD, AND IN THE JAGGED, ANGULAR LINES BINDING THE COLOUR SURFACES.

E. L. KIRCHNER (1880-1938). WOMAN ON A BLUE DIVAN, 1907. 31½×35½".
KIRCHNER ESTATE, BASEL.

K. SCHMIDT-ROTTLUFF (1884). LOFTHUS, 1911. 34½×37½". HAMBURG, KUNSTHALLE.

SCHMIDT-ROTTLUFF SPENT THE SUMMER OF 1911 IN NORWAY. THE SOFTLY FLUENT OUTLINE OF THE COLOUR SURFACES AND THE STRONG CONTRASTS OF LIGHT AND SHADE BRING SCHMIDT-ROTTLUFF, IN THIS PICTURE, MORE INTO LINE WITH NOLDE THAN WITH 'DIE BRÜCKE.'

SCHMIDT-ROTTLUFF

Karl Schmidt, who like Heckel and Pechstein hailed from Saxony, was born at Rottluff, near Chemnitz. Robuster than Kirchner and Heckel, he was not, like them, rudely shaken by the war and its disasters. He it was who acted as the bridge ('*Die Brücke*') enabling the Dresden group to enlist Nolde in their ranks. Schmidt-Rottluff stood midway between his friends Heckel and Kirchner, highly strung city-dwellers, and that taciturn, rather stolid countryman Nolde, whose acquaintance he had made in 1906 at Alsen. When *Die Brücke* entered on its active phase, Schmidt-Rottluff's ruling interest was in landscape, especially the lonely desolation of the seaboard and the dunes. His feeling for the grandiose side of nature is evident in his monumental treatment of his subjects, in which the line, now fluctuating, now concise, demarcates within smoothly rolling contours contrasting surfaces of pure colour, whose undulations remind us of the lava-fields round a volcano.

Schmidt-Rottluff, who had acquainted his friends with the technique of lithography, devoted himself almost exclusively, after 1910, to woodcuts. The angularity of his line, which looks as if it had been hacked out inch by inch with a hatchet, also determined the new, very personal handling of forms we find in his painting.

MUNICH 1900-1911

January 1896 witnessed the publication by Georg Hirth of the first issue of that famous magazine *Die Jugend* (Youth), to which the best writers and black-and-white artists in Germany contributed. By reason of its lay-out and the tendencies for which it stood, it gave its name to an art movement roughly corresponding to that of the 'Nineties' in England which found its figurehead in the art of Beardsley. In Vienna this movement was sponsored by the leaders of the 'Secession'—Klimt, Wagner and Hoffmann ; hence its name 'Secession Style.' But it is at Barcelona that we find what is perhaps the most impressive manifestation of this movement : in Antonio Gaudis' *Holy Family Cathedral*. The term 'Jugendstil,' deriving from the name of the Munich magazine, has entered into the vocabulary of the German-speaking countries, while the French refer to it, always with a touch of irony, as *l'Art Nouveau*. Munich, Vienna and Barcelona were the headquarters of the movement. The scant esteem subsequently accorded to *l'Art Nouveau* does less than justice to its historical importance. True, we must admit that it failed to solve the host of problems which art was facing at the dawn of the new century, the reason being that it all too soon lost its way in tangles of lush ornamentation. Still, it stands to the credit of this movement that, in Germany, it laid low the barriers of tradition and opened the path for new developments in art. Also, its indirect influence and its intercourse with the European art of 1900 went farther than is usually admitted. Those flexible, flowing outlines characteristic of 'Jugendstil' are to be found not only in Munch's and Hodler's work, but also in Gauguin's and Vallotton's woodcuts, in Toulouse-Lautrec's posters and in some Fauve pictures.

The outstanding exponents of Jugendstil in German painting were Stuck, the Munich group 'Die Scholle,' and (at Vienna) Klimt. It was in the ambiance of 'Die Scholle' that Kandinsky, who came to Munich in 1896, produced his early works. After studying under Stuck and Azbe, Kandinsky opened in 1902 his own art school ; in the same year he founded with other painters 'Die Phalanx,' whose president he subsequently became. This group organized in 1904 a large-scale Neo-Impressionist Exhibition, at which Seurat, Luce and Signac were represented by numerous works ; it was almost certainly under their influence that Kandinsky took to using pure colour straight from the tube. At first he employed it in quaint anecdotal compositions, in which his memories of Russian folklore and of popular art played a leading part. Only very slowly did he eliminate the elements of descriptive *Art Nouveau*, giving even freer play to colour, reaching indeed a point where objects were submerged by it. During the period when his first 'improvisations' were taking form, and Kandinsky was soon to implement his leanings towards abstract art, the 'New Association of Munich Artists' was founded by Adolf Erbslöh, Alexei von Jawlensky, Wassily Kandinsky, Alexander Kanoldt, Alfred Kubin, Gabriele Münter, Marianna von Werefkin, Heinrich Schnabel and Oskar Wittenstein. Amongst its members were Vladimir von Bechtejeff, Erma Bossi, Moissei Kogan, Alexander Sacharoff (1909), Pierre Girieud, Le Fauconnier (1910), Franz Marc, Otto Fischer (1911) and Alexander Mogilewsky (1912). Also Karl Hofer and Paul Baum belonged to the Association for a while. It invited the following painters to figure in its exhibitions : Braque, Derain, Van Dongen, Picasso, Rouault, Vlaminck ; also the sculptors Haller and Hoetger.

The 'New Association' had no cut-and-dry programme, no special bias ; it merely proposed to band together all the younger men who were striking out new directions in creative art.

But, in December 1911, differences regarding a jury led to a break ; Kandinsky, Kubin, Marc and Gabriele Münter withdrew, and, on December 18, 1911, organized the first exhibition held under the auspices of *Der Blaue Reiter*.

W. KANDINSKY (1866-1944). LANDSCAPE WITH HOUSES, 1909. 30×39".
DÜSSELDORF, STÄDTISCHE KUNSTSAMMLUNG.

THIS PAINTING BELONGS TO THE SERIES OF LANDSCAPES DONE AT MURNAU, NEAR MUNICH. IT MARKS THE CLOSING PHASE OF
KANDINSKY'S OBJECTIVE WORK. HERE COLOUR ALREADY LEADS AN INDEPENDENT LIFE, EMANCIPATED FROM THE SUBJECT.

KANDINSKY and JAWLENSKY

Wassily Kandinsky was born in 1866, in Moscow. He studied political economy,
law, statistics and, as a promising young scientist, took part in an expedition to north-
eastern Russia, his reports on which won for him high esteem in scientific circles. However,
in 1896, having decided to make painting his life's work, he threw up science, and settled
down at Munich. Even in his student days Kandinsky showed no readiness to pin his faith
to the doctrines of the Academy. Against the ideals of western academic painting he set up
a personal way of viewing the world, conditioned by memories of his childhood and what he had
seen of Russian folk-art. For Kandinsky the *ne plus ultra* was colour, colour immanent with
shimmering vitality. And thanks to his Russian temperament he felt at ease in an atmosphere of chaos and intimations of infinity ; thus plastic form meant nothing to him and it
was natural enough that, in later years, when trying to defend his art against the perils of
anarchy, he found the only solution in a resort to geometrically rigid forms. He attached
little importance to that beauty of form, as the West conceives it, whose volumes and
proportions are always found, in the last analysis, to derive from aspects of nature.

After beginning with illustrations of the folkore type, and after seeking vainly to find
himself by way of travel in Tunisia, Holland and Italy, and visits to Paris, he at last, in 1908,
saw daylight. And, now he had found his path, a rapid evolution brought him within
three years to non-representational painting. During this period Kandinsky was the moving
spirit of the Munich ' New Association of Artists,' from which stemmed *Der Blaue Reiter*.

Alexei von Jawlensky, who was born in 1864, in the Tver Province of Central Russia, on the ancestral estate, went, in 1896, the same year as Kandinsky, to Munich, and Anton Azbe was his first teacher. In the course of his travels Jawlensky saw canvases by Cézanne and Van Gogh. But it was Matisse, whom he knew personally, who made the deepest impression on him. Unlike Kandinsky, Jawlensky succumbed gladly to the influence of modern French painting. From Matisse he took over his use of unmixed colour and his composition by broad contrasting planes, though not the French artist's mobility of forms. At one time the emotional drive of Kandinsky and Marc—during the *Blaue Reiter* period—roused in him tendencies towards the monumental, and he now created that series of large heads which have a curious affinity with Nolde's religious works. The 1914 war obliged him to leave his friends and take refuge in Switzerland, where he stayed first at St. Prex (on the Lake of Geneva), and later in the canton of Ticino. The solitude which was his lot in Switzerland worked a great change in him, and his later art is strongly imbued with mysticism.

PAINTED IN THE SAME YEAR AS KANDINSKY'S MUNICH LANDSCAPE, THIS PORTRAIT SHOWS JAWLENSKY'S CLOSER RELATION WITH
HIS SUBJECT. THE FACE IS MODELLED, WHILE THE REST OF THE PICTURE IS BUILT UP WITH FLAT SURFACES.

A. VON JAWLENSKY (1864-1941). WOMAN WITH FLOWERS, 1909. 40½×30".
WUPPERTAL, KUNST- UND MUSEUMSVEREIN.

Paula Modersohn, the " Die Brücke " group, Kandinsky and Jawlensky (the last-named as members of the Munich " Neue Künstlervereinigung," or New Association of Artists) figure in this volume between the Fauves and the Expressionists properly so called. Their productions of the period 1906-1911 form so to speak a German parallel, though with a time-lag, to the works of the Fauves. We shall meet Kandinsky and Jawlensky again in our third volume, amongst the leaders of the " Blaue Reiter " (Blue Rider) group, which included the artists who were the first in Germany to solve, in their own manner, the problems of Cubism and Abstract Art.

In the pages devoted to Expressionism which follow, we deal with the painters who in different countries went furthest on the way of " Suggestive Expression," in other words those who focussed their attention not on art itself and stylistic problems, but on Man, his anxieties and his revolt.

Not all these artists belong to the same generation. Munch and Ensor, for example, whose activities in the nineteenth century led us to mention them in our first volume will be found here in their more natural setting, in which the emphasis is laid on the expressionist rather than the symbolist aspect of their art. These artists never belonged to any definite group ; they are great lonely figures whose influences nevertheless combined to leave an indelible imprint on the art of the twentieth century.

EXPRESSIONISM

IN

NORWAY - SWITZERLAND - BELGIUM - GERMANY - THE UNITED STATES

MUNCH - HODLER - ENSOR

NOLDE - KOKOSCHKA - WEBER

BY

ARNOLD RÜDLINGER

Director of the Kunsthalle - Bern

EXPRESSIONISM

IN FRANCE

ROUAULT - SOUTINE

BY

JACQUES LASSAIGNE

1886-1917

The summary which follows will enable the reader to trace the course of Expressionism from its outset, and to follow the evolution of its leading painters.

1886 Munch joins the " The Bohemians of Christiania," a group whose central figure is the poet Hans Jäger, and whose general outlook and rebellious attitude towards society and its sexual problems shape the future trend of Munch's work (first important paintings).

1888 In his **Entrance of Christ into Brussels** James Ensor creates his masterpiece.

1890 Munch visits Paris, where he sees works by Pissarro, Seurat, Lautrec, and, at Theo Van Gogh's gallery, Gauguin and Vincent Van Gogh.

1891 Rouault enrols at the Ecole des Beaux-Arts in Elie Delaunay's class.
Gustave Moreau succeeds Delaunay.
Retrospective Van Gogh Exhibition at Salon des Indépendants.
Hodler exhibits **Night** at the Champ-de-Mars.

1892 Rouault wins the prize in Moreau's class, with a series of religious subjects.
Munch sends 55 pictures to the exhibition of the Berlin Artists' Association; all are rejected.

1893 Rouault paints **Samson tournant sa meule**: his first important work.

1894 Munch's first engravings.

1895 The Magazine **Pan** is launched, and comes quickly to the forefront of art periodicals published in this period Illustrated matter contributed by Munch, Lautrec, Vallotton, Signac.
After Rouault's failure to get the Prix de Rome, Moreau advises him to leave the Ecole.
Rouault exhibits at Salon des Artistes Français.

1896 Munch's first woodcuts.
S. Bing opens the ' Art Nouveau ' Gallery in the rue de Provence. Munch Exhibition.

1897 Rouault paints a series of imaginative landscapes, embellished with sacred and profane scenes. Among them is **Le Chantier,** in which Rouault shows for the first time his interest in social problems. Munch's **Frieze of Life** is exhibited at Salon des Indépendants.

1898 Death of Gustave Moreau. Rouault becomes curator of the Moreau Museum.

1899 Nolde enrols at the Académie Julian.
A special issue of the Belgian review **La Plume** is devoted to James Ensor.

1902 Rouault takes part in the meetings preparatory to the foundation of the Salon d'Automne.

1903 Rouault's experimental period ends. New subjects appear in his work.

1904 At Salon d'Automne Rouault exhibits 3 paintings, and 82 watercolours and pastels (clowns, circus folk, acrobats, etc.). Rouault's extremely dark tones are severely criticized.

1905 Max Weber comes to Paris.

1907 Kokoschka: first pictures and expressionist plays. **Die Träumenden Knaben** (The Dreaming Children), poems with illustrations by himself, brought out by the Wiener Werkstätte. At the first Vienna 'Kunstschau' Kokoschka's works are violently attacked by critics and public alike; which soon leads to his expulsion from the School of Arts and Crafts.

1909 Nolde paints his first great religious pictures: **The Last Supper** and **Pentecost.**

1910 Big Rouault Exhibition at Druet's: 121 pictures. 54 original ceramics at A. Méthey's.
Kokoschka visits Berlin. Meets Cassirer, who organizes his first one-man show. Introduced by Adolf Loos to the **Der Sturm** group. He is soon one of the chief contributors to the periodical. Kokoschka does the portraits of Herwarth Walden and the **Sturm** poets, in which psychological and expressive aspects are strongly emphasized.

1911 Nolde travels in Belgium and Holland. Greatly impressed by Van Gogh's pictures. Meeting with James Ensor. Soutine comes to Paris.

1912 Nolde: period of intense creative activity. His cycle of pictures on **The Life of Christ,** first shown at the Folkwang Museum in Hagen, is withdrawn from the Exhibition of Religious Works at the Brussels World's Fair upon the protest of the Catholic authorities.
Berlin: at the " Sturm" Gallery, H. Walden puts on Kokoschka's second one-man show, concurrently with the first Berlin exhibition of the " Blaue Reiter."

1916 Ambroise Vollard becomes Rouault's sole agent and advises him to concentrate on illustration.

1917 From 1917 to 1927, Rouault devotes himself to engraving. It was during this period that he did his masterly series of etchings, **Le Miserere.**

EXPRESSIONISM

In contrast to the notion of Impressionism, which to-day has become a well-defined conception of art applicable to a limited number of artists, the term Expressionism still applies to various artists and tendencies widely differing in character. Herwarth Walden, the editor of *Der Sturm* in Berlin, used the word to cover nearly all the revolutionary manifestations in art that took place between the years 1910 and 1920. Most German writers on art follow this practice.

What Expressionism is, may best be understood if we realize at the outset that the problems it dealt with are pre-eminently human, rather than aesthetic or academic. Thus any attempt at finding a common ' manner ' in a movement hardly less diversified in its manifestations than are men's minds and mores, can serve but little purpose. The artists called Expressionists are far less concerned with art as such, than with themselves and their fellow-men, as seen in a definite psychological predicament. And there is a world of difference between them and those who, following Cézanne and Seurat, seek for an object-ive intuitive perception of the outside world and new ways of rendering it.

Rouault, Nolde, Kokoschka and Soutine had little contact with one another. They formed no group, as did the Impressionists, the Fauves, and the Cubists. All that, in the last analysis, they seem to have in common is a fervent emotional sympathy with their subject, carried even to self-effacement and identification with it. The picture, be it landscape, still life, or portrait, becomes a mirror of the painter's psychic stimulus and his response to an emotion intensely felt. Hence the directness of the artist's personal expressive imprint, which stands for no aesthetic precepts, no rigid laws of composition, no technical premeditation. Expression is everything.

Expressionistic art arises in all ages when purely pictorial problems have given way to those of the psyche and the inward life. The evolution of art in Europe has always shown expressionist tendencies in times of great psychological tension.

Gauguin, Van Gogh, Toulouse-Lautrec, Ensor, Munch and Hodler were, between 1885 and 1900, the harbingers of an expressionist revolt against Impressionism and the objective outlook of Cézanne and Seurat. Hodler, Munch and Ensor took part not only in the express-ionist reaction at the end of the XIXth Century ; they were also active in the second, more decisive outbreak which began with Rouault round about 1905. Picasso took part in it during his ' blue period ' and his ' negro period,' and in some of his pictures Matisse showed similar tendencies. Towards 1910 the movement was taken up enthusiastically in the German-speaking countries by Nolde, Kokoschka and Kirchner ; and, a little later, in Paris, by Soutine. Thus what we may call Expressionist Cubism, an attempt to amal-gamate expressive with constructive elements, emotion with geometry, was, between 1910 and 1923, one of the forms of art most characteristic of the trend of European painting during the period.

Of the essence of Expressionism is its predilection for black-and-white. Daumier, Gauguin, Toulouse-Lautrec, Ensor and Rouault were the pioneers of modern graphic art. In the work of Munch, Kirchner and Nolde, the drawings, woodcuts and etchings rank on at least an equal footing with the paintings, the former often surpassing the latter in pregnancy and expressive power. Black and white furnish dramatic means of expression, compelling concentration, reduction and transliteration. Wood-engraving in particular, as a coming to grips with stubborn material, is a great test of the imagination's power to recast and reform. It was not due to mere chance that this art was taken up in the 1890's by Vallotton, Gauguin and Munch, and given a new lease of life. And Japanese prints, which had already influenced the impressionist painters, now acquired a new significance for Western European artists.

EDVARD MUNCH (1863-1944). KARL JOHANS GATE, 1892. 33½×48½". RASMUS MEYER COLLECTION, BERGEN.

LIKE IBSEN IN HIS PLAYS, MUNCH UNMASKS THE NORWEGIAN MIDDLE-CLASS, STRESSING ITS SUPINENESS AND FEAR OF LIFE.

EDVARD MUNCH

No more painting of interiors with women knitting and men reading! I want to show men who breathe, feel, love and suffer. I want to bring home to the spectator the sacred element in these things, so that he takes his hat off just as he would in church."
Written at Saint-Cloud in 1889, this entry in Munch's journal has the same ring as the letters of Van Gogh, who set forth the aim of his painting in like terms. Ten years later Paula Modersohn was to voice similar views. They reveal a passionate striving towards the essential man—the focal point about which expressionist painting turned and developed.

Like Hodler's, Munch's early years were darkened by the presence of death. At the age of five, Hodler lost his father, at fourteen his mother; during his youth, nearly all his brothers and sisters died of consumption. The same disease carried off Munch's mother when he was only five years old, and his sister Sophie when he was thirteen. Hodler reacted to death with a tenacious will to live, allowing access to fear only in his dreams—witness the picture *Night*. Whereas Munch's waking life, all his thoughts and feelings, were overshadowed by the constant fear of death. *The Sick Girl, Death-Chamber, The Dead Mother, Death and Woman, Murder, Death of Marat*—these are the themes that haunted Munch throughout his life, and continually forced their way into expression in his art.

Sickness and death obsessed him. He would have nothing to do with sport in any form, lest he should get his feet wet. He took immense care to ensure that the room temperature was kept between 60 and 70 degrees. Told he was not looking too well, he would promptly take to his bed. In his old age he could not bear the sight of sick or ageing people. He

THE LITHOGRAPH OF THIS SAME SUBJECT BEARS AN INSCRIPTION WRITTEN IN MUNCH'S OWN HAND: "ICH HÖRE DAS GESCHREI
DER NATUR" (I HEAR THE SCREAM OF NATURE). WHAT WE ARE SHOWN HERE IS THE EFFECT OF ALMOST CRAZY PANIC A TERRIFYING
LANDSCAPE CAN PRODUCE ON A HIGHLY STRUNG MAN.

EDVARD MUNCH (1863-1944). THE SCREAM, 1893. 35¾ × 28¾". NATIONAL GALLERY, OSLO.

EDVARD MUNCH (1863-1944). THE DEATH CHAMBER, 1892. 59×65¾". NATIONAL GALLERY, OSLO.

HIS SISTER SOPHIE'S DEATH LEFT ITS SHADOW ON ALL MUNCH'S YOUTH. HERE THE ISOLATION, THE IMMOBILITY, THE PRO-
FOUND DEJECTION OF EACH OF THE PERSONS IN THE ROOM CONVEY THE HELPLESSNESS OF MAN CONFRONTED BY DEATH.

loathed hyacinths because their perfume brought to his mind the odour of death. He never attended a funeral. " When my cousin Edvard Didriks died, I drove over but didn't go in. I stayed in the car. But I saw the smoke—thick, yellow smoke."

Other experiences of his youth left their imprint on his life and work. Munch was extremely sensitive, and the straitened circumstances in which his mother's death left the family preyed on his mind. His father, a doctor in the slum quarter of Oslo, took no payment for his treatment of the poor, and his income suffered accordingly. A man of gloom, stern and moody, he stifled any possibilities of cheerfulness in his surroundings. Munch hardened his heart against his father, and in time lost any real feeling for him. This atmosphere of sickness, gloom and poverty produced in Munch that morbid craving for isolation which always made it so hard for him to enter into cordial relations with any man.

The casual love-affairs of Bohemian life in Oslo and Berlin left their mark on Munch's relations with women. For him the partner of his life was art. Ever jealous of his independence, he pictured woman as a vampire who robs man not only of his personal freedom and strength, but even of life itself (Death of Marat). On one occasion, in a love quarrel, a woman fired at him with a revolver, wounding a finger. Ever afterwards, Munch hated

hands and almost always wore gloves. " Nothing is nakeder or more disgusting than fingers.
I can't bear people who're always fiddling with their hands." To draw the hand in *Self-
Portrait with a Cigarette* Munch asked a friend to pose for him. In his *Alpha and Omega*,
a mythological tale written in Copenhagen in 1909 and illustrated by him with lithographs,
he represents the human species as arising from an inter-breeding of man and beast.

In 1886, after a few lessons with the painters Christian Krogh and Heyerdal, Munch
painted *The Sick Girl*, *Puberty*, and *The Day After*. The twenty-three-year-old painter woke
up to find himself acclaimed as a highly original personality with a bold artistic vision. At
this time, Munch moved in a circle of writers and Bohemians who foregathered at the café
of the Grand Hotel in Oslo and, emulating Ibsen, harried by word and deed the pretensions
of ' bourgeois ' morality and orthodox piety. Association with this group, and particularly
with its moving spirit, Hans Jäger, confirmed and clarified Munch's own outlook. His
friends gave him social and moral support and stood up for him when, in 1889, his first exhibition in Oslo provoked a storm of abuse. However, thanks to the good offices of his teacher
Christian Krogh, he obtained a grant of money enabling him to spend four months in Paris
during the winter of 1889-1890, studying art. There Munch discovered the works of the
Impressionists and of his contemporaries, Gauguin, Van Gogh, Seurat, Toulouse-Lautrec.
In the next few years, further art scholarships gave him an opportunity of travelling in the
South of France, in Italy and in Germany. In 1891 Munch worked in Paris with the Neo-
Impressionists and now his palette underwent a very needful brightening up. Here he
first conceived the idea of his *Frieze of Life*, a pictorial pageant narrating the struggles, joys
and sufferings of mankind. The *Frieze of Life* became the ruling interest in all Munch's
work and remained so throughout his career. Some pictures from the *Frieze* were exhibited
in Oslo in 1892. As a result, Munch received an invitation from the Berlin Artists' Association to join in their annual exhibition. He brought 55 works with him to Berlin but they

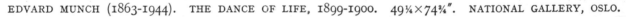

THIS PICTURE, WHICH FORMS PART OF THE FIRST *FRIEZE OF LIFE*, SHOWS DIFFERENT ASPECTS OF THE ZEST FOR LIFE. MUNCH
REVERTED TO THIS THEME IN 1921, IN A VERSION BOTH MORE VARIED AND MORE SUMPTUOUS.

EDVARD MUNCH (1863-1944). THE DANCE OF LIFE, 1899-1900. 49¼×74¾". NATIONAL GALLERY, OSLO.

EDVARD MUNCH (1863-

WHEN THEY WERE IN BERLIN TO[...]
WOMAN, THE WIFE OF THEIR F[...]
MY NERVES STOOD THE STRA[...]
THINKING, 'DOESN'T HER [...]
WENT TO PARIS TO ARR[...]

drew down on his he[...]
promptly retaliated wit[...]
with advanced ideas to his [...] for
recognition. While in Berlin, [...] con-
noisseur Albert Kollmann and o[...]zewsky,
Bierbaum, Dehmel, Holz, Scheerbar[...] dquarters
at E. T. A. Hoffmann's tavern 'The B[...]eier-Graefe,
Pastor and Servaes issued their challenging [...] *Munch*. The
same year saw the appearance of his first etching[...], printed by Clot
in Paris, and 1896, the first woodcuts. In Paris [...]ented the circle of
Mallarmé and did the sets for *Peer Gynt* (produced at [...] Oeuvre). In 1897 he
exhibited his *Frieze of Life* at the Salon des Indépendant[...] as he then was figures
in Strindberg's *Inferno*, as both the Danish painter and the [...]some Heinrich.

Until 1908 Munch led a wandering life, sharing his time between Germany, Norway
and France. It was in Germany, however, in increasing measure, that he found friends,
recognition and security, so that his centre of gravity, so to speak, tended more and more to
fix itself there. And after the turn of the century, Munch was no more to be seen in Paris.

Seen in its historical perspective, the real significance of Munch's art seems to lie in
the first two decades of his activity, *i.e.* in the years during which he took part in the revolt
against Impressionism, as a contemporary of Gauguin, Van Gogh, Toulouse-Lautrec and
Ensor. Like Toulouse-Lautrec, Munch's milieu was that of writers and Bohemians, whose
ideas on art and society influenced his painting. Toulouse-Lautrec, however, felt at home

THE BLACK FORMLESS SHADOW LOOMING UP BEHIND THE FIGURE SYMBOLIZES THE NAMELESS FEAR THAT COMES ON THE
YOUNG GIRL AT THE MOMENT OF THE PROFOUND CHANGE, OF BODY AND SOUL, THAT IS TAKING PLACE IN HER.

EDVARD MUNCH (1863-1944). PUBERTY, 1895. 47¼×55½". NATIONAL GALLERY, OSLO.

in the world of the circus and the cabaret, and practically lived his life there. For Munch, on the other hand, the Grand Hotel in Oslo and the ' Black Pig ' in Berlin were only stopping-off places, where from time to time he could sharpen his wits in argument, and find brief solace in convivial surroundings. But his was too complex a personality to get any real satisfaction there. He was intellectually and spiritually unfitted to form close ties in an ' artistic '—or indeed any—milieu. Thus his pictures have no documentary value as regards his surroundings, as have those of Toulouse-Lautrec for Paris Bohemian life, or the work of Bonnard and Vuillard for middle-class life at the end of the XIXth Century.

His *Frieze of Life*—that vast cyclical portrayal of mankind's trials and triumphs—will probably take its place as the greatest realization of the programme laid down by the French Symbolists. It succeeded because the abstract idea of the *Frieze* took body from the artist's own outlook and experience. Munch's symbols have their roots directly in his intuition and are not a distillation of mental processes. Thus, in turn, they waken in us an immediate intuitive response and need no written commentary. Ibsen and Strindberg make themselves felt as the literary background to Munch's pictures of the 1890's—but no more than a background.

The change in Munch's personality and painting dates from his illness of the winter of 1908-09. He became increasingly touchy, reserved and mistrustful in his relations with all those about him, not excepting his friends. From this time on he rarely left Norway. After 1908 he lived first in Kragerö, then on Jelöy Island, later in Hvitsen in the Oslo

THIS WOODCUT EXISTS IN SEVERAL DIFFERENT STATES WITH DIFFERENT COLOUR COMBINATIONS. MUNCH SAWED THE PLATE INTO THREE PIECES.

E. MUNCH (1863-1944). WOMEN ON THE SEASHORE, 1898. 17¾×19¾". WOODCUT IN FOUR COLOURS.

Fjord and finally at Ekely, near Oslo. He bought four houses which he used as repositories for his paintings, fitting them out with studios and working turn by turn in each. In his work the depressive themes of the 1890's sometimes reappear ; but he reverted to them only for making copies of pictures he had sold. He liked to have all his pictures around him—his children, as he was fond of calling them. Thus it is that many of his best-known works exist in two or three versions. After 1908, his handling of colour was freer, less controlled ; the brushwork adapted itself spontaneously to the creative impulse, and the violence of colour sometimes brings to mind the work of the Fauves. This change in his art stands in direct relation to the monumental murals which he executed for the University of Oslo between 1909 and 1911. In their train followed a series of pictures of artisans and workers, and a cycle of self-portraits that make a harrowing record of the artist's growing isolation and old age. On January 23rd, 1944, Munch died of a heart-attack at Ekely.

During the last thirty years of his life, Munch was averse from holding exhibitions. Outside Scandinavia, the only large Munch exhibitions took place in Zurich (1922), Mannheim (1926), Berlin (1927), and Amsterdam (1938). Only after a full inventory of the Munch bequest—left in its entirety to his native city Oslo—is available will any methodical classification and appraisal of his later work be possible.

HODLER
Ferdinand Hodler was born in the same month and year as Van Gogh : in March, 1853. Later, in Geneva, Hodler underwent the same solitude and privations that Van Gogh was to know in Borinage and Nuenen. And as Van Gogh painted ' potato-eaters,' weavers and peasants, so Hodler depicted those he saw around him ; the washerwoman, the joiner, the cobbler, the watchmaker. But from the first Van Gogh found his direct expression in the vividness of his brushwork, while Hodler's means of expression lay in contour and drawing. In Paris, Van Gogh made happy contacts with the French painting of his time ; Hodler missed these, and developed his art apart from such influences—an art which forms one of the most distinctive ensembles of modern painting.

Hodler was an artist of the first rank, and equalled in power the best of his contemporaries. This power was developed, however, along a private path whose curves wind like youthful arabesques round the direct and beaten track of evolution in painting, touching it only intermittently and mostly with a time-lag. His spiritual isolation and the hostility of the provincial, reactionary critics in Geneva forced Hodler into an attitude of defiance, owing to which he found it ever more difficult to make contact with his environment. He failed to measure himself with contemporary painting and with those minds that left their stamp on the time. To set up against his opponents, he had only his indomitable will and a full-blooded personal conception of art—a strange mixture of intellectualism, intuition and eclecticism. By a sweeping, vigorous, strongly marked realism he sought to express the supersensuous, and landed consequently in allegory. In him, literary outlook and artistic intuition were constantly at odds ; hence that feeling of strain and stress which Hodler's over-wrought compositions often convey to us. Sometimes he would idealize his struggle, setting himself up as champion of an ideal, defiantly facing the enemy. And, in the end, Hodler overcame his opponents. The laurels which the ' Rose-Croix ' had bestowed on him in Paris did not miss their effect in Switzerland ; and once the dispute over the Marignano murals for the Swiss National Museum in Zurich was won, after long controversy, the way to glory lay open. From Vienna, whose *Secession* toasted Hodler as the master of Jugendstil, he received the enthusiastic recognition of all Germany. He seemed the romantic artist-myth of the XIXth Century come to life ; as a Promethean creative spirit he seemed to have forced his intuitions on the world about him. Yet it was a Pyrrhic victory, resting on the confusion of a formulated literary outlook and an artistically formed intuition.

Deadly Sins and *La Panne Beach*. In these canvases the narrative element supersedes the pictorial. Perhaps it was living in the provinces that gave Ensor's art this trend.

From 1900 on, the thrills he gets from the antics of his grotesques replace the quiet joy of a delicate perfection. His painting loses its iridescence, grows motley and obstreperous. Indeed Ensor's last works are mere caricatures of his masterpieces.

THE ENTRANCE OF CHRIST INTO BRUSSELS

1888

The Entrance of Christ into Brussels *is Ensor's greatest work, not only by reason of its dimensions—it covers over ten square yards of canvas—, but also by reason of the magnificent painting that has gone to the making of this fantastic scene. This notion of picturing how his contemporaries would react if Christ came to Brussels was for Ensor a splendid opportunity for giving free rein to his fantasy. Like Victor Hugo in his description of the " Mysteries " in* Notre Dame de Paris, *Ensor depicts a huge concourse of all types of humanity. Here the Flemish genius for narrative, a keen sense of satire, and the skill of a great craftsman and colourist merge in a pageantry at once burlesque and grandiose. We see Christ riding on an ass in the midst of a motley crowd whose excitement is whipped up by the drums and trumpets of the " Belgian Bigots'*

JAMES ENSOR (1860-1949). THE ENTRANCE OF CHRIST INTO BRUSSELS, DETAIL (1888). PRIVATE COLLECTION, OSTEND.

JAMES ENSOR (1860-1949).   THE ENTRANCE OF CHRIST INTO BRUSSELS, DETAIL (1888).
PRIVATE COLLECTION, OSTEND.

Band." A streamer inscribed " Up with the Socialist State! " is slung across the street. Another welcomes Christ with the words, " Long live Jesus, King of Brussels! " And with what gusto Ensor caricatures these worthy people who to-day are singing Hosannas and to-morrow will be shouting " Crucify Him! " To vent his scorn of them he replaces their faces with grotesque masks—for their true expression is the leer, in which stupidity, vulgarity and greed, and all the other ignobilities that flesh is heir to, are plain to see.

Ten years later Ensor transposed this picture into an etching, in which some new inscriptions bring the scene up to date. Thus behind the " Bigots' Band " we see the " United Pork Butchers of Jerusalem " ; " Wagnerian Blaresmen " make an unholy din; the " Flemish Vanguard " competes with the socialists, exalting in one breath their leader Anseele and Christ their King; then come the " Vivisectionists " and the " Tough Belgians." And, crowning all, is a poster of Colman's Mustard.

GEORGES ROUAULT (1871). LA NOCE A NINI-PATTE-EN-L'AIR, 1905. 23¼×26¼".
PRIVATE COLLECTION, PARIS.

GEORGES ROUAULT

Of all modern masters Rouault alone has honestly recognized the need for schooling in technique, has dutifully applied himself to studying the traditional rules of art, has believed in the possible existence of an institution, benevolent and beneficent, capable of imparting crafts-manship and culture, and, despite much disillusionment, has retained the feeling of regret (which he attributes also to Degas) for an ideal School which perhaps will never again exist. Yet, amazingly enough, his work is at the furthest remove from all accepted patterns of art ; though backed by tradition and authentic knowledge, it seems to well up from a pure, primitive source, it has no affinities, and stands or falls alone. So remote, indeed, is it from any venture of contemporary art that we cannot well see how any painter save Rouault himself could practise such painting or be inspired by such conceptions.

Rouault had an early training as a stained-glass worker. Even when in the nine-teenth century it had fallen on evil days, stained-glass art still retained its usage of the crucible and of mixtures whose outcome was something of a gamble. Stained glass combines transparency and intensity, and the lead strips enclosing each piece of glass ensure not only structural stability but are constructive elements in the visual lay-out. His classical training may at first have hindered Rouault from realizing the possibilities of this technique as applied to pictorial art, but they must have hovered in the background of his mind. Thus when, later, he radically changed his style of painting, at the prompting of his inner vision, memories of that earlier experience helped him to co-ordinate his methods of expression. And in the full flowering of his maturity Rouault referred back to the stained-glass window with the happiest results ; his painting worked the miracle of building-up with tiny flat surfaces those same magical effects of figures poised in air, enlarged in space, riddled by light.

But there were many stages on the way towards this plenitude. From twenty to thirty he lived in the stuffy atmosphere of official art. True, he had the luck to profit almost at once by the generous help of Gustave Moreau, an intelligent, cultured and broad-minded teacher. Yet the narrow discipline of the School, its absurd conventions, its tedious hierarchy, must have weighed heavily on the mind of a naïve, conscientious young man like Rouault. Anyhow, he got from it all that was to be had in the way of ' classical ' draughtsmanship, traditional mixtures of pigments, and the methods of the Masters—even if, once his eyes were open, he discarded these, seeing the inhibitions they entailed.

Nevertheless, Rouault took no part in the experimental work then being carried out by the Neo-Impressionists, or in the gatherings of the Nabis, where Gauguin's ' message ' was so eagerly debated. Even with his fellow-students (amongst whom for a while was Matisse) he felt that he had no community of outlook or of aim, and his only real friend at this time, despite the difference of age, was his teacher. Nor, in 1905, did he take any part in the ' demonstration ' of the Fauves, whom as a matter of fact he had forestalled by sending to the previous Salon a work quite as revolutionary as any of theirs.

During the five or six years intervening between his leaving the Ecole des Beaux-Arts and the first exhibitions of the new painting, Rouault was undergoing a profound spiritual crisis and following a purely subjective course. Gustave Moreau's death in 1898 had been a terrible blow, but at least it served to force him out of the blind alley which was checking his advance. For the expression of emotions—it never even crossed Rouault's mind that a painting could be merely decorative or a recreation for the eye—it is essential that the emotions should be embodied in a communicable form. In the world of to-day, the ancient allegories, symbols and myths are but shadowy things, lacking the consistence that would give them value in themselves. For that, they need to be revivified with modern signs, and it is for the artist to transfuse into them his passion, his own substance, his very lifeblood. Likewise the methods employed should have the driving force of youth—whether natural or regained—behind them. Obviously the concoctions of the School, its mixtures based on brown and its treacly impasto, were quite useless. And thus there came to Rouault a realization of the futility of these intractable materials, and what it was that held him back from self-fulfilment. So he decided to review both his technical knowledge and his aims ; to make a wholly new approach.

He began by deepening his inner life, and found an inspiration in the writer, Léon Bloy. Bloy, it is true, knew little of the problems of creative art, but he felt that it could serve to exalt the divine element latent in man, though his judgement in those matters was obscured by prejudices in favour of the lifelike, the resembling, and that anecdotal art which is the supreme betrayal of the supramundane. Nevertheless, Bloy gave the painter the example of a dedicated life, and a life's work wholly applied to the service of the faith within him. By this contact with Bloy, Rouault strengthened his own faith and charity, and he now confronted the world with more humility and love. He accepted the ' message ' of certain landscapes because they were imbued with sadness or mystery ; he deliberately devoted himself to certain particularly wretched types of humanity, revolting yet pathetic creatures, in whom, nevertheless, is manifested at its clearest the imperfection of the flesh. And, finally, he completely revised his technique, limiting his drawing to the essential lines ; abandoning chiaroscuro, the modulations of ' high art,' perspective, sequences of planes, he set out to grasp the subject of the picture in its stark immediacy, with colours chosen solely for their high expressive value.

GEORGES ROUAULT (1871). THE COUPLE, 1905. 27¼×20¾″. PRIVATE COLLECTION, PARIS.

GEORGES ROUAULT (1871). THE DANCER, 1905. 27½ × 21¼″. PRIVATE COLLECTION, PARIS.

GEORGES ROUAULT (1871). THE TRAGEDIAN, 1906. 15¼×11¾″. HAHNLOSER COLLECTION, WINTERTHUR.

GEORGES ROUAULT (1871). THE SUBURBS, 1911. 11½×7". HAHNLOSER COLLECTION, WINTERTHUR.

could draw at will for the basic elements of that supreme art, wider in scope and purged of all impurity, which for ever haunted his imagination.

In fact the process of creation which usually operates for individual pictures subserves in Rouault's case the *ensemble* of his art, and extends over his whole career. He began by visualizing this *ensemble* under all its aspects and in all its ramifications ; then, in the full-ness of time, he set about bringing it into being. This explains the surprising homogeneity of his evolution, that steady and so to speak collective maturation, never complete so long as the artist felt something could be added. (Here may be a clue to the astounding contract he made with Vollard, in which he pledged to that dealer his uncompleted works.)

In 1928 Rouault set about the immense task of completing, adding the final touches to, such of the hundreds of works still 'on the stocks' as seemed to him the most important ; those as near to him then as they had been at the crucial moment when he wrenched them, as it were, from his living flesh. The love he bore for them demanded that they should be brought to full fruition. He strengthened them, shoring them up with heavy black lines that trued the planes of colour into equilibrium. And these planes, being given their independ-ence, attained their full significance. On each the painter lavished the most sumptuous, yet most appropriate tones, vibrant with iridescent gleams, and charged with that depth-beyond-depth of which he had the secret. Even his darkest colours carry undertones of brightness. So now he was master of a technique adequate for those great religious themes which, in his humility, he had reserved for the time when he would be worthy of them.

EMIL NOLDE (1867). CHRIST AND THE WOMAN TAKEN IN ADULTERY, 1914. 34×42″.
PRIVATE COLLECTION, BERN.

THIS PICTURE WAS FORMERLY IN THE KRONPRINZEN PALACE COLLECTION, BERLIN. PUT UP TO AUCTION AT LUCERNE IN 1939
WITH OTHER 'DECADENT' WORKS, IT WAS BOUGHT BY ONE OF NOLDE'S EARLIEST PATRONS.

EMIL NOLDE

Born in 1867, Nolde, whose real name was Emil Hansen (which he replaced by that of
his birthplace), was three years younger than Toulouse-Lautrec, three than Munch, and four
years older than Rouault. His place is midway between the generation of great isolated
figures and that of the Fauves. But, as regards his art, he clearly belongs to the twentieth
century. Nolde developed slowly, hesitantly. At Flensburg (in Schleswig) he learned the
craft of wood-carving, which he practised at Munich, Karlsruhe and Berlin, meanwhile
continuing his studies in the Schools of Art and Crafts in these cities. In 1892, he held a post
of draughtsman at Saint-Gall, the headquarters of the Swiss embroidery industry. In 1899 he
went to Paris, by way of Munich, but does not seem to have come in contact there with modern
art; it was in Germany he saw the works by Van Gogh and Gauguin that pointed him in
the right direction. His familiarity with black-and-white art, especially with etching, both
sharpened his power of expression and helped him to give precision to his painting.

EMIL NOLDE—PENTECOST (DETAIL).

THE LAST SUPPER AND *PENTECOST* ARE EARLY WORKS. THIS DETAIL REVEALS A CERTAIN AWKWARDNESS IN THE ARTIST'S
MANNER; HE DOES NOT HESITATE TO SACRIFICE PLASTIC VALUES TO THE EXPRESSIVE ELEMENT.

When, in 1909, he was beginning to make his name, he had already painted the *Last Supper* and *Pentecost*, compositions that betoken his intense devotion to the spirit of primitive Christianity, and are expressed in an appropriately primitive idiom. There are discords in this painting ; it deliberately offends the aesthetic sense so as the more exclusively to stimulate the religious sense. During the years which followed, up to 1912, Nolde painted his cycle, *The Life of Christ*, which, liberating religious painting from the tradition of the Western Church, aspires to bring it back to the fountain-head, and to invest it with the splendour of the East, the dawn of Christendom.

Encouraged by Ensor, whom he visited in 1911, Nolde painted a series of Still Lifes with masks ; these bring out clearly the extreme originality of his work. Ensor's masks have their being in a limbo of life and not-life ; where a half-mocking, half-demoniacal spirit somehow animates the inertia of these objects, and human faces stiffen into masks, masks come to hideous life. Indomitably Nolde tried to conjure up this demon and to penetrate further the hinterland of magic, using all the devices at his command, exaggeration no less than simplification. But the stress he lays, in his mask pictures, on the grotesquer aspects of the human visage, shows, in the last analysis, that Nolde confused the primitive with the barbarian mind.

The most authentic message Nolde has to give us is to be found in his landscapes and flower pictures, in which his feeling for nature finds poignant and direct expression. It is in his Baltic landscapes that Nolde truly evokes those ' powers ' of the elemental and the primitive which he vainly tried to conjure up in his compositions.

Under the spell of Picasso in 1908, both Derain and Vlaminck deserted Fauvism for the new and more exciting problems of Cubism. It was in the autumn of 1911, after moving from Dresden to Berlin, that Kirchner, Heckel and Schmidt-Rottluff gave up painting in unmodulated colours, bringing the first phase of *Die Brücke* to an end. Thus the time-lag of about three years behind the Fauves holds good not only for the beginning of the first *Brücke* style, but for its end as well. The same year, 1911, saw the formation in Munich of a new group of artists headed by Kandinsky and Marc, known as *Der Blaue Reiter*. In 1911, too, Kandinsky published his book *Über das Geistige in der Kunst* (The Art of Spiritual Harmony), laying the theoretical groundwork for the abstract art to come. At the same time he was painting the first of his own abstract works. Marc, for his part, was occupied with the problems of Orphism, the colour Cubism of Delaunay and Gleizes. Thanks to the presence of Kandinsky and Klee, Munich became the focal point of a movement whose significance in XXth-Century painting proved to be indeed far-reaching. In Berlin, the artist's chief concern was man as a subject of psychological and aesthetic interpretation. Kirchner, Heckel and Schmidt-Rottluff followed the middle way between two extremes : the factual, psychological Expressionism of Kokoschka, and the purely formal conceptions of Kandinsky. Using a language of forms tinged with Cubism, these painters tried to grasp the reality of man and voice his feelings and experiences.

In this venture, Kirchner and his friends were not alone. In New York Max Weber was working towards a similar synthesis : his *Geranium* could just as well have been painted in Berlin. Vlaminck and Derain were pursuing much the same aims in Paris. A language of forms took shape, a kind of expressionist Esperanto, soon to be learnt by countless eager pupils, and its influence, especially in Germany, determined the course of modern painting well into the 1920's.

The artists' war experiences left their mark on many of the chief works produced by German Expressionism between 1914 and 1920 : Kokoschka's *Knight Errant*, Heckel's *Madonna of the Bivouac*, Marc's sketches for his *War Journal*, and Kirchner's illustrations for *Peter Schlemihl*.

E. L. KIRCHNER (1880-1938). WOODCUT FOR "PETER SCHLEMIHL," BY ADALBERT VON CHAMISSO, 1915-1916. 12½×8¼". PRIVATE COLLECTION, BERN.

After his first nervous breakdown, and subsequent release from military service, Kirchner lived in constant dread of being called up again and sent to the front. It was in this neurotic state, attended by partial paralysis, that Kirchner did the woodcuts for Adalbert von Chamisso's *Peter Schlemihl*. By way of the story of Schlemihl—who sells his shadow to the devil for gold, and is so cruelly hounded and browbeaten by its purchaser that he redeems his shadow with his soul—Kirchner was able to give artistic form to his own persecution mania, an affliction that dogged him even after he took refuge in Switzerland, and from which he found relief only after the signing of the armistice.

During the war a younger generation of artists had sprung up, seizing on expressionist forms as an instrument of social criticism. They railed against the senseless continuation of the war, against German militarism and the war's crop of parasites and profiteers. Expressionism became an art of pamphleteers, an arm in the social struggle preceding the revolution of 1918.

Max Beckmann, George Grosz and Otto Dick took the lead. With ruthlessly deliberate vulgarity they caricatured the underworld of profiteers and hangers-on. Eclectically combining the most varied techniques of Futurism and Expressionism, Grosz's *Deutschland, ein Wintermärchen* (Germany, A Winter's Tale)—painted in 1918—marks the turning point of post-war Expressionism. In much the same way as Brecht and Weill's *Beggar's Opera*, the painting and graphic art of this period gives a striking picture of the inflation and chaos of post-war Germany.

Class bitterness, hollow revolutionary gestures, a romantic glorification of the demimonde—these post-war reactions combined to produce a kind of anecdotal art that marked the end of a great movement.

MAX WEBER

The new directions taken by modern art after 1910 were, as we know, not confined to Europe. The movement was international in scope and in America it was Max Weber who most capably promoted it.

Weber was born in 1881 at Bialystok, in Russia, the son of a tailor. When he was ten years old the family emigrated to New York and, at the age of sixteen, Weber began drawing and painting lessons at the Pratt Institute in Brooklyn. There he found an invaluable teacher in Arthur Wesley Dow, who had worked with Gauguin in France and was very much at home in contemporary French art. And so in 1905 Weber went to Paris, where he soon made the acquaintance of Le Douanier Rousseau. In company with the German painter, Hans Purrmann, he took lessons from Matisse. In 1907 he met Picasso. Thus by the time he returned to New York in December, 1908, Weber was thoroughly versed in the problems and trends of modern art.

In the next few years, Weber's efforts were concentrated on evolving an art that turned to good account his experiences in Europe. Building up an Expressionism of his own on Cubist lines, he came to grips with the same problems as those then occupying Kirchner, Heckel, Schmidt-Rottluff, Derain and Vlaminck. *The Geranium*, painted in 1911, marks the peak of his work during this period.

The years to come were spent in close, persistent analysis of the problems involved in Cubism and Futurism. Pursuing this line of research, Weber came to the brink of purely abstract painting. By the 1930's, however, by devious ways his art had worked its way back to a more personal idiom, a vigorous Expressionism.

Holger Cahill commented on his work as follows: " Max Weber has lived the history of modern painting in America." His importance as a link between two continents is almost equal to his significance as a painter.

MAX WEBER (1881). THE GERANIUM, 1911. 39¾×32¼″. MUSEUM OF MODERN ART, NEW YORK.

LIKE SOME OF HIS CONTEMPORARIES AT BASEL AND PARIS, MAX WEBER WAS TRYING, IN 1911, TO EFFECT A UNION BETWEEN
CUBIST TECHNIQUE AND THE EXPRESSION OF EMOTION.

KOKOSCHKA

It was in Vienna, at the turn of the century, that 'Jugendstil' was carried to its purest and most elegant level. Ceramics, furniture, jewellery and fine craftwork of all kinds were produced by the artists of the Wiener Werkstätte—the visible signs of a culture whose refined taste delighted in precious objects. Undisputed leader of the city's art life was Gustav Klimt. His murals for the University of Vienna, painted in 1899 and 1900, combined on the same stretch of wall highly decorative figures and abstract forms, built up with precious substances inset in the wall like a mosaic. There is a fine sensitivity in this painting, which, while representational in character, aspires to recapture something of the glittering magnificence of Byzantine art.

It was in the atmosphere of the Viennese *fin-de-siècle*, the exotic flowering of the 'Jugendstil,' that Hugo von Hofmannsthal wrote his poems and playlets, Gustav Mahler composed *Das Lied von der Erde* (The Song of the Earth) and the *Kindertotenlieder* (Children's Death Songs), and Peter Altenberg wrote *Die Märchen des Lebens* (Tales of Life). An abounding joy in life and the pleasures it offers went hand in hand with the decadence, tinged with melancholy, and the over-refinement of the age. In *Die Fackel* Karl Kraus published his biting criticisms of society and politics. And in 1900 Sigmund Freud brought out his *Traumdeutung* (The Interpretation of Dreams).

This was the cultural atmosphere into which young Kokoschka plunged when he entered the Vienna School of Arts and Crafts in 1904. Three years later—at the age of twenty-one—he wrote the plays *Sphinx and Straw Man* and *Woman's Hope* with a precocious competence reminding us of the early maturity of Hofmannsthal. In 1908 the Wiener Werkstätte published *The Dreaming Children*, his book of poems and illustrations, a delightful autumn fruit of Jugendstil and Symbolism. Struck by his abilities, Adolf Loos, the architect, and the writer Karl Kraus stood by Kokoschka when he was expelled from the School of Arts and Crafts, following the scandal created by his pictures and plays.

By a strange coincidence, the same time and place saw both Freud and Kokoschka—psychologist in science and psychologist in art—laying the foundations of all their future work. Between 1908 and 1914 Kokoschka painted a series of portraits, and such was the artist's psychological grasp of his subjects that each is a human document of extraordinary interest and significance. Among those portrayed are the writers Karl Kraus, Peter Altenberg, Herwarth Walden, Alfred Kerr, Paul Scheerbart, Richard Dehmel, Gustav Meyrink, Peter Baum, Albert Ehrenstein ; the actor Rudolf Blümner and the actresses Else Kupfer, Tilla Durieux, Gertrud Eysoldt ; the musicians Egon Wellesz and Anton von Webern ; the dancer Nijinsky, the architect Adolf Loos and the psychiatrist Auguste Forel.

Kokoschka responded like a seismograph to the psychic characteristics of the sitter. In those remarkable pictures, the *Portrait of Forel* and the *Portrait of the Countess de Rohan-Montesquieu*, one feels that the artist has an almost supernormal faculty of identifying himself with his model, whose innermost life he understands and shares. The subtlest idiosyncrasies of the face and the eloquent language of the hands are so forcibly brought out that, as it were, a double portrait is evoked, one of hands and one of head. All the artist's power is concentrated in the human qualities of his subject ; problems of colour and form are wilfully ignored. Here practically all is effected by the drawing ; the colour is little more than a groundcolour, keyed to the prevailing mood and giving the merest hints of a spatial dimension.

By 1913-14, Kokoschka's interest had moved beyond the purely psychological and he entered on a world of vaster intimations. It was now he painted *The Tempest*, whose surging rhythms exalt his love for Alma Mahler.

Then came the war. Serving in the Austrian army on the Eastern Front, Kokoschka was severely wounded in the lungs and head in 1915. *Knight Errant* is the summing-up of this war experience : the seemingly interminable journey by hospital train from Russia back to Vienna.

OSKAR KOKOSCHKA (1886). PORTRAIT OF HERWARTH WALDEN, 1910. 39¼×26¾″. NELL WALDEN COLLECTION.

IN 1910 KOKOSCHKA MADE THE ACQUAINTANCE OF HERWARTH WALDEN IN BERLIN. IN THE SAME YEAR WALDEN BEGAN EDITING
'DER STURM,' A WEEKLY MAGAZINE WHICH DID YEOMAN SERVICE TO THE CONTEMPORARY 'AVANT-GARDE.'

OSKAR KOKOSCHKA (1886). THE TEMPEST, 1914. 27¼×33¾″. KUNSTMUSEUM, BASEL.

HERE THE TEMPEST SYMBOLIZES THE LOVE OF KOKOSCHKA AND ALMA MAHLER, WIDOW OF THE FAMOUS COMPOSER ; TOGETHER
THEY ARE BEING BORNE ON THE WINGS OF LOVE'S WHIRLWIND THROUGH THE ABYSM OF SPACE.

Discharged from the army, he settled in Dresden in 1917 and a deep change came over his art. Psychological curiosity gave way to a wider, more general outlook on life. The autobiographical obsession—from which sprang *Tempest* and *Knight Errant*—now lost its hold and in Kokoschka's art landscape took on a new meaning. Not only was the subject of the picture a problem for psychological interpretation, but the treatment of the picture itself became a problem. Colour and line, formerly dealt with separately, became one. The colour, broadly applied with a thick brush or palette-knife, became the real hinge on which his composition turned. The dynamic quality of the brushwork is reminiscent at times of Van Gogh, but is lusher, more baroque. Thus his art now ranged far beyond that of the group of his friends in Vienna and Berlin.

During the 1920's, Kokoschka travelled a great deal, for the most part in southern countries, whose effect was to make his pictures brighter and more strongly coloured. Previously he had painted the faces of men ; now he painted the faces of cities, in vast, almost topographical views that bring out all the multifarious details which go to make a city's physiognomy. Thus he gives us ' portraits ' of Dresden, Paris (Louvre, Opéra, Jardin des Tuileries), Biarritz, Marseilles, Aigues-Mortes, Lyons, Segovia, Toledo, Jerusalem, Amsterdam, Dover, London and Prague.

After the assassination of Dollfuss, Kokoschka fled Vienna and took refuge in Prague. In 1938 he went to London. In England during the war, he painted his historical pictures, *What We Are Fighting For, Loreley, The Anschluss* and others, which raise a problem of considerable interest—how far allegory is feasible in modern painting.

OSKAR KOKOSCHKA (1886). SELF-PORTRAIT, 1917. 30×24½″. VON DER HEYDT COLLECTION, WUPPERTAL.

HERE THE VACILLATING, UNDECIDED POSTURE SUGGESTS THE ARTIST'S STATE OF MIND IN 1917, WHEN HE WAS ABOUT TO REPLACE
HIS 'PSYCHOLOGICAL' MANNER BY A MORE 'COSMIC' OUTLOOK.

II. 82

MARC CHAGALL (1887). MY STUDIO, 1910. 23½×28″. OWNED BY THE ARTIST.

BEFORE POINTING TOWARDS SURREALISM, CHAGALL'S ART PASSED THROUGH A PHASE OF EXPRESSIONISM. ITS BEGINNINGS
HAD SOMETHING OF THAT CHAOS, "WITHOUT FORM AND VOID," WHICH IS THE PRELUDE TO ALL CREATION.

SOUTINE

In 1910 the painters who were joining forces in Germany, with a view to cultivating an art of more intense significance—by means of expressive 'distortion,' a bolder use of colour, and simplified construction—looked eagerly towards France, and indeed regarded themselves as following the same aims as the early Cubists. Meanwhile, the younger painters living in Paris, though they had followed a somewhat similar line of development, were devoting themselves to experimental work conducted on a more scientific basis, in which the problem of form was paramount. Obviously they could not be expected to take an equal interest in what was happening abroad. Had not the Fauves said the last word on the subject of light ? Had not Rouault given the greatest possible depth to colours bound by thick contour-lines, thus carrying Gauguin's doctrines to their utmost limit ? Nevertheless, there yet were numerous and indeed far-reaching discoveries in the field of colour to be made by the successors, whether deliberate or instinctive, of the Impressionists and Seurat. And now French art was to benefit by the influx into its blood-stream of something wholly new and foreign to it—with the coming of Jewish painters from Eastern Europe.

It was to his encounter with French Impressionism that Van Gogh owed his ' discovery ' of light ; yet the colour impressions then revealed to him were those he had brought, so to speak, within him, and were quite unlike those of his contemporaries. Whence he had

CHAÏM SOUTINE (1894-1943). SELF-PORTRAIT, 1918. 21½×18″. PEARLMAN COLLECTION, NEW YORK.

WHAT SOUTINE AIMED AT HERE WAS NOT MERELY A PSYCHOLOGICAL EVOCATION OF THE ANGUISH WRITTEN ON HIS FACE; THIS PORTRAIT ISSUES AS NATURALLY FROM HIS BRUSHSTROKES AS THE SOUND OF HIS VOICE FROM HIS LIPS. USUALLY THE EXPRESS-IONISTS DID NOT TROUBLE MUCH ABOUT TECHNIQUE; SOUTINE HOWEVER, IF QUITE INSTINCTIVELY, PROBES PERSISTENTLY THE VITAL STUFF OF PAINTING, SO AS TO WREST FROM IT THE SECRETS OF ITS BEING; LIKE AN ANATOMIST EXPLORING THE SECRETS OF A BODY.

got those colours (so revolutionary for their time) seems somewhat of a mystery, especially if we try to trace an origin for them in traditional Dutch art. Perhaps, borrowing a term from chemistry, we might call them a 'precipitate.' Chagall's palette, and Soutine's too, were quite new factors. Their origin was much remoter, in both Space and Time, than was Van Gogh's; they came from those borderlands of Russian and German culture, that zone of racial ambivalence, in which the Jewish centres—neither quite towns nor yet quite villages, but partaking of both—had until now preserved a mode of living that then seemed destined to last unchanged for ever. Heart-breaking poverty was allied with a spiritual ferment, that having been so long kept under, was ready to burst forth at any moment. For historical and other reasons their art had no precedent, but implicit in it was a centuries-old lore that now, for the first time, was to take form and fructify. Thus when these 'displaced persons' of an earlier day came westwards, they brought with them a secret vision that not only enabled them to endow the simplest elements of their memories with a strange magnificence, but was powerful enough to bend to its hegemony all the new sights that reached their eyes. On the technical side they had little to learn; their craftsmanship, if incommunicable, was innate. While Chagall's art underwent long, subtle transformations (to be described in another volume), Soutine's, with its passionately reiterated affirmations, displays an unbroken continuity. And neither has anything in common with the works of his contemporaries.

When he came to Paris at the age of twenty-one, Chagall already knew all that needs be known of painting. His art had been shaped by observation of the life of the common folk, so rich in picturesque material, of a Jewish village. These elements, familiar from his childhood, were for him an ever-present psychical reality, a world within, self-contained and complete in all its aspects. In even his earliest paintings (done while he was still in Russia), he showed his gift for combining these, and making them express something other than their outward appearance. His colours were then rather dark, though certain strongly resonant passages hint at a future lavishness of colour; but (as Chagall said in a lecture delivered in the United States) it was in Paris that he " washed his eyes." *My Studio* is one of the most revealing works of this transitional period; here the rippling colour brings objects to life, imposing on them a rhythm that profoundly modifies their natural lay-out. Chagall came in contact with Canudo, Walden, Cendrars, Apollinaire—also with the painters Delaunay and La Fresnaye, and proceeded to apply in his own manner the theories then being built up around Cubism, finding in them an encouragement towards the vast structures on which his heart was set.

When, after studying at the Wilno Academy, he came to Paris (in 1911), entered the Ecole des Beaux-Arts and was assigned to Cormon's studio, Soutine was little more than a boy. Indeed, for a long while yet he was to have that curious face we see in Modigliani's memorable portrait (1917), with its effect of inscrutability, as though the eyes were intent on some inner, secret vision. Characteristic, too, were his small, finely shaped, pale hands commented on by Elie Faure, who has also described his childish shyness and his way of taking to his heels at the first signs of a shower of rain. He went through those years of testing with the same quiet faith in himself as he had displayed when he talked his poverty-stricken family and shocked village elders into belief in his vocation. What knowledge he had amassed was due to his unaided efforts; to haphazard reading of novels, poetry, philosophy, and to observation of the great masters' works from Rembrandt to Cézanne, no less than to early ventures into art, hidden so mistrustfully from others' eyes that practically none are extant. In short, this early period was not so much one of learning his *métier* as one of mental and moral preparation, a 'probation' almost like a monk's.

What he needed was 'a stroke of luck'—like all who have been through misfortune he believed in 'luck,' and he had a liking for the word. That stroke of luck came in 1919 when Zborowski (whom he got to know through Modigliani) sent him to paint at Céret. Soutine stayed there nearly three years. And in the dazzling sunlight of the South the long-awaited miracle took place. His colours gradually came alive, losing their opacity and inertia. He succeeded in infusing them with his emotions, his passions; one might almost

CHAÏM SOUTINE (1894-1943). THE HERRINGS, 1916. 25½×19½". KATIA GRANOFF COLLECTION, PARIS.

NOTEWORTHY ARE THE DULL, DISPIRITED TONES IN WHICH SOUTINE PAINTS THESE HUMBLE FISHES, SYMBOLS OF POVERTY.

say he sought to transmute them into animal or vegetable tissues. And, to achieve this, he fiercely probed the living flesh ; broke up the lines and masses of landscapes so as to extract from them their secret essences. What lies behind Soutine's art is, doubtless, an immense love of " all things great and small " ; he cannot endure the incommunicability of beings— and how he suffers by it !—, nor immobility : the unresponsiveness of death ; and when he directs his attention to decaying flesh, it is to discover in it germs of renewal, resurrection.

Awareness of his imperfection and a sense of rankling frustration lead him to hark back, dissatisfied, to the same themes again and again ; to destroy whatever does not come up to his exacting standard. Yet in that hopeless quest of a fusion, never achieved in art, between the living thing and the lifeless matter art employs, Soutine perhaps comes nearest of all artists to a solution. But at the cost of a cruel, total sacrifice of—himsef.

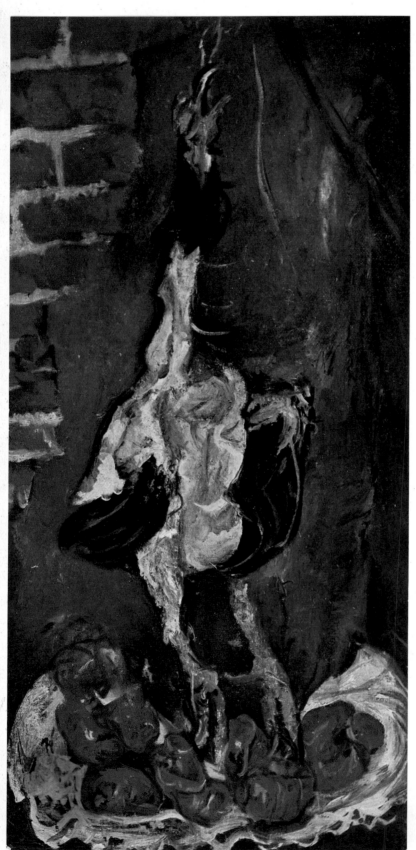

CHAÏM SOUTINE (1894-1943). THE COCK, 1925. 39½×17¾". PRIVATE COLLECTION, PARIS.

IT WAS AN OBSESSION WITH SOUTINE TO CARRY 'NATURALISM' TO FANATICAL EXTREMES. HE LIKED PAINTING DECOMPOSING FLESH ; FOR THE BODY'S DISSOLUTION MEANT, TO HIM, THE JOURNEY'S END, AN ULTIMATE RELEASE FROM A WORLD FROM WHICH HE WAS SEEKING TO ESCAPE, WITH ALL THE PASSION OF THE " OUT-CAST PAINTER " HE FELT HIMSELF TO BE.

CHAÏM SOUTINE (1894-1943). LANDSCAPE, 1926. 23½×28″. PRIVATE COLLECTION, PARIS.

THERE IS ALWAYS A STRONG ELEMENT OF HALLUCINATION IN SOUTINE'S APPROACH TO NATURE ; HIS MORBIDLY EXASPERATED
SENSITIVITY LEADS HIM TO VISUALIZE THE OUTSIDE WORLD ACROSS THE SEETHING, STIFLING CHAOS OF A NIGHTMARE.

Painting cost Soutine a terrible expenditure of nervous energy ; to begin with, in bracing himself for the initial ' shock,' and then in responding to it. He had to rouse himself from a sort of coma, indispensable no doubt for the recruiting of his strength. Thus, after periods of total sterility, suddenly he would fling himself, as it were, at the canvas—and it was amazing, the amount of work he got through on these occasions. He brought back from Céret no less than two hundred pictures ! This method of working explains why he regarded any kind of preparation as positively harmful ; for it well might disperse, fritter away his inspiration. He never ' drew ' in the technical sense of the word, he only blocked out some passages with charcoal—the merest scaffolding for the work to come ; notations meaningless to anyone except himself. When it came to filling out a form, curving an outline, giving it the warmth of life, his only medium was paint, pigments he squeezed in masses from his tubes and compounded with a sort of calculated frenzy. Nevertheless, Anne Collié, a reliable and exceptional witness (' exceptional ' because Soutine hated being watched when painting) assures us that he never lost sight of his subject, and also never placed a brushstroke without measuring it up against the one preceding it—and always at a high nervous tension that left him quite exhausted, the day's work done. Several times that ' luck ' which cost him so dear befell him. After Céret, there was Cagnes (where his feverish exploration of the secrets of the living being reached its climax), then Chatelguyon, then Paris (whose pearly skies he loved), and lastly Champigny-sur-Vende, the village in Touraine where he hid in 1942, and to whose lofty trees he bade a sorrowful farewell, in the shadow of the death awaiting him.

CHAÏM SOUTINE (1894-1943). CHOIRBOY, 1927. 24¾×14½″.
PRIVATE COLLECTION, PARIS.

LIKE THE POSTURES OF THE BODIES, THE HUMAN FACE IN SOUTINE'S ART ALWAYS CONVEYS A SENSE OF UTTER HOPELESSNESS.
THE OUTCOME OF A SORT OF MASOCHISM, NOW RESIGNED, NOW SEETHING WITH REVOLT. HERE THE PAGEBOY'S RED UNIFORM
IS PURPOSEFUL; THUS FOR VAN GOGH RED SIGNIFIED "THOSE TERRIBLE THINGS, MEN'S PASSIONS."

CHAÏM SOUTINE (1894-1943).   THE PAGEBOY.   38½×31½".   PRIVATE COLLECTION, PARIS.

THE DESTINIES
OF FAUVISM AND EXPRESSIONISM

Our readers have now been given a general conspectus of Fauvism and Expressionism presented in the setting of their period. It remains for us briefly to indicate their after-effects on the course of modern art.

The generation following that of Matisse, Munch and Rouault, sought to implement by new methods the lessons of these two great movements. After taking stock of what was best or, rather, most durable in them, the younger artists cast about for ways of remedying their weaknesses or inadequacies. Thus Fauvism seemed to call for more solid composition, while Expressionism obviously needed discipline and technical amendment.

Before embarking on our third volume, we would draw attention to certain already perceptible indications of an impending change. The post-Fauve work of Vlaminck, Derain and Friesz, for instance, foreshadowed a new direction art was soon to take. The German " Die Brücke " movement had applied Fauve methods to its evocations of social problems and mystical experiences. And, shortly after, Soutine showed a subtle insight into the poss-ibilities of colour, and a penchant towards pure tones, which Expressionism, properly so called, had disregarded. Then, again, in the case of Pascin (whose work we shall examine later), we find Expressionism qualified by vigorous, clean-cut drawing. In the United States Beckmann recorded his almost feverishly sensitive impressions in the setting of a somewhat lyrical composition. Modigliani's expressive portraits are stiffened by the application of constructive rules. Picasso in his expressionist phase (his " Blue Period ") rendered his visions of suffering humanity by way of a highly expert calligraphy.

Thus the two methods of expression, which had tended to be reciprocally exclusive, interpenetrated and overlapped each other, forming a relatively homogeneous whole. What was aimed at was, in fact, a sort of eclecticism, whose supreme manifestation we may find in Picasso's *Guernica*. Thus the evolution of the Fauve and Expressionist aesthetics culmi-nated in a synthesis. No cut-and-dry definition will meet the case ; the form this synthesis took varied with the artist's temperament. To quote some instances, Gruber inured his ' patheticism ' to rigid graphic rules ; while Manessier gave utterance to his mysticism in terms of colour, and similar methods served the sense of the fabulous in such an artist as Sutherland. Many other illustrations could be given of this interaction of Form and Content, so character-istic of the present generation. That popular catchword " a return to the human " briefly, if clumsily, suggests certain tendencies at work to-day : a move away from the purely plastic conceptions sponsored by Abstract Art, which was an offshoot of Cubism as practised by Picasso, Braque, Gris and Léger, and the non-figurative art of Mondrian and Kandinsky. But we will not further anticipate the themes to be dealt with in our third volume of the History of Modern Painting ; our purpose here was merely, in concluding, to evoke what destinies the future held in store for Fauvism and Expressionism.

BIOGRAPHICAL
AND
BIBLIOGRAPHICAL NOTICES
INDEX OF NAMES

BIOGRAPHICAL NOTICES

Mr. Hans Bolliger, of the Zurich Public Library, compiled specially for this volume a fully documented bibliography relating to the Expressionists, and the information contained in it has been of invaluable help in the preparation of our text. Unfortunately, lack of space prevents us from including more of it than the brief extracts following the biographies.

BRAQUE, Georges (1882)

Georges Braque painted only some twenty pictures in the Fauve style. After 1907, he took his place as one of the pioneers of Cubism, and his manner changed accordingly. Thus it is in the third volume of our History of Modern Painting that a study of Braque's work will be found, together with a biography of the artist and the pertinent documentary information.

DERAIN, André (1880)

1880   Born June 10 at Chatou, where his father kept a pastry-shop. Wished to see his son an engineer and had him study for the Ecole Polytechnique. But as early as 15, Derain was already painting.

1898-99   Attends the Académie Carrière where he meets Matisse.
Makes friends with Vlaminck, also living at Chatou.

1900   As he is copying Ghirlandaio's *Bearing of the Cross* at the Louvre, the attendants take exception to his interpretation and turn him out.

1901-02   At the Van Gogh Exhibition, he introduces Vlaminck to Matisse. At Chatou, he and Vlaminck work in the same studio. They do landscapes at Saint-Germain en Laye, Carrière-Saint-Denis, Le Pecq. First illustrated book : *D'un Lit dans l'Autre*, a novel by Vlaminck.

1904   Studies at Académie Julian.

1905   Military service ; afterwards he joins Matisse in the South of France. In 1905 all the pictures in his studio are bought up by Vollard. Matisse visits Derain and Vlaminck at Chatou and advises them to exhibit at Salon des Indépendants.
Shows some landscapes at Salon d'Automne with Matisse, Rouault, Vlaminck, Manguin. Exhibits at Berthe Weill's.

1907   Makes a contract with the Kahnweiler Gallery. Concurrently with a study of wood-engraving, he tries his hand at sculpture.
Works towards a simplified form ; studies volumes.
Stays at Martigues where he comes to grips with the problem of composition.

1908   Does ceramics, fired by Méthey, and paints *Les Baigneuses* ; strong influence of Cézanne and of Cubism.
Abandons pure colour and breaks with Fauvism.

1909   Stays at Montreuil-sur-Mer. Does woodcuts for Apollinaire's *L'Enchanteur Pourrissant* : one of the best XXth-century illustrated books.

1910   Stays at Cagnes. Paints *Le Pont de Cagnes*, typical of his lifelong interest in building the picture on 'architectural' lines.
Autumn : first trip to Spain where he meets Picasso (Cadaqués). Paints his first still lifes.

1912   Beginning of his 'Gothic' period. Leanings towards stylization. Paints landscapes in the Lot 'Department.' Returns to Paris in the winter. Figure studies.

1914   Portrait of Paul Poiret. Paints one of his masterpieces : *Saturday* (Museum of Modern Art, Moscow), as well as *The Two Sisters*, *The Chevalier X...* and *The Drinker*. Paints *The Last Supper*, which marks the end of Cubist influence in his work.

1914-18   Called up during the war, he makes masks from shell-cases. First exhibition organized in 1916, at Paul Guillaume's.

1919   Commissioned to do sets for the Russian Ballet, *La Boutique Fantasque*.

1920-30   Rambles throughout the South of France. Landscapes at Bandol, Sanary, Cahors. Trip to Italy ; stays for some time on the Riviera.

1924   Paints *Arlequin et Pierrot* and *La Table de Cuisine*.

1928   Carnegie Prize awarded him for *La Chasse* (Pittsburgh Museum).

1931   Large exhibition at Paul Guillaume's.

1945   Portraits, sanguines. Illustrates Rabelais' *Pantagruel* (colour woodcuts).
Does stage-sets in London.

BIBLIOGRAPHY

Basler, *Derain*, Edition Crès, Paris ; A. Salmon, *Derain*, in *Chroniques du Jour*, Paris, 1929 ; Daniel Henry, *André Derain*, Leipzig, 1920 ; Album of the *Chroniques du Jour* No. 3 devoted to Derain ; *Pour ou contre André Derain*, in the *Chroniques du Jour* No. 8, Paris, 1931 ; *Album d'Art Druet* No. 31, Paris ; Elie Faure, *Derain*, Editions Crès, Paris, 1923 ; Carlo Carrà, *Derain*, Rome, 1924.

DUFY, Raoul (1877)

1877   Born June 3 at Le Havre. Has eight brothers and sisters.

1891   The family has a hard time making ends meet and, at 14, Dufy has to take a clerk's job in a coffee importing firm.

1895   First drawing lessons at Ecole des Beaux-Arts, Le Havre, under Professor Lhullier, former pupil of Cabanel and admirer of Ingres. Dufy and Friesz (also from Le Havre) paint together.

1899   On military service.

1900   Comes to Paris on a grant of 100 francs a month allotted him by the Le Havre Municipality. Enrols in Bonnat's class, Ecole des Beaux-Arts.
His *Fin de Journée au Havre* exhibited at Salon des Artistes Français.
At the Louvre, he feels 'crushed' by the masterpieces. Henceforward he avoids the museums and spends his time in front of Durand-Ruel's windows where the Impressionists are shown. At Vollard's he sees pictures by Cézanne.

1901   The Van Gogh Exhibition at Bernheim's makes a lasting impression on him.

1903   Exhibits at Salon des Indépendants.

1905 At Salon d'Automne, Matisse's *Luxe, Calme et Volupté* opens his eyes to a new world.

1906 First exhibition at Berthe Weill's and at Salon d'Automne.

1907 Abandons pure colour. Getting his bearings, Dufy moves in the direction already indicated by Cézanne and applies himself to the problems of colours investigated by Matisse and Picasso. His palette changes; in the period 1907-11 his pictures show a great severity of style. Interest in architectural construction. Their bright, gay colours gone, his pictures no longer sell.

1908 He and Braque work together at l'Estaque.

1909 Visits Munich, accompanied by Friesz.
Paints his first boating scenes on the Marne.

1911 Friendship with the poets Fernand Fleuret, Vincent Muselli, Roger Allard, Guillaume Apollinaire. Does woodcuts for the latter's *Le Bestiaire*.
From this work and his friendship with the fashion-designer, Paul Poiret, he conceives the idea of doing woodcuts for printing on textiles. Poiret is won over and advances him 2500 francs to set up a small plant, boulevard de Clichy. Installs a steam boiler for 350 francs; hires a chemist at 500 francs a month, and one other employee (formerly a waiter at the Hotel Ritz), whom he instructs in handling the vaporizer. Dufy made the designs, engraved the plates, decided on the colouring; with the resultant fabrics Poiret made up dresses which were an immediate success.
Impressed by the venture, the big Bianchini firm takes Dufy on its staff.

1920 Stay at Vence, where he paints a great many landscapes.
Does ceramics in collaboration with the Catalan potter, Artigas.

1921 Does tapestries in 'corrosive colours' (artistic application of a mechanical process).

1922 Trip to Sicily, where the small Sicilian carts and waggons, so gaily splashed with colour, enchant and stimulate his painter's eye.

1923-25 Bianchini advises him to go to the horse-races, so as to observe the dresses of the women; but Dufy has eyes only for the horses. His racing pictures date from this time.
Tired of the work at Bianchini's, Dufy gives up his copyright in exchange for cancellation of his contract.

1925 Travels to Morocco with Poiret, where he does a series of paintings.

1926 Exhibition at the Bernheim Gallery.
Paints a triptych representing the road from Vallauris to Antibes.
Sets for the ballet *Palm Beach*.

1927 Series of watercolours of Nice.

1928 Paints for the most part in the Bois de Boulogne (Paris).

1929 Deauville.

1932 Does pottery with Artigas.
Designs a drawing-room suite for the great Beauvais tapestry factory.

1936 Illustrates *Mon Docteur Le Vin* for the Parisian wine-merchant, Nicolas.

1937 Works on large-scale decorations for the Palais de l'Electricité at the Paris Exhibition.

1940 Dufy moves to Perpignan.
Executes large-scale decorations for the entrance-hall of the monkey-house at the Jardin des Plantes, Paris. The work—not yet installed—comprises two large panels.

1942 Makes a copy of Renoir's *Moulin de la Galette*.

1944 Scenery for Salacrou's *Les Fiancés du Havre*.
To-day our great colourist maintains that "colour is not painting." In contrast with Matisse, who has never wearied of chromatism, Dufy confines himself to what he calls' tonal painting,' i.e. reducing the number of colours to a minimum. Thus he has painted pictures in a single tone, as for example *The Red Violin*, reproduced earlier in the book, in which apart from the white—red is the sole colour employed.
Dufy has also painted a *Dark Seascape*. This picture calls to mind a remark once dropped by Matisse, to the effect that, with black, a painter can convey all colours.

BIBLIOGRAPHY

Raoul Dufy, *Sélection*, 1928 ; C. Zervos, *Cahiers d'Art*, Paris, 1928 ; M. Berr de Turquie, Paris, 1930 ; F. Fleuret, Paris, 1931 ; Claude Roger-Marx, in René Huyghe's *Histoire de l'Art Contemporain*, Paris, 1935 ; R. Escholier, *La Peinture Française au XXᵉ Siècle*, Paris, 1937 ; *Trésors de la Peinture Française*, Geneva, 1946 ; Pierre Camo, Lausanne, 1947 ; Bernard Dorival, *Etapes de la Peinture Française Contemporaine*, Paris, 1948 ; René Huyghe, *Les Contemporains*, Paris, 1949 ; Maximilien Gauthier, Paris, 1949.

ENSOR, JAMES (1860-1949)

James Ensor presents a problem for his biographers. From its beginning to its recent close, his life was one of tranquil domesticity, quite devoid of any exceptional events.

1860 Born April 13 at Ostend of an English father and Flemish mother. The family runs a small business, selling 'Souvenirs of Ostend.' The shop is filled with *bric-à-brac*—jewelcases made of sea-shells, Japanese and Chinese vases, tiny ships fitted inside bottles—that stir the boy's imagination.
First drawing lessons from a little known Ostend artist, named Van Cuick.

1877 Attends the Académie des Beaux-Arts, Brussels, until 1879. Does drawings from the antique.

1879 Returns to Ostend, where he makes his home for the rest of his life. His first sketches show the influence of Van Gogh.

1880 His personal style asserts itself.

1881 Joins the art society *La Chrysalide*.

1882 Joins the *Essor* group.

1883 A section of the *Essor*, including Ensor, breaks away and forms the group known as the *XX* (17 painters and 3 sculptors).

1884 First exhibition of the *XX* at Brussels; the group puts on a number of exhibitions in the years to come.

1886 First etchings.

1888 Paints his famous *Entrance of Christ into Brussels*.

1891 *Libre Esthétique* group.

1899 The magazine *La Plume* puts out a special issue on Ensor, with contributions by Camille Lemonnier, Edmond Picard, Emile Verhaeren, Maurice Maeterlinck.
Retrospective Exhibition, Palais des Beaux-Arts, Brussels.

1900 'Discovers' negro art at the Palais de Tervueren.

1930 A Baronetcy is conferred on Ensor by King Albert I.
Ensor Exhibition in Paris (Galerie des Beaux-Arts). To get his *Entrance of Christ* into the gallery, a balcony has to be dismantled.

1949 Rumours of Ensor's death had gone round and obituary notices were frequent. Actually he died on November 19, in his 90th year.

BIBLIOGRAPHY

Eugène Demolder, *James Ensor*, Brussels 1892 and Paris 1899 ; Vittorio Pica, *James Ensor*, Bergamo, 1902 ; Emile Verhaeren, *James Ensor*, Brussels, 1908 ; Herbert von Garvens-Garvensburg, *James Ensor, Maler, Radierer, Komponist*, Hanover, 1913 ; Paul Colin, *James Ensor*, Potsdam, 1921 ; Grégoire Le Roy, *James Ensor*, Brussels and Paris, 1922 ; Firmin Cuypers, *James Ensor, l'Homme et l'Oeuvre*, Paris, 1925 ; Paul Desmeth, *James Ensor*, Brussels, 1926 ; Alexandre Dörner, H. von Garvens-Garvensburg and Wilhelm Fränger, *James Ensor*, Hanover, 1927 ; Paul Fierens, *James Ensor*, Paris, 1929 ; André de Ridder, *James Ensor*, Paris, 1930 ; Paul Colin, *James Ensor*, Leipzig, 1931 ; Jean Teugels, *Variations sur James Ensor*, Ostend, 1931 ; Lucien Schwob, *Ensor*, Brussels, 1936 ; Paul Desmeth, *Paysages Bruxellois, suivis d'une Etude sur James Ensor*, Brussels and Paris, new edition 1937 ; Leo van Puyvelde, *L'Ardente Peinture d'Ensor*, in the *Gazette des Beaux-Arts*, Paris, 1939 ; Jozef Muls, *James Ensor, Peintre de la Mer*, Brussels, 1942 ; Paul Fierens, *James Ensor*, Paris, 1943 ; Paul Fierens, *Les Dessins d'Ensor*, Brussels and Paris, 1944 ; Firmin Cuypers, *Aspects et Propos de James Ensor*, Bruges, 1946.

FRIESZ, EMILE OTHON (1879-1949)

1879 Born at Le Havre of a family of shipwrights and sailors. His father's side of the family came from Scandinavia and Holland (Friesz means ' Frisian '), his mother from Normandy. Friesz's father was a sea-captain.

1885 Enters the Lycée where he soon strikes up a friendship with Raoul Dufy.

1891 Drawing is already his favourite pastime.

1895-96 Learns the rudiments of painting at the Ecole des Beaux-Arts, Le Havre, under the supervision of Charles Lhullier, a follower of Ingres. In the same class are Raoul Dufy and Georges Braque.

1897 Thanks to the good offices of Lhullier, he receives a grant of 1200 francs a year from the Municipality of Le Havre, enabling him to proceed to Paris.

1898 In October he enrols at the Ecole des Beaux-Arts, Paris. Works at first in Bonnat's class (where Dufy joins him in 1900), then in Gustave Moreau's class, where he meets Matisse, Marquet, and Rouault.
At the Louvre, he ' interprets ' Veronese, Delacroix, Rubens, Corot.
At the Durand-Ruel Gallery, his eyes are opened to the Impressionists.

1900 First exhibition at the Salon des Artistes Français.

1901 Makes the acquaintance of Pissarro, and stays in the Creuse ' Department,' doing a good many landscapes ; here he meets Guillaumin.

1903 Exhibits at Salon des Indépendants.

1904 Exhibits at Salon d'Automne, with Marquet, Matisse, Manguin, Puy, and others. Works at Cassis.

1905 Takes part in the Salon d'Automne, in the *Cage des Fauves*.

1906 Visits Antwerp ; then La Ciotat, accompanied by Braque.

1907 La Ciotat. Interest in arabesques and architectural composition. Druet becomes his exclusive buyer.

1908 Paints the *Cathedral of Rouen*, now at the Moscow Museum.

1908-10 Still much interested in problems of structure ; his tones become darker.

1909 Trip to Italy, via Munich ; greatly impressed by Giotto.

1911 Trip to Portugal.

1912 Breaks off relations with Druet.

1913 Successful large-scale exhibition at Paul Cassirer's in Berlin.

1914 Appointed to professorships at the Académie Moderne, the Académie Scandinave and the ' Académie de la Grande Chaumière.'

1915 Paints the famous portrait of Mme Othon Friesz.

1919 Stays in Provence and at Toulon.

1924 Awarded the Carnegie Foundation prize.

1935 *La Paix* : tapestry design for *Les Gobelins* (state factory for Gobelin tapestry).

1937 He and Dufy are commissioned to do decorations for the Palais de Chaillot : *La Seine*.

1938 Becomes a member of the Carnegie Foundation. Visits the United States.

1949 Dies in Paris, in January.

BIBLIOGRAPHY

F. Fleuret, preface to catalogue (exhib. Druet Gal.), Paris, Nov. 1907 ; A. Salmon, *Nouvelle Revue Française*, Paris, 1920 ; L.G. Cann, *The Arts*, New York, Nov. 1926 ; F. Fleuret, C. Vildrac, A. Salmon, *Chroniques du Jour*, Paris, 1928 ; R. Brielle, Paris, 1930 ; F. Neugass, *Die Kunst*, Munich, Sept. 1928 ; M. Le Sieutre, Paris, 1931 ; F. Neugass, *L'Amour de l'Art*, Paris, July, 1933 ; M. Gauthier, Paris, 1949.

HODLER, FERDINAND (1853-1918)

1853 Born March 14 in Bern. Childhood in conditions of extreme poverty.

1857 Family moves to La Chaux-de-Fonds.

1858 His father dies of consumption.

1861 His mother marries the house-painter Schüpbach in Bern.

1867 His mother dies of consumption. Hodler works with his step-father to help support the large family.

1869-70 Lessons at Thun with the painter Ferdinand Sommer, who earns a livelihood selling small genre paintings of the Bernese Oberland to tourists.

1871 Relations becoming strained, Hodler leaves Sommer and goes to his uncle, the cobbler Neukomm at Langenthal. Hodler hesitates between painting and studying natural science. Fame of the geologist and zoologist Karl Vogt draws him to Geneva. Copies works by Calame and Diday. Makes a living selling small genre pictures and doing occasional house-painting. Does his best to acquire the breeding and education hitherto denied him.

1872 First self-portrait, reflecting his keen desire to ' realize ' himself.

1873 Studies with Menn, a friend of Corot and Delacroix.

1874 Menn's influence first seen in his self-portrait, *The Student.* Studies Dürer's theory of proportions and Leonardo's *Treatise on Painting.*

1876 Prize-winner in the competition of the 'Société des Arts' with his *Turnerbankett.* During his earlier stay in Langenthal he had contacts with religious groups, whose influence lingers. Hesitates for a while between the call of art and that of religion.

1878-79 Trip to Spain. Open-air landscapes.

1880 His religious emotion finds expression in his big composition *Das Gebet im Kanton Bern.* The self-portrait *Angry Man* is Hodler's retort to the hostile attitude of the Geneva critics and public. During the 1880's Hodler works out his theory of parallelism (rhythmic repetition of the leitmotif).

1887 First one-man show at Bern.

1890 Hodler paints his *Night,* which marks the 'divide' between his early work and the monumental allegorical paintings of his later period. It is his *Night* that establishes his reputation, despite much opposition.

1892 Paints *Disillusioned Souls* (shown in March in the Salon de la Rose-Croix in Paris), *The Life-Weary* (shown in the same year at the Champ-de-Mars) and in 1895 *Eurhythmy.*

1896 Exhibits figures of warriors on the pillars of the Swiss National Exposition in Geneva, in connexion with the competition for the ' Hall of Weapons ' murals at the Swiss National Museum in Zurich.
After violent controversy, Hodler's *Retreat from Marignano* is awarded first prize in the Zurich competition. The Marignano murals form the starting-point of modern historical painting. Hodler now paints his great historical pictures : *Tell,* in 1903 ; *Departure of the Jena Volunteers* for the University of Jena in 1908 ; *Oath of the Hanover Reformation* (also called *Unanimity*) for the town-hall in Hanover, 1913-14.

1897 Lectures at Fribourg (Switzerland) on *The Mission of the Artist* (published in E. Bender's *Die Kunst Hodlers,* Zurich, 1912).

1904 Upon his participation in the exhibition of the Vienna Secession (31 pictures), Hodler's fame spreads to Germany and Austria. *Day* (1900), *Truth* (1902-03), *Emotion* (1902-03), *Young Man Admired by Women* (1903), *Glance into Infinity* (three versions, 1915-16) : these typify Hodler's allegorical compositions.

1908 New development in his landscape painting inaugurated with his pictures of the Bernese Oberland and the Lake of Geneva.

1909 Portraits of the dying Augustine Dupin, mother of his only son, Hector.

1913-15 Series of portraits of Madame Darel, during her fatal illness.

1914-18 In his last four years Hodler breaks away from his fixed theory of parallelism. Last landscapes and portraits do not conform to any theoretical principles. 1917-18 : Landscapes of Lake of Geneva with Mont-Blanc. Hodler died in Geneva, May 19, 1918.

BIBLIOGRAPHY

The standard work is C. A. Loosli's article on Hodler in the *Schweizerisches Künstlerlexikon,* Volumes II and IV, Frauenfeld, 1908 and 1917 ; E. Bender on Hodler in the Thieme-Becker : *Allgemeines Lexikon der Bildenden Künstler,* Volume 17, Leipzig, 1924 ; C. A. Loosli, *F. Hodler : Leben, Werk und Nachlass,* Bern, 1924, four volumes ; fourth volume contains a nearly complete bibliography up to 1924, and a general catalogue of Hodler's works (2337 items) and all his writings ; for his correspondence, see Volumes I and IV ; W.Y. Müller, *Die Kunst F. Hodlers,* Zurich, 1941 (contains a catalogue of the landscapes).

JAWLENSKY, ALEXEI VON (1864-1941)

1864 Born March 26 in the Tver province of Russia (near Moscow). Military school in Moscow.

1889 Attends Art Academy, St Petersburg. Influenced by Ilya Repine.

1896 Moves to Munich and enrols in Anton Azbe's art school, where he meets Kandinsky. Becomes acquainted with Matisse and with Hodler ; studies their works.

1903 First exhibition with the Munich Secession.

1905 Paints in Brittany (Carantec) and Provence.

1909 One of the founders of the ' New Association of Artists,' Munich.

1911 Stays at Prerow, on the North Sea : portraits and landscapes.

1912 Meets Nolde and Klee.

1914 On the outbreak of war, he takes refuge at St. Prex (Switzerland).

1917-21 Paints his series of mystical portraits, figures of Christ, abstract heads. Stays in Zurich, then at Ascona.

1920 Retrospective exhibition at Gurlitt Gallery, Berlin.

1921 Settles at Wiesbaden (Germany).

1924 He, Feininger, Kandinsky and Klee found the group known as *Die Blauen Vier* (The Blue Four), whose largest exhibition takes place in 1929 at the Möller Gallery, Berlin.

1929-30 Abstract heads influenced by Cubism. His last works are reminiscent of Russian icons.

1941 Dies March 15 at Wiesbaden, after a protracted illness.

BIBLIOGRAPHY

W. A. Lutz, *Der Cicerone,* 1921 ; R. Reiche, *Das Feuer,* Weimar, 1921 ; W. Grohmann, *Cahiers d'Art,* 1934 ; W. Moufang, Catalogue, Gal. Ralfs, Braunschweig, 1948 ; In preparation : Monograph by Wilhelm Moufang, Heidelberg.

KANDINSKY, WASSILY (1866-1944)

Allied for a time with the ' Die Brücke ' group, Kandinsky soon began to move in the direction of non-representational art. In 1911, he was one of the founders of ' Der Blaue Reiter.' A study of this group will appear in our third volume, as well as extensive information on Kandinsky's life and work.

KIRCHNER, ERNST LUDWIG (1880-1938)

1880 Born May 6 at Aschaffenburg, where his father was an engineer. The family moves to Frankfurt-on-the-Main. Kirchner's early attempts at drawing and painting encouraged by his father.

1887-89 The family moves to Perlen, near Lucerne. Kirchner senior manages a local paper factory, until he is appointed to a professorship at Chemnitz. Elementary and high school in Chemnitz.

1898 Study trip to Nuremberg. Much impressed by Dürer and the old wood engravings and incunabula.
Makes his first woodcuts.

1901 Studies architecture at the Technical Institute in Dresden. Painting on the side.

1902 Works at art with his friend Fritz Bleyl, another architecture student. First etchings.

1903 Studies two semesters under W. Debschitz and Hermann Obrist in Munich. Rembrandt's sketches stimulate his drawing.

1904 Resumes his architecture studies in Dresden. Collaboration with Heckel and Bleyl. Studies the theories of colour expounded by Goethe, Helmholtz, Newton and Rood. Tries to break away from the naturalistic use of colour. Paintings in the pointillist style (influenced by Neo-Impressionist Exhibition of the 'Phalanx,' Munich, 1904).
Admiration for Seurat; studies the work of Beham, Cranach and other mediaeval German masters. Stimulated by Japanese prints on show at Arnold's, the book-and-art dealer. Kirchner now discovers negro art and carvings by the Palau islanders in the Ethnological Museum. Heckel transforms an empty butcher's shop on the Berlinerstrasse into a studio. In Kirchner's living-room and Heckel's studio the artists work together.

1905 Through Heckel, meeting with the architecture student Karl Schmidt-Rottluff. Together they form the art group styled 'Die Brücke' (The Bridge). Kirchner gets his degree in architecture and now devotes himself entirely to painting. First lithographs.

1906 Meeting with Cuno Amiet, Axel Galén, Nolde, Pechstein. Heckel lets him use his studio. Works with Pechstein during the summer, near Dresden. Draws up the programme of 'Die Brücke.' First and second exhibitions of 'Die Brücke' at Dresden-Löbtau.

1907-09 Summer months with his friends on the Lake of Moritzburg, north of Dresden, where they paint from the nude in the open air. In the winter they live and work together in Heckel's and Kirchner's studios on the Berlinerstrasse.

1910 Meeting with Otto Müller. Trip with Müller to Northern Bohemia and Moritzburg. The 'Die Brücke' album of 1910 is his work. Exhibits with the New Secession of Berlin.

1911 Moves in the spring to Berlin. *Der Sturm* publishes illustrations by Kirchner. He and Pechstein found the MUIM Institute *(Moderner Unterricht in Malerei)* in Berlin-Wilmersdorf. Not a single pupil enrols.

1912 Kirchner and Heckel do frescos for the 'Chapel' in the International Exhibition of the 'Sonderbund' at Cologne. Under the influence of city life, Kirchner's style evolves towards psychological expressionism.
Takes part in the second 'Blaue Reiter' Exhibition at the Goltz Gallery in Munich; also in the 'Blaue Reiter' Exhibition at the *Der Sturm* Gallery in Berlin. Meeting with Erna Schilling, who becomes his devoted friend. His friends commission Kirchner to write a *Chronik der Brücke* (Chronicle of The Bridge).

1913 Summer at Fehmarn. His friends reject the *Chronik der Brücke* as being too subjective. Only a few copies printed. Break-up of the group.

1914 Summer at Fehmarn. At the outbreak of war, Kirchner enlists as an artillery-driver.

1915-16 Military training at Halle. Found to be physically and mentally unfit for service, Kirchner is released and sent to Dr Kohnstamm's sanatorium at Königstein, in the Taunus. Paint his first murals for the staircase of the sanatorium. Lives in dread of being called up again.

1917 Goes to Davos on May 8, where with enormous energy he sets to work once more. On September 15, he goes to Dr Binswanger's sanatorium at Kreuzlingen.

1918 Returns to Davos on July 9, after a partial cure. It is amazing how quickly Kirchner, city-bred painter though he is, achieves expression of a world quite new to him, that of countryfolk and mountains. His impressions are recorded in thousands of drawings, woodcuts and lithographs, and landscape finds new forms of expression in his large pictures, more and more abstract in their conception. With the Armistice, Kirchner's physical recovery is complete.

1922 From 1922 to 1938, the weaver Lise Gujer works with Kirchner, making carpets from his designs.

1923 Exhibition in the Basel Kunsthalle, where his paintings make a deep impression on the younger Basel artists.

1924 Publication of the book *Umbra Vitae* by Georg Heym, with illustrations by Kirchner. With this book Kirchner made one of the most significant contributions to modern German book-illustration.

1925-26 The Basel painters Camenisch, Albert Müller and Hermann Scherer work under Kirchner's guidance. Together they form the 'Red-Blue' group.

1929-33 Meeting with René Crevel.
Commissioned to decorate the Folkwang Museum at Essen. The German government prevents Kirchner from carrying out the order. Member of the Academy of Plastic Arts in Berlin (1931).

1937 In Germany 639 of his works are confiscated as 'degenerate.' 32 of them are shown in the so-called 'Degenerate Art' Exhibition in Munich.

1938 Suffering from a steadily worsening intestinal disease and in despair over the political and intellectual developments in Germany, Kirchner committed suicide in Switzerland on June 15.

BIBLIOGRAPHY

G. Shiefler, *Die Grafik E. L. Kirchners bis 1916*, Berlin, 1920; *Das Graphische Werk bis 1924*, Berlin, 1926; W. Grohmann, *Kirchners Zeichnungen*, Dresden, 1925; W. Grohmann, *Das Werk E. L. Kirchners*, Munich, 1926; R. Schapiro on *E. L. Kirchner*, in the Thieme-Becker *Allgemeines Lexikon der Bildenden Künstler*, volume 20, Leipzig, 1927; with bibliography.
Kirchner's views on art and outlook on life are set forth in some twenty articles he published in the course of his career, some under his own name, some with the pseudonym 'Louis de Marsalle.'

KOKOSCHKA, Oskar (1886)

1886 Born March 1 at Pöchlarn-on-the-Danube (Austria).
As a student, Kokoschka was deeply impressed by the South Sea masks and negro art shown at ethnographic exhibitions in Vienna.

1904-08 Student at the School of Arts and Crafts. Friendship with Egon Schiele, his schoolmate.

1907 First oil paintings : *The Trance Player* and the *Portrait of Frau Hirsch*. First poetic writings : the dramas *Sphinx and Straw Man* and *Woman's Hope*. These works rank high in the literature of Expressionism.

1908 The first Vienna Kunstschau exhibits Kokoschka's work for the first time : colour illustrations from his book *The Dreaming Children* (published by the Wiener Werkstätte), and the life-size drawings *Bearers of Dreams*. The works exhibited rouse the ire of the official critics. With the result that Kokoschka is expelled from the Art School. He now meets the well-known architect Adolf Loos, who becomes his friend and guide. Through Loos he meets the poets Peter Altenberg and Karl Kraus, whose magazine *The Torch* lends its support to the young painter.

The illustrations of *The Dreaming Children*, in their sensitivity of line and decorative use of colour and planes, bear the stamp of Gustav Klimt, to whom the work is dedicated. Also perceptible is the influence of Hodler. *The Dreaming Children* is one of the outstanding art-books of ' Jugendstil,' as well as one of the most significant in XXth-century German book illustration.

1909 Takes part in the second Kunstschau. At the exhibition's open-air theatre the plays *Sphinx and Straw Man* and *Woman's Hope* are performed and give rise to violent protests. Leaves Vienna for Switzerland. Paints the portraits of Bessie Loos, the Countess of Rohan-Montesquiou, and of the Swiss savant, Auguste Forel ; also *Winter Landscape*.

1910 Trip to Berlin. Introduced by Loos to the *Der Sturm* group. Becomes one of the chief collaborators, also writing occasionally for the magazine. Friendship with Herwarth Walden and his then wife, the poetess Else Lasker-Schüler. First one-man exhibition in the Paul Cassirer Gallery.

Soon after, makes a contract with Cassirer. Portraits of the early *Sturm* poets : R. Blümner, Richard Dehmel, Paul Scheerbart, H. Walden. In the early portraits, strong emphasis is laid on the psychologically significant.

From 1910 to 1914, numerous journeys between Berlin and Vienna.

1911 25 pictures and several drawings in the ' Hagenbund ' exhibition in Vienna. Official criticism once again sharply challenges Kokoschka's work, culminating in the remark of the heir to the Austrian throne : " The fellow deserves to have every bone in his body broken."

1912-14 H. Walden organizes Kokoschka's second one-man exhibition in the *Sturm* Gallery, at the same time as the first ' Blaue Reiter ' exhibition.

Takes part in the ' Sonderbund ' Exhibition at Cologne. Friendship with Alma Mahler. The influence of this talented and beautiful woman results in the *Portrait of Alma Mahler, Double-Portrait* (1913), *The Tempest* (1914), as well as lithographic illustrations.

On the outbreak of war, serves in the Dragoons.

1915-16 Wounded on the Eastern Front in the lungs and head, he is sent to a hospital in Vienna, then returned to the front. Continued lung-trouble and mental unbalance due to the head-wound send him back to hospital.

1917 Consults a brain specialist in Stockholm. Paints *Stockholm Harbour*.

Swiss première of his play *Sphinx and Straw Man* at the Dada Gallery in Zurich on April 14. The actors are Hugo Ball, W. Hartmann, E. Hennings, F. Glauser. Joint exhibition with Max Ernst, Kandinsky, Klee and others in the Dada Gallery.

Moves in a circle of young poets and actors who forgather in the ' White Stag ' Café, Dresden. Paints at this time the great portrait compositions *Exiles* and *Friends* (1917-18).

1918 Writes the play *Orpheus and Eurydice*. Orders from a woman artist a life-size female doll in whose company he is often to be seen at the theatre in Dresden. Kokoschka's letters on the genesis of the doll are in P. Westheim's *Der Fetisch*, included in *Künstlerbekenntnisse*, Berlin 1925, and, in English, in E. Hoffmann's *Kokoschka, Life and Work*, London, 1947.

1919 Performances of *Hiob* and *The Burning Bush* in Max Reinhardt's Kammerspiele in Berlin with scenery by Kokoschka. Appointment to professorship at the Academy of Art, Dresden.

1921 Returns to Biblical themes with *Saul and David, Lot and his Daughters* (1923), etc. ' Expressive ' landscapes of the city of Dresden.

1924 Gives up his teaching post. A stay at Blonay, near Vevey (Switzerland). Landscapes. Death of his father. Return to Vienna. Portrait of the composer Arnold Schönberg. Visits Bordeaux, Biarritz, Avignon, Aigues-Mortes, Marseilles, Toledo, Madrid, Lisbon, Amsterdam. Landscapes and paintings of cities.

1926 First stay in London. Paintings : *Waterloo Bridge* and *The Mandrill*.

1927 Exhibitions at Cassirer's in Berlin and Zurich.

1928-30 Tunisia, Italy, Istanbul, Jerusalem, Ireland, Egypt, Algeria, Italy.

1931 Exhibition at Georges Petit's in Paris. Contract with Cassirer cancelled. Returns to Vienna.

1932 Takes part in the Venice Biennale.

1934 After assassination of Dollfuss, Kokoschka flees to Prague.

1937 First retrospective exhibition in Vienna, May and June. In Germany 417 of Kokoschka's works are confiscated as "degenerate." 16 works shown in the " Degenerate Art " Exhibition in Munich. The events in Germany and Austria and the tragic collapse of the Spanish Republic make a deep impression on him. In Prague he paints Thomas Masaryk, the ageing President of Czechoslovakia.

1938 Following the events at Munich, he leaves for London.

1940 After a stay in Cornwall, returns to London during the darkest days of the Battle of Britain. In articles and allegorical pictures he expresses his horror at what the war is making of the world, and man's degradation. *Alice in Wonderland* (1942), *What We Are Fighting For* (1943). With the money thus earned, he helps war victims. Becomes an honorary citizen of Vienna in 1946.

1947 Trip to Switzerland. Big Kokoschka Exhibition at the Basel Kunsthalle, continued at the Zurich Kunsthaus. In the Valais he paints boldly conceived landscapes of intense colour and strength.

Exhibitions in Amsterdam in November 1947, at the Venice Biennale of 1948, and in the United States during 1949: at Boston, New York, St Louis and San Francisco. Kokoschka now lives and works in London.

BIBLIOGRAPHY

P. Westheim, *O. Kokoschka*, Potsdam, 1919 (2nd edition, revised and enlarged, 1925); G. Biermann, *O. Kokoschka*, in *Junge Kunst*, No. 52, Leipzig, 1929; H. Heilmaier, *O. Kokoschka*, Paris, 1929; Kokoschka, Handzeichnungen (1906-1932), with letterpress *Lebensgeschichte von O. Kokoschka*, and 126 plates, Berlin, 1935; M. Masciotta, *Disegni di Kokoschka*, Florence, 1942; H. Platschek, *O. Kokoschka*, Buenos-Aires, 1946 (in Spanish); E. Hoffmann, *Kokoschka, Life and Work*, containing two essays by Kokoschka and foreword by Herbert Read, London, 1947 (most important book thus far written on Kokoschka, with catalogue of his works, 1907 to 1945, and nearly complete bibliography).

MARQUET, ALBERT (1875-1947)

1875 Born March 27 at Bordeaux, where he first goes to school.

1890 Comes to Paris. Attends the Ecole des Arts Décoratifs, then moves on to the Ecole des Beaux-Arts.

1897 Enrols in Gustave Moreau's class, where he quickly gets to know Rouault and Matisse; forms a lifelong friendship with Matisse. Has an extremely hard time of it for a while, doing hack-work at the Grand Palais, and tedious opera sets at Jambon's.

1898 First landscapes in the 'Fauve' manner. Paints with Matisse in the mornings in the Luxembourg Gardens, in the afternoons at Arcueil.

1901 Exhibits at the Salon des Indépendants yearly from 1901 to 1910.

1902 Exhibits at the Berthe Weill Gallery.

1903 Exhibits at Salon d'Automne.

1904 Paints André Rouveyre's portrait.

1907 First one-man show at Druet's.

1908 Enters the Académie Ranson, where he becomes acquainted with Frantz Jourdain.

1910 Begins to travel more widely.

1912 Visits numerous seaports: Le Havre, Naples, Hamburg, Rotterdam, Rouen, Tangier, Sète, Bordeaux, Dunkerque. Trip to Norway.

1915 Settles at Marseilles.

1925 Works more in watercolours than in oils.

1940 For the duration of the war settles at Algiers, where he is in touch with Saint-Exupéry and André Gide.

1945 Returns to Paris.

1946 Journey to Russia.

1947 Dies on June 14.

BIBLIOGRAPHY

C. Sterling and G. Bazin in René Huyghe's *Histoire de l'Art Contemporain*, Paris, 1935; C. Roger-Marx, *Gazette des Beaux-Arts*, Paris, March, 1939; F. Schmalenbach, Basel, 1941; *Marquet: Dessins*, in *Le Point*, Paris, Dec. 1943; G. Besson, Paris, 1947; James W. Lane, *Gazette des Beaux-Arts*, Paris and New York, May-June, 1947.

MATISSE, HENRI (1869)

1869 Born December 31 at Le Cateau (in the North of France). His father was a grain-merchant at Bohain. His mother was artistic and used to spend her leisure painting china. At 12, he entered the Saint-Quentin Lycée and did well at classics; he was, however, an indifferent pupil and his attention was always wandering. It was his father's wish that he should study law.

1890 Goes to Paris to carry on his law studies, but prefers spending his time in the Louvre. Back at home with his parents, convalescing from an illness, he happens to read Goupil's *How to Paint*. His first picture is a *Still Life with Books*.

1891 His father puts him to work in a solicitor's office; at the same time, on the sly, Matisse enrols in the Ecole Quentin de la Tour, where he works in the morning, before going to the office. In the end, his parents consent to his devoting himself wholly to painting.

1892 Matisse returns to Paris and enrols at the Académie Julian. He works under Bouguereau and Ferrier, members of the Institute, and studies especially Chardin and Goya.

1893 Ecole des Beaux-Arts, in Gustave Moreau's class. This teacher gives him much kindly advice and help. He meets Rouault, Marquet, Piot, Camoin, Manguin. At the Louvre he copies the Masters.

1896 Exhibits for the first time at Salon de la Société Nationale, showing four pictures. During this period, Matisse still uses the dark tonalities of museum art. It is not long, however, before he discovers Daumier, Degas, Lautrec, the Japanese and—most important!—the Seine. He and Marquet set up a studio together at 19, quai Saint-Michel. Begins his copy of Chardin's *The Ray*.
Stays in Brittany (Belle-Ile) with the painter Véry, pupil of Bonnat; does land- and seascapes. He utilizes to the full the lessons of Impressionism, but soon moves beyond them.
Matisse now goes alone to Beurec-Cap-Sizun (Finistère), where he paints a *Church* and *Woman with a Pig*.

1897 Takes to using brighter colours. Paints *La Desserte*; meets Camille Pissarro.
Exhibits five pictures at the Société Nationale.

1898 Matisse 'discovers' Provence. Great admiration for Renoir and Cézanne. Stays in Corsica during the winter. Returns to Paris, with the intention of re-entering Moreau's class. His old teacher has passed away, however, succeeded by Cormon. Matisse studies a short time under Cormon, then enters Carrière's class, applying himself to the study of the human figure. Meets Derain, Laprade, Puy. When Carrière closes down his studio, he works at Jean Biette's, rue Dutot. Does a large male nude, painted wholly in blue.
Begins to have a hard time of it financially, finding few buyers for his pictures. He and Marquet get work doing decorations for the 1900 World's Fair.
Matisse now uses pure colour (*Nature Morte Orangée*). Exhibits *La Desserte* at Salon de la Société Nationale.
He and Marquet spend the mornings painting at the Luxembourg, the afternoons at Arcueil. Buys Cézanne's picture *Les Baigneuses* at Vollard's.

1900 Turns his attention to problems of sculpture, working in a municipal studio, rue Etienne-Marcel.

KOKOSCHKA
MARQUET
MATISSE

1901 At the Van Gogh Exhibition in Bernheim-Jeune's Gallery, Derain introduces Vlaminck to Matisse. Matisse visits the two painters at Chatou, to have a look at their pictures.

1902 Exhibits at Berthe Weill's, rue Victor-Massé, alongside Marquet, Manguin, Camoin.

1903 Salon d'Automne is founded by Rambosson, Desvallières, Rouault, Piot. Director is Frantz Jourdain; Matisse, Marquet and Bonnard are the 'shock-troops.'

1904 First exhibition at Ambroise Vollard's (preface by Roger Marx). Sells his picture *Phlox* to Olivier Saincère. Has a brief fling at Pointillism, soon gives it up, all idea of 'system' being repellent to him. The landscapes painted during the winter at Collioure and Saint-Tropez are done in broad tracts of flat colour.

1905 It is at this year's Salon d'Automne, grouping a large number of works by Matisse, Vlaminck, Derain, Manguin and Rouault, that Vauxcelles' famous remark baptises the young painters with the name 'Fauves.' Matisse exhibits *Luxe, Calme et Volupté*.

1906 Matisse gives up his studio at 19, quai Saint-Michel, moving to the former Couvent des Oiseaux in the rue de Sèvres, where he opens an academy. Purrmann and Bruce are among the early pupils. Paints *Le Bonheur de Vivre*, an early revelation of his commanding personality. Severe criticism is hurled at the Fauves, particularly at Matisse, who is looked upon as the ringleader. Matisse moves his growing academy to the former Couvent du Sacré-Cœur, boulevard des Invalides. More and more pupils flock to him.
Makes the acquaintance of Picasso at Gertrude Stein's. Shows Picasso a negro statuette he has picked up at Père Sauvage's shop, in the rue de Rennes. Beginning of a lifelong friendship between the two painters.

1907 Exhibits at Cassirer's in Berlin. Paints his remarkable *Blue Nude* (Souvenir of Biskra).

1908 In the *Grande Revue* he publishes his *Notes d'un Peintre*, an epoch-making article destined to have a considerable effect on European art.

1909 Returns to the theme of *La Desserte*, painted in 1897, and makes two new versions: *Red Harmony* and *Blue Harmony*.
In this same year he paints *Poissons Rouges et Statue de Terre Rose*.

1910 First Retrospective Exhibition at Bernheim-Jeune's. Sends in *La Danse* and *Musique* to the Salon d'Automne.

1911-13 Moves to Issy-les-Moulineaux. Makes two trips to Morocco, accompanied the second time by Camoin and the Canadian painter Morice. The African landscape gives Matisse a taste for the bare and formally patterned. He rejects the casual for what is permanent. He returns from Morocco with several pictures now reckoned among his masterpieces.
He now takes up sculpture. Interested in recent developments of Cubism.

1915-16 Paints several of his best works in these years: *The Piano Lesson, Young Girl Bathing, Moroccan Women, Still Life with Colocynths*. In these pictures the spareness of construction is in perfect harmony with his geometric vision.

1917 Moves to Nice, where he gets to know Renoir. Paints his famous *Interior at Nice* (now in the Copenhagen Museum). This, he says, is "one of my most beautiful pictures."

1918 A certain realism reappears in his work. Paints the series of *Odalisques*. Moving away from both Fauve and Cubist methods, he harks back to Delacroix. Now sees Morocco from a more orientalist angle.

1919 *The White Plumes.*
Large exhibition at Bernheim's.

1920 Visits Etretat. Sets for the ballet *Le Chant du Rossignol*.

1929 His *Le Compotier* is awarded first prize at the Pittsburgh International Exposition. In 1930 he is invited to be a member of the jury.

1930 Retrospective Exhibition in Berlin.

1931 After a series of journeys—in Italy, Spain, Germany, England, Russia—Matisse sets out for the South Seas. Stays three months at Tahiti where he is fascinated by the utter novelty of everything he sees, and stores up innumerable impressions, haunted by memories of Gauguin. On the return journey, he stops in the United States, where Dr Barnes commissions him to decorate the largest hall in his museum at Merion (Pa.). Matisse undertakes the task. Through an error in measurement, he has to do the decoration twice (for an area of 52 square yards), only finishing in 1933. The first version is bought by the city of Paris.
This period is marked by a change in Matisse's work, a second flowering, so to speak. His conceptions of art have reached their most advanced stage. The supreme visions of his creative genius now are bodied forth in terms of a geometrical architecture which gives them their fullest significance. Retrospective Exhibition at the Georges Petit Gallery, Paris, and at the Museum of Modern Art, New York.

1932 Illustrations for Mallarmé's *Poésies* (Editions Skira).

1936 From now on, Matisse draws on the accumulated knowledge of long years of work to revive certain tendencies of his 'Fauve period'; the resulting works are among the most serene and significant of his career. Retrospective Matisse exhibitions are put on in Paris, New York, Stockholm.

1939 Retires to the Var Valley (Vence).
Drawn to illustration and typography, he illustrates several books whose entire format is his creation.

1943 After successfully undergoing a dangerous operation, he branches out in several new directions. As a corollary to his usage of flat colour, he now assembles compositions consisting of pieces of coloured paper cut out with scissors. Begins preliminary studies for his illustrations of Ronsard's *Amours*.

1944 Large-scale Matisse Exhibition at Salon d'Automne.
Does illustrations for Montherlant's *Pasiphaé*.

1945 Matisse Exhibition at Victoria and Albert Museum, London.

1947 Matisse Exhibition at Palais des Papes, Avignon.
Illustrations for Baudelaire's *Fleurs du Mal*.

1948 Large-scale exhibition of his pictures, drawings and sculpture at Museum of Art, Philadelphia (271 items).

1949 Matisse Exhibition at the Kunstmuseum, Lucerne.
At Vence, he undertakes the decoration of a Dominican chapel whose lay-out is designed

by him. Matisse intends it to be at once a résumé and a solution of the problems engrossing him throughout his career.

BIBLIOGRAPHY

M. Sembat, Paris, 1920 ; F. Fels, Paris, 1929 ; H. Purrmann, Berlin, 1922 ; A. H. Barr, *Catalogue, Museum of Modern Art*, New York, 1931 ; G. Scheiwiller, Milan, 1933 ; P. Courthion, Paris, 1934 ; A. Romm, Moscow, 1937 ; R. Escholier, Paris, 1937 ; P. Fierens, Bergamo, 1938 ; L. Swane, Stockholm, 1944 ; I. Grunewald, Stockholm, 1944 ; Aragon, *Catalogue, Philadelphia Exhibition*, 1948.

MODERSOHN-BECKER, Paula
(1876-1907)

1876 Born February 8 in Dresden.

1888 The family moves to Bremen.

1892 Spends almost a year with relatives in a suburb of London. First lessons in drawing and painting at a London art school.

1893-95 Following her father's wishes, she attends the schoolteachers' seminary in Bremen.

1896 Art-school in Berlin.

1897 First stay at Worpswede in the summer. Under the supervision of Fritz Mackensen, she sketches peasants, inmates of the poorhouse, and the landscape. Returns in the autumn to Berlin.
Worpswede : a picturesque village on the moorland near Bremen. Mackensen settled here to paint in 1884, followed later by Otto Modersohn, in 1892 by Fritz Overbeck, in 1894 by Heinrich Vogeler and others. The ' Worpswede Society of Artists ' was founded in 1895 ; a school of naturalistic ' genre ' painters strongly influenced round about 1900 by ' Jugendstil.'

1898 Trip to Norway. Settles at Worpswede in the autumn, working in the spirit of the painters there. Becomes a close friend of the sculptress, Clara Westhoff, later, wife of the poet R. M. Rilke.

1899 She has her first doubts about the art practised at Worpswede, now that she is trying to chart a course more naturally her own. Short trip to Switzerland in the summer.
In December, her first exhibition of sketches at the Bremen Kunsthalle has a devastating reception from the critics.

1900 Goes to Paris on January 1. Attends the Académie Colarossi (at the Grande Chaumière), studying under Collin, Courtois, Girandot ; anatomy course at the Ecole des Beaux-Arts. Much impressed by Cottet and Lucien Simon, whose art runs parallel to that at Worpswede. Wins the medal at the Académie Colarossi. She and Clara Westhoff—now a student of Rodin—meet Nolde.
" He has had the happy idea," she writes in a letter, " of drawing the mountains in the form of grotesque human faces, and had them printed as postcards. Some have been published in *Jugend*." In a letter to Clara Westhoff, dated October 21, 1907, she writes : " I've thought so hard about Cézanne to-day, for he is one of the three or four giants who have swept me off my feet, like a great rushing wind. Do you remember how already at Vollard's, in 1900...? "

1901 Marries Otto Modersohn May 25 ; at nearly the same time as Clara Westhoff's marriage with Rilke. She and Modersohn visit Prague and Munich, spend a short time with the poet Karl Hauptmann, and visit the playwright Gerhart Hauptmann.
She and her husband work together. She turns away from the naturalism of her Worpswede friends, towards a new, more personal style. Second stay in Paris.

1903 February and March in Paris. From her *Journal*, February 15 : " Saw to-day an exhibition of old Japanese painting and sculpture. The night side of life, the terrible, the lovely, the feminine, the playful—all these it seems to express in a forthright yet childlike way, so different from ours. First things first ! "
Rilke's monograph on Worpswede painting comes out ; contains no mention of Paula Modersohn.

1905 Third stay in Paris, February-April. Still drawn to Cottet's work ; enrols in his class at Académie Julian. In her *Journal* she speaks of Vuillard, Denis, Bonnard. Of the Salon des Indépendants (May 24) she writes : " Fatuous conventionality alongside fantastic pointillist experimentalism. " On February 20 she moves from rue Cassette to 65 rue Madame.

1906 Centennial Exhibition in Berlin. Deeply impressed by Böcklin, Feuerbach, Leibl, Marées, Trübner.
During her first year of married life, she is filled with the joy of living and working with her husband. But when her work begins to draw away from his, marriage in her eyes becomes a threat to her art. In February 1906 she goes off to Paris, resolved to make her way alone. Anatomy course at Ecole des Beaux-Arts.
At the beginning of May, in the sculptor Bernhard Hoetger, whose work she greatly admires, she finds an equally great admirer of her own art. " Your belief in me is all the more beautiful, because I believe also in you. You have given me the most wonderful thing in the world : faith in myself." (Letter to Hoetger after his visit to her studio.)
She sees the Gauguin Memorial Exhibition at Salon d'Automne.
Autumn : her husband comes to Paris. Her feeling that now at last she has found her own way leads to a reunion, and they work together during the winter. In November at the Bremen Kunsthalle, joint exhibition of pictures by Paula and Otto Modersohn. Paula's work is hardly noticed.
In this year she produces her best work : portraits, still lifes, and a series of pictures whose central theme is motherhood.

1907 In the spring she returns with her husband to Worpswede. Gives birth to a daughter on November 2. Not yet 32, she dies suddenly of a heart-attack, on November 21.
At the age of 24, she wrote : " I know I'm not going to live very long. But is that so sad a thing ? Is a festival more beautiful because it lasts longer ? "

BIBLIOGRAPHY

R. M. Rilke, *Worpswede* (Knackfuss Monographs of Artists, No. 64), Leipzig, 1903 (no mention of Paula Modersohn) ; R. M. Rilke, *Requiem für Eine Freudin*,

Leipzig, 1909, 2nd edition, 1912 ; C. E. Uphoff, *P. Modersohn-Becker*, with a contribution by B. Hoetger, *Erinnerungen an Paula Modersohn* (from *Junge Kunst*, vol. 2), Leipzig, 1919 ; reproduced in *Der Cicerone*, 1919, and in *Jahrbuch der Jungen Kunst*, 1920 ; re-issued with letterpress by G. Bierbaum, Leipzig, 1927 ; S. D. Gallwitz, *30 Jahre Worpswede*, Bremen, 1922 ; H. Franck, *Meta Koggenpoord* (roman à clef), Heilbronn, 1925 ; K. Tegtmeier, *P. Modersohn-Becker*, a short biography with unpublished letters to M. and H. Vogeler, Bremen, 1927 ; W. Müller-Wulckow, *Bernhard Hoetgers P. Modersohn-Becker-Haus in der Bôttcherstrasse in Bremen*, Bremen, 1927 ; W. Müller-Wulckow, *Das P. Modersohn-Becker-Haus in Bremen* (with guide and map), Bremen, 1930 ; R. Hetsch, *P. Modersohn-Becker : Ein Buch der Freundschaft*, Berlin, 1932, with contributions by F. Mackensen, O. Modersohn, C. Rilke-Westhoff, R.M. Rilke, et al. ; M. Hausmann, *P. Modersohn-Becker*, Meisterbilder, Biberach/Riss, 1947 ; G. Busch, *Handzeichnungen*, Bremen, 1949.

MUNCH, EDVARD (1863-1944)

1863 Born December 12 at Löyten, Norway. His father, Christian Munch, was a doctor. The early death of his mother and two sisters left a lasting impression on Munch's mind, as did the difficulties of his father's work as doctor in a slum district of Oslo.

1881-84 School of Arts and Crafts in Oslo. Painting lessons from Christian Krogh.

1885 First visit to Paris ; stays three weeks.

1886 Joins the group styled ' The Bohemians of Christiania,' whose leading figure is the poet Hans Jäger. The rebellious, independent spirit of the group decisively shapes Munch's future work. First important paintings : *The Day After, Puberty, The Sick Girl, The Men of Letters.*

1889 First stay at Aasgaardstrand in the summer ; landscape painting. First one-man exhibition at Oslo. A government grant enables him to spend the winter in Paris.

1890 Four months in Léon Bonnat's class. Sees Japanese woodcuts, pictures by Pissarro, Seurat, Toulouse-Lautrec and, at Theo Van Gogh's gallery, Gauguin and Vincent Van Gogh. First trip to Germany.

1891 Journey to France, the Riviera, Italy. Paints in the pointillist style, under the influence of the Neo-Impressionists.

1892 First part of the *Frieze of Life* exhibited at Oslo. Invited to take part in the Exhibition of the Berlin Artists' Association, Munch comes to Berlin with 55 pictures. Exhibition opens November 5 in the Architektenhaus. Controversy over Munch's work leads to the decision to shut down the exhibition. As a reprisal, Munch puts on a one-man show at a gallery on the Friedrichstrasse. For him the scandal is a godsend. His name, bandied about in the newspapers, is soon on everyone's lips. Within the Association several members form a ' New Free Association,' in protest against the treatment of Munch.

1893 Meeting and friendship with Strindberg, and with Dagny and Stanislas Przybyszewsky. Moves in the literary group including Bierbaum, Dehmel, Meier-Graefe, Przybyszewsky, Scheerbart, Strindberg, whose headquarters is the ' Black Pig ' Café on the Wilhelmstrasse.

1894 First etchings. First book on Munch, written by Przybyszewsky.

1895 First issue of *Pan*, with illustrated matter contributed by Munch, Signac, Toulouse-Lautrec, Vallotton, and others.
First lithographs printed by A. Clot in Paris, who also prints Toulouse-Lautrec.

1896 First woodcuts. In Paris he frequents the circle of Mallarmé and *Le Mercure de France*. Sets for Ibsen's *Peer Gynt* at the Théâtre de l'Œuvre. Exhibition at the ' Art Nouveau ' Gallery.
Strained relations with Strindberg owing to their simultaneous infatuation with the wife of one of their friends. This ' affaire ' obsesses Munch for many years.

1897 His *Frieze of Life* exhibited at Salon des Indépendants. Works in the spirit of the Pont-Aven school.
His graphic work has a marked influence on his painting. Until about 1902, strong emphasis on decorative elements ; often with the symbolic, decorative edgings of ' Jugendstil.'

1898-1901 Travels in Germany. A period of rankling unease and economic troubles. Begins the series of life-size male portraits : *The Frenchman, Albert Kollmann*, etc.

1902 He meets the Lübeck oculist, Max Linde, who becomes his friend and patron. Commissioned to do portraits, as well as a second *Frieze of Life*. Album of etchings and lithographs *Aus dem Hause Linde* (From the Linde House). Through Meier-Graefe, he meets Paul Cassirer, secretary of the Secession. At the Berlin Secession Exhibition, Munch shows 28 pictures, 22 of them from his first *Frieze of Life*.

1903-04 Spring and winter in Germany : Lübeck and Hamburg.
Summer at Aasgaardstrand. Works on the second *Frieze of Life* for Linde. Completed, these pictures are not accepted, and are sold singly.

1905 Berlin and Hamburg. December at Elgersburg, in Thuringia. Etching : portrait of Schiefler.

1906 Stays with Count Kessler at Weimar. Portrait of Kessler. Meets Elisabeth Förster-Nietzsche, sister of the philosopher so much admired by Munch. Portrait of Nietzsche after photographs. Sets for Max Reinhardt's production of Ibsen's *Ghosts*. Reinhardt commissions him to do a third *Frieze of Life* for the foyer of the Berlin Kammerspiele.

1907 Berlin and Lübeck. Summer at Warnemünde. His picture *Men Bathing* (1907-08) foreshadows the later style of his Oslo University murals.

1908-09 The state of his nerves brings him to Dr Jacobsen's sanatorium in Copenhagen. Sketches and lithographs of animals in the Zoological Gardens, Copenhagen. *Alpha and Omega*, a book of poetry and lithographs.
Back on his feet, he returns to Norway. At Kragerö on the Oslo Fjord he does preliminary work on the murals for the University of Oslo. Change in his style : colour is brighter, contour less important for him as a structural element. Literary and psychological problems, the ' human interest,' become more prominent in his work.
Increasing grandeur of form.

1911-13 Purchases a home near Hvitsen, on the Oslo Fjord. Takes part in the Sonderbund Exhibition, Cologne ; one gallery with 32 pictures devoted to Munch (1912). Visits Copenhagen, Paris, London. *Woman* (1913).

1915 Completes his murals for the University of Oslo. Chief pictures: *History, Alma Mater, Sun Rising over the Fjord.*

1916 Purchases a home at Ekely, near Oslo. Now owns four houses, with 43 studios.

1920-22 Travels to Berlin, Paris, Italy. Large-scale exhibition in Zurich. Murals for the workers' dining-hall at the Freia Chocolate Factory, Oslo.

1937 Has many pictures in the Norwegian Pavilion at the Paris World's Fair. Three pictures and eight prints in Berlin, 82 works in the rest of Germany, confiscated as 'degenerate.'

1940 Norway occupied by the Germans, April 9. Munch refuses to join an 'Honorary Art Council' being formed by the Quisling Government. Munch's last years are clouded by sickness and bitterness at the turn taken by world events. Revelatory self-portraits done in his last years.

1944 Dies of a heart-attack on January 23.

BIBLIOGRAPHY

S. Przybyszewsky, *Das Werk des Edvard Munch,* with four contributions by S. Przybyszewsky, F. Servaes, W. Pastor, J. Meier-Graefe, Berlin, 1894; H. Esswein, *E. Munch* (Modern Illustrators, No. 7), Munich, 1905, and *Das Graphische Werk,* 1906-26, Berlin, 1928; C. Glaser, *E. Munch,* Berlin, 1917, 2nd edition, 1922; G. Schiefler, *E. Munchs Graphische Kunst,* Dresden, 1929; C. Glaser, *E. Munch,* in Thieme-Becker: *Allgemeines Lexikon der Bildenden Künstler,* vol. 25, Leipzig, 1931, with bibliography; P. Gauguin, *E. Munch,* Oslo, 1933, 2nd edition, 1946; J. Thiis, *E. Munch og hans Samtid,* Oslo, 1933; J. Thiis, *E. Munch,* Berlin, 1934; R. Stenersen, *E. Munch,* Stockholm, 1944, German edition, Zurich, 1949; P. Gauguin, Grafikeren E. Munch, *Litografier,* Trondheim, 1946; P. Gauguin, Grafikeren E. Munch, *Tresnitt og Etsninger,* Trondheim, 1946, with woodcuts and etchings; J. P. Hodin, *Edvard Munch, Der Genius des Nordens,* Stockholm, 1948, with detailed documentation and bibliography.

NOLDE, EMIL (1867)

1867 Born August 7 at Nolde, on the Danish frontier. Came of old peasant stock (the family name is Hansen).

1884-88 Student at Sauermann's Wood-Carving School, Flensburg. Works as a wood-carver at Munich and Karlsruhe.

1889 Student at the Applied Arts School, Karlsruhe.

1890-91 Works in Berlin as a designer of ornaments and furniture.

1892 Teacher at the Trade and Industry Museum, St. Gall. Gives lessons in colour and decorative drawing. Hans Fehr is Nolde's pupil and friend.

1896 Nolde's first large picture, *The Mountain Giants,* is rejected for the Annual Exhibition in Munich. He draws picture postcards showing the Swiss mountains in grotesque human form. The Munich magazine *Die Jugend* reproduces two of the cards, and later many of Nolde's illustrations. The success of the cards, the sales of which run to one hundred thousand copies, enables him to devote himself entirely to painting.

1898 Gives up his teaching post at St. Gall. Spends a year in Munich at the Friedrich Fehr Art School. First etchings.

1899 Studies under Adolf Hölzel at Dachau. First visit to Paris. Enrols at Académie Julian. Copies Titian in the Louvre.

1900 Admiration for Daumier, Rodin, Degas, Delacroix, Manet and the "seraphic calm of Millet, and his thick impasto." "The sweetness of Renoir, Monet and Pissarro cannot touch my tougher, Nordic senses."
Meeting with Paula Modersohn.
The fruits of his Paris stay are a few School studies. "Paris has given me so little, and I had hoped for so much." Returns to Nolde, his native town. Trip to Copenhagen, where he meets the actress Ada Vilstrup.

1901-03 Stays in Berlin, Copenhagen, Flensburg, and on Alsen Island. Marriage with Ada Vilstrup.

1904-05 Assumes the name Emil Nolde. His impressionist pictures of flowers and gardens announce a new style in his work.
Trip to Italy and Sicily. "We made few stops; sorrow and sickness were our companions." Thus did Nolde sum up the journey. In Berlin he does the *Phantasien* etchings.

1906 Following an exhibition at the Arnold Gallery, Dresden, in which he took part, Nolde is invited to join *Die Brücke*: "In tribute to the storm of your colour." He becomes a member of *Die Brücke.* Does his first woodcuts. He and Schmidt-Rottluff paint together on Alsen Island. Meeting and friendship with Osthaus, founder of the Folkwang Museum at Hagen, and with Christian Rohlfs. Takes part in the exhibitions of the *Deutscher Künstlerbund* and the Berlin Secession. Paints *Free Spirit.* Begins his series of grotesque and religious pictures.

1907 Takes part in the Die Brücke Exhibition at Dresden-Löbtau, and in a show at the Richter Gallery. Quits the group.
First lithographs.

1909 After a serious illness, he paints his first great religious picture, *The Last Supper.* "The picture of *Christ Scorned* saved me from sinking into a mire of religious emotion... Then, once more, I descended into the mystical depths of the half-Man, half-God, and my *Pentecost* was sketched out... The pictures of *The Last Supper* and *Pentecost* mark the transition from a superficial aesthetic feeling to one of innermost fulfilment." Paints luminous land- and seascapes on Alsen Island, where he leads a secluded life.

1910 Hamburg: etchings of the harbour. Berlin: sketches at the cafés, dance-halls, theatres. At the instance of Liebermann, the jury of the Berlin Secession rejects *Pentecost.* Work of 26 other artists rejected, among them the painters of *Die Brücke* and the 'New Association of Artists' in Munich. They organize the 'Exhibition of Artists Rejected for the Berlin Secession' at the Macht Gallery, and unite to form the 'New Secession.' On December 10, in an open letter to the magazine *Kunst und Künstler* Nolde attacks Liebermann's dominating position in the Berlin Secession, for which action he is expelled from the group.

1911 Trip to Belgium and Holland. Van Gogh's pictures leave a strong impression on him. Meeting with Ensor. Paints grotesque still lifes with masks.

1912 Period of great productivity: *Triptych of Santa Maria Egyptiaca, Resurrection, Soldier with his Wife,* and the big, nine-fold altar-

piece *The Life of Christ*. The latter work, first shown at the Folkwang Museum, is sent to the Religious Exhibition at the Brussels World's Fair by Osthaus, organizer of the exhibition. Upon the protest of the Catholic authorities, the work has to be withdrawn. Nolde takes part in the Sonderbund Exhibition, Cologne. Meeting with Macke and Lehmbruck. At an exhibition in the ' New Art Salon,' Munich, he meets Jawlensky.
Takes part in the *Blaue Reiter* Exhibition at the Goltz Gallery, Munich.

1913 Accompanies the Külz-Leber South Sea expedition, travelling across Russia, China, Japan, to the South Seas.

1914 War breaks out during his return journey. His South Sea pictures are confiscated at Suez.

1915-21 Winters in Berlin, summers at Alsen.
Visits Paris and England in February, 1921. At Plymouth he recovers the pictures confiscated 6 years before at Suez. Returns to Alsen via Paris, Spain, Switzerland.

1927 Jubilee Exhibition in Dresden. 60th birthday tribute with written contributions by Klee, Schiefler, Westheim and others.

1931 Publishes *Das Eigene Leben*, the autobiography of his early years, and in 1934 the sequel, *Jahre der Kämpfe*, covering his life up to 1914.

1937 1052 works by Nolde confiscated in Germany as ' degenerate.' 26 paintings—including the nine-part *Life of Christ*—, 4 watercolours and 9 prints figure in the ' Degenerate Art ' Exhibition at Munich in the summer.

1941 Forbidden to paint by the Nazi authorities. During the war his Berlin studio destroyed by air-raids.

1946 Appointed to a professorship in Schleswig-Holstein.
Now has his home at Seebüll, near the Danish frontier.

BIBLIOGRAPHY

G. Schiefler, *Das Graphische Werk E. Noldes bis 1910*, Berlin, 1911 ; *Das Graphische Werk 1910-25*, Berlin, 1927 ; M. Sauerlandt, *Emil Nolde*, Munich, 1921 ; *Festschrift für Emil Nolde zum 60. Geburtstag*, with contributions by Paul Klee, Sauerlandt, Schiefler and others, and the catalogue of the Dresden exhibition, Dresden, 1927 ; P. F. Schmidt, *E. Nolde*, in *Junge Kunst*, No. 53, Leipzig, 1929 ; W. Grohmann, on *Emil Nolde* in Thieme-Becker : *Allgemeines Lexikon der Bildenden Künstler*, vol. 25, Leipzig, 1931, with bibliography ; W. Haftmann, *Holzschnitte von E. Nolde*, Bremen, 1947 ; W. Haftmann, *Radierungen von E. Nolde*, Bremen, 1948.

ROUAULT, GEORGES (1871)

1871 Born May 27 in a Paris cellar during the bombardment of the city in the troubled days of the ' Commune.' His father, a cabinet-maker, hailed from Brittany ; his mother was Parisian. His maternal grandfather, Champdavoine, was extremely fond of Manet, Courbet and Daumier ; he collected prints and reverently showed them to his young grandson. Attends a Protestant primary school.

1885 Apprenticed to a stained-glass maker named Hirsch. Restores old stained-glass windows. Out of loyalty to his employer, he turns down a chance to work with Albert Besnard on the windows of the Ecole de Pharmacie. Evening classes at the Ecole des Arts Décoratifs.

1891 Ecole des Beaux-Arts, in Elie Delaunay's class. This teacher dies soon afterwards ; succeeded by Gustave Moreau.

1892 With a series of religious subjects he wins first prize at the Ecole.

1893 First important picture : *Samson tournant sa meule.* Fails to take the Prix de Rome. Meets Matisse in Moreau's class.

1894 Awarded the Chenavard Prize for *L'Enfant Jésus parmi les Docteurs*, but the decision of the judges is annulled.

1895 Awarded instead the Fortin d'Ivry Prize, in addition to an award at the Salon. Competes for the Prix de Rome with *Le Christ mort pleuré par les Saintes Femmes*, but fails once again. Acting on the advice of Gustave Moreau, he leaves the Ecole.

1898 Death of Moreau. Rouault is appointed Curator of the Gustave Moreau Museum, at 2400 francs a year, not enough to support those dependent on him. He is in constant pecuniary difficulties. Passes through a spiritual crisis ; breaks with Academicism. Back from a convalescent stay in Savoy, he is filled with antipathy for his ' brown ' manner.

1902 Present at the first meetings preparatory to founding the Salon d'Automne. Works out new techniques for the new trends in his art. Ill again, he convalesces at Evian (Savoy). Shows an interest in the movement which later becomes Fauvism.

1903 Religious conception of the world. Becomes acquainted with Huysmans, who wants to form a group of Catholic artists and persuades Rouault to visit the Abbaye de Ligugé, in Poitou. Meets Léon Bloy, whose influence is strong for a time *(La Femme Pauvre)*. A series of pictures of prostitutes, performers at fairs and circuses. He stresses the dark side of life by violent contrasts of tones and colours evocative of night.

1903 Takes part in the first Salon d'Automne, with Matisse and Marquet.

1904 Salon d'Automne : eight pictures, 32 watercolours and pastels, all in his new style.

1905 Salon d'Automne : exhibits three important works—not, however, in the Fauve gallery.

1906 First *Odalisque*. From 1906 on, he exhibits at Berthe Weill's.

1907 The *Clowns*. Pictures more varied in tone. At the instance of Vollard, paints ceramics and glazed earthenware (fired by Méthey). Stays at Bruges.

1908 Marries Marthe le Sidaner. Begins his series of *Judges* and *Tribunals*.

1910 First one-man show at Druet's.

1911 Social themes : peasants, workers, family life. Portraits.

1913 Returns to religious subjects.

1916 Now his sole agent, Vollard advises him to concentrate on illustration. He fits out a studio in his own home, to enable Rouault to complete some hundreds of unfinished works. Turns whole-heartedly to the illustration of books. Paints few pictures between 1917 and 1927.

1917 Works on the illustrations for Jarry's *Ubu Roi*, followed by Vollard's *Réincarnations du Père Ubu*, and *Le Miserere*. Illustrations for *Les Fleurs du Mal* remain unfinished.

1924 Receives the ' Légion d'Honneur ' for his services as Curator of the Gustave Moreau Museum.

1928 Resumes a number of unfinished works, restyling them according to his new ideas.

1929 Sets and costumes for a ballet by Diaghilev: *The Prodigal Son*, music by Prokofiev.

1930 Stays in Switzerland, in the Valais. His colours become more intense and varied. Etchings in colour: *Le Cirque de l'Etoile Filante*, *La Passion*. Illustrations for *Le Cirque*, by Suarès, are not issued.

1932 After 1932 Rouault ceases to date his works.

1937 Exhibition of some of his most important works at Salon des Indépendants (Petit Palais). Does tapestries under the supervision of Mme Cuttoli.

1939 Death of Ambroise Vollard.

1940 Devotes himself almost entirely to religious painting.

1947 Involved in a law-suit with the Vollard heirs. The court decides in Rouault's favour, that pictures unsigned and unsold by him remain his property.

1948 In the presence of the bailiff, Rouault burns the 315 pictures restored to him by decision of the court. Makes his first journey to Italy.

1948 Makes stained-glass windows for the village church at Assy (Upper Savoy).

1949 Trip to Belgium and Holland.

BIBLIOGRAPHY

M. Puy, Paris 1921. G. Charensol, Paris 1926. R. Cogniat, Paris 1930. A. Jewell, New York, Paris 1945-47. R. Marx and G. Geffroy were the first to hail Rouault's work at the Salon des Indépendants, 1895 to 1901; A. Alexandre, L. Vauxcelles and T. Sisson at the Salon d'Automne, 1903 to 1908. The standard work on Rouault is that of Lionello Venturi: *Georges Rouault*, New York 1940; reissued Paris 1948.

SCHMIDT-ROTTLUFF, KARL (1884)

1884 Born December 1 at Rottluff, near Chemnitz.

1897 High School at Chemnitz.

1901 Meeting and artistic collaboration with Erich Heckel.

1905 After obtaining his school-leaving certificate, he moves to Dresden. Begins studying architecture. Meeting with Kirchner, through Heckel. Collaboration with Heckel, Kirchner and Bleyl. Formation of 'Die Brücke' (The Bridge). Name suggested by Schmidt-Rottluff, who also introduces the group to the technique of lithography.

1906 Stays on the island of Alsen. Meeting with Nolde. First and second exhibitions of 'Die Brücke' at Dresden-Löbtau.

1907-08 Spends the summer months on the Dangaster Moor (Oldenburg). Winter in Dresden.

1909 Summer and autumn at Dangast, winter in Dresden. The 'Die Brücke' album of 1909 is his work.

1910 Takes part in the 'New Secession' exhibitions in Berlin (1910-12). Exhibition of 'Die Brücke' at Arnold Gallery, Dresden.

1911 Hamburg. Exhibits at Commeter Gallery. Summer in Norway. Moves in the autumn to Berlin. Collaborates on the magazine *Der Sturm*. Meeting with Otto Müller and Feininger. Increasing massiveness of form. Pronounced tendencies towards abstraction.

1912 Hamburg. Summer at Dangast. Takes part in the 'Sonderbund' Exhibition in Cologne and in that of the 'Blaue Reiter' in Goltz Gallery, Munich. First Berlin exhibition of 'Die Brücke' at Gurlitt Gallery.

1913 Hamburg. Summer at Nidden (coast of Courland). Break-up of the 'Die Brücke' group.

1914 Hamburg. Summer at Hohwacht. Collaboration on the magazine *Die Aktion*, in which many of his woodcuts appear during 1914, 1915, 1916, 1918, etc.

1915-19 Service on the Eastern Front from May 1915 until the end of the war. Series of woodcuts on religious themes during 1918. Returns in 1919 to Berlin, where he now makes his home. Exhibits at Goltz Gallery, Munich.

1920-22 Summer and autumn at Jershöft (Pomerania).

1923 Trip to Italy with the sculptor Kolbe.

1924 Stays in Paris with Kolbe. Summer and autumn at Jershöft.

1925 Trip to Dalmatia.

1925-31 Spends summers and autumns at Jershöft. Exhibits at Nierendorf's in Berlin (1927). Spring of 1928 and 1929 in the Ticino (Switzerland). Three months at the German Academy in Rome in the spring of 1930. Exhibition at Hanover. Appointed in 1931 to the Academy in Berlin.

1932-43 Several stays in the Taunus, in spring. Summers and autumns on the Lebasee (Pomerania).

1933 Expelled from the Academy.

1935 Exhibition at K. Buchholz Gallery, Berlin.

1936 Exhibition at the Westerman Gallery, New York.

1937 In Germany 608 works by Schmidt-Rottluff are confiscated as 'degenerate.' 51 of them figure in the 'Degenerate Art' Exhibition at Munich.

1941 Forbidden to paint. Under police surveillance.

1946 Appointed to a professorship at the Institute of Plastic Arts in Berlin, where he now lives.

1948 Exhibition at the Kunsthalle, Bern (P. Modersohn and the 'Die Brücke' painters).

BIBLIOGRAPHY

R. Schapiro, *Schmidt-Rottluff als Graphiker*, in *Das Graphische Jahrbuch*, Darmstadt, 1920; W. R. Valentiner, *K. Schmidt-Rottluff*, in *Junge Kunst*, Vol. 16, Leipzig, 1920; V. Dirksen, *K. Schmidt-Rottluff* in *Kleine Führer der Kunsthalle*, No. 21, Hamburg, 1921; W. Niemeyer, *Kündung*, Hamburg, 1921; R. Schapiro, *K. Schmidt-Rottluffs Graphisches Werk bis 1923*, Berlin, 1924, with descriptive catalogue; W. Grohmann, *K. Schmidt-Rottluff*, in Thieme-Becker's *Allgemeines Lexikon der Bildenden Künstler*, vol. 30, Leipzig, 1936, with abundant documentation; *Katalog der Ausstellung der Städtischen Kunstsammlung Chemnitz*, with articles by A. Behne, W. Grohmann, C. G. Heise, O. Jäger, W. R. Valentiner and others, Chemnitz, 1946.

SOUTINE, CHAÏM (1894-1943)

1894 Born at Smilovitch, near Minsk, Lithuania, the tenth of eleven children. His father, a tailor, wished him to take up the same trade. The family lived in the ghetto in great poverty. While still a youngster, Soutine ran away from home. Already at Minsk, he showed an interest in painting.

1910 Enrols at the School of Fine Art, Wilno, earning his living as assistant to a photographer.

1911 Through the kindness of a doctor, whose acquaintance he has made, Soutine is enabled to go to Paris. He attends the Ecole des Beaux-Arts, in Cormon's class.

1912 Lives at *La Ruche* (The Hive), the well-known community house in the rue de Dantzig, near the Vaugirard slaughter-houses. Makes friends with the butchers and slaughterers, who lend him quarters of meat from time to time, to serve him as models.

Strikes up friendships with many artists and writers living at *La Ruche* : Chagall, Laurens, Lipschitz, Kremegne, Blaise Cendrars, Fernand Léger, and others.

Down and out, in despair he tries to hang himself. His compatriot, the painter Kremegne, prevents this.

He meets Modigliani and they become fast friends. Through Modigliani, he gets to know the art dealer Zborowski, who buys his first pictures.

1919 On Zborowski's advice, he moves to Céret. His landscapes of this period are among the tensest, most highly strung of his career.

1920 Profoundly affected by Modigliani's death.

1922 Returns to Paris, bringing back with him more than 200 pictures.

1923 January 1 : Dr Barnes, who is getting together his famous collection, buys about a hundred pictures by Soutine.

1925 Stays at Cagnes.

1927 Does many portraits, including a series of choirboys.

1929 Stays at Chatelguyon. Meets M. and Mme Castaing, with whom he lives in the Château de Lèves, near Chartres. The affection and tranquillity he finds here is reflected in the growing calmness of his pictures. Nevertheless, his art remains at bottom one of profound despair. He is obsessed by a craving for solitude. No longer to be seen at Montmartre, he also refuses to take part in exhibitions.

1943 A refugee at Champigny-sur-Vende, in Touraine. Rushed to Paris for an emergency operation for perforated intestine. Operation unsuccessful, and Soutine dies on August 9.

BIBLIOGRAPHY

Maurice Raynal, *Anthologie de la Peinture en France*, Paris, 1927 ; New York, 1928 ; Elie Faure, *Soutine*, Paris, 1928 ; Waldemar George, in *Le Triangle*, 1928 ; Basler and Kunstler, *La Peinture Indépendante en France*, Paris, 1929 ; Drieu La Rochelle, in *Formes*, 1930 ; Raymond Escholier, *La Peinture Française au XXe siècle*, Paris, 1937 ; R. H. Wilenski, *Modern French Painters*, London, 1944 ; Bernard Dorival, *Les Etapes de la Peinture Française Contemporaine*, Paris, 1948 ; Marcel Zahar, *Panorama des Arts*, Paris, 1948 ; James Thrall Soby, *Contemporary Painters*, New York, 1948 ; Maurice Raynal, *Peintres du XXe Siècle*, Geneva, 1948 ; René Huyghe, *Les Contemporains*, Paris, 1949.

VLAMINCK, MAURICE (1876)

1876 Born April 4 in Paris. His father was Belgian ; his mother came of a Protestant family in Lorraine : both were musicians.

1879 The family settles at Le Vésinet.

1894 Vlaminck gets married, becomes the father of two girls.

1895 Becomes a cycling enthusiast ; his athletic abilities gain him a certain amount of success. Takes drawing lessons from an obscure member (Robichon) of the Salon des Artistes Français. Studies with Henri Rigal, visiting the Island of Chatou in his company. Much attracted by the impressionist pictures exhibited by the Paris art-dealers.

1896 Military service.

1899-1900 Discharged, he earns a living giving music lessons. For two months, near the end of the World's Fair, he is a ' gipsy ' bandsman at the Restaurant des Cadets de Gascogne. He next finds a job as violinist at the Théâtre du Château d'Eau.

Meeting with Derain. They fit up a studio in an abandoned house on the Island of Chatou, where they work together. Levasseur, owner of the place, lets it to them for ten francs a month. Vlaminck wrote : "The building creaked in all its limbs and seemed always on the verge of lurching over into the Seine. The beams and joists holding up the floor sagged underfoot. It was winter and we imported a small stove. But there was no fuel. Armed with a saw and a hatchet, we turned our attention to the chairs and tables stored in an adjoining room, feeding them piece by piece into the stove. Needless to say, the owner was kept in the dark as to the fate of his furniture."

Makes the acquaintance of Claude Monet at Durand-Ruel's.

1901 With Derain, he visits the Van Gogh Exhibition at Bernheim's. Enraptured with what he sees.

Derain introduces him to Matisse. Vlaminck paints his *Little Girl with a Doll*, which is shown at Salon des Indépendants—his first appearance there.

1901-02 Writes his first novel, *Grains au Vent*, the title which his publisher substituted for its original name *D'un Lit dans l'Autre*. For this book Derain does thirty-odd sketches ; Félicien Champsaur writes the preface. Two other novels follow later : *Tout Pour Ça* and *Ame de Mannequin*.

1905 Joins the group of artists of the ' Bateau-Lavoir ' at the Café Azon, Montmartre. Here he meets Van Dongen, Picasso, Max Jacob, Guillaume Apollinaire, and others.

Encouraged by Matisse, Vlaminck and Derain exhibit for the first time at the Salon des Indépendants. Each of them sells a picture for 100 francs to an art-lover and patron from Le Havre who is known to loathe modern painting. The story goes that he visited the exhibition with the avowed intention of buying the ugliest canvases he could find, with a view to making a present of them to his son-in-law.

Exhibition at Berthe Weill's, and at Salon d'Automne in the famous ' Cage des Fauves.'

1906 Ambroise Vollard buys up all the pictures in Vlaminck's studio.

1908 Vlaminck abandons pure colour ; his palette grows darker. He now comes under the influence of Cézanne.

1914 During the war, he works in the Loucheur Factory.

1918 Sees much of Zborowski, André Salmon and Francis Carco.

1919 Large-scale Exhibition at Druet's.

1920 Settles at Auvers-sur-Oise.

1925-50 Moves to Rueil-la-Gadelière, where he still lives.

BIBLIOGRAPHY

G. Bazin, *L'Amour de l'Art*, Paris, June 1933 ; F. Fels, Paris, 1928 ; W. Gaunt, New York, 1939 ; W. Grohmann, Leipzig, 1940 ; H. D. Kahnweiler, Leipzig, 1920 ; K. G. Perls, New York, 1941 ; M. Gauthier, Paris, 1949.

WEBER, Max (1881)

1881 Born at Bialystok, Russia. His father was a tailor. Passes his early years in the atmosphere of Bialystok's Jewish community.

1891 The family emigrates to the United States.

1897 Enrols at the Pratt Institute in Brooklyn, where his teacher is Arthur Wesley Dow (a former pupil of Gauguin in Paris).

1905 Goes to Paris where he enters the Académie Julian. Makes the acquaintance of Le Douanier Rousseau.

1906 Enrols at the Académie de la Grande Chaumière and the Académie Colarossi. Greatly impressed by the Retrospective Cézanne Exhibition. Becomes acquainted with Matisse. He and Hans Purrmann organize a group of young painters who work under the guidance of Matisse. He travels in Europe, notably to Madrid and in Italy.

1908 Travels in Holland.

In December he goes back to the United States, taking with him first-hand knowledge of the new tendencies and problems in French painting (Fauvism and Cubism).

1911 He is the pioneer of Cubist Expressionism in America *(The Geranium)*.

1912-17 His work is instrumental in the development of Cubism and Futurism in America *(Rush Hour New York*, and *The Two Musicians*, 1917).

1918 Reverts to figurative painting.

1926-36 Various compositions of women bathing *(Eight Figures*, 1927 ; *At The Lakeside*, 1935).

1937 Enters on a period of completely personal Expressionism *(Fugitives*, 1939 ; *Chassidic Dance*, 1940 ; *The Workers*, 1942).

BIBLIOGRAPHY

H. Cahill, New York, 1930 ; Catalogue of the Museum of Modern Art, New York, 1930 ; American Artists' Group, New York, 1945 ; L. Goodrich, New York, 1949.

GENERAL BIBLIOGRAPHY

For the data given below, we have drawn on the bibliography, the most complete that has so far appeared, compiled by Bernard Karpel, Librarian of the Museum of Modern Art, New York. It was published in 1949 in *Les Fauves* by Georges Duthuit (Geneva, Editions des Trois Collines ; New York, Wittenborn, Schultz, Inc., 1950).

FAUVISM

BOOKS

G. Apollinaire, *Il y a*, Messein, Paris 1925. A. Basler and C. Kunstler, *La Peinture Indépendante en France*, G. Crès, Paris 1929. A. Breton, *Les Pas Perdus*, Paris 1924. F. Carco, *Le Nu dans la Peinture Moderne*, G. Crès, Paris 1924. G. Coquiot, *Cubistes, Futuristes, Passéistes*, Ollendorf, Paris 1923. G. Coquiot, *Les Indépendants*, Ollendorf, Paris 1920. P. Courthion, *Panorama de la Peinture Française Contemporaine*, Simon Kra, Paris 1927. G. Diehl, *Les Fauves*, Editions du Chêne, Paris 1943. B. Dorival, *Les Etapes de la Peinture Française*, vol. II : *Le Fauvisme et le Cubisme*, Gallimard, Paris 1944. G. Duthuit, *Les Fauves* (Braque, Derain, Van Dongen, Friesz, Manguin, Marquet, Matisse, Puy, Vlaminck), Trois Collines, Geneva 1949 ; Wittenborn, Schultz, New York 1950. A. J. Eddy, *Cubists and Post-Impressionism*, A. C. McClurg, Chicago 1914. C. Einstein, *Die Kunst des 20. Jahrhunderts*, 2nd edition, Propyläen-Verlag, Berlin 1926. R. Escholier, *La Peinture Française au XXe Siècle*, Floury, Paris 1937. H. Focillon, *La Peinture aux XIXe et XXe Siècles, du Réalisme à nos Jours*, H. Laurens, Paris 1928. M. Georges-Michel, *Les Grandes Epoques de la Peinture ' Moderne ,'* Brentano's, New York and Paris 1944. J. Gordon, *Modern French Painters*, Dodd, Mead, New York 1923. O. Grautoff, *Die Französische Malerei seit 1914*, Mauritius-Verlag, Berlin 1921. R. Huyghe, *Histoire de l'Art Contemporain : La Peinture* (Le Fauvisme, Les Coloristes, Les Peintres Pathétiques, Le Réveil des Traditions : chaps. IV, V, VI), Félix Alcan, Paris 1935. R. Huyghe, *La Peinture Française : Les Contemporains*, Bibliothèque Française des Arts, Editions Pierre Tisné, Paris 1939 ; new impression, Tisné, 1949. W. Pach, *The Masters of Modern Art*, B. W. Huebsch, New York 1924. M. Raynal, *Anthologie de la Peinture en France, de 1906 à nos Jours*, Editions Montaigne, Paris 1927 ; English translation by Ralph Roeder : *Modern French Painters*, Brentano's, New York 1928. M. Raynal, *Peintres du XXe Siècle*, Albert Skira, Geneva 1947. C. Terrasse, *La Peinture Française au XXe Siècle*, Editions Hypérion, Paris 1939. L. Venturi, *Pittura Contemporanea*, Ulrico Hoepli, Milan 1947. B. Weill, *Pan! Dans l'Oeil!... ou Trente Ans dans les Coulisses de la Peinture Contemporaine, 1900-1930*, Lipschutz Paris 1933. R. H. Wilenski, *Modern French Painters*, Reynal and Hitchcock, New York 1940. C. Zervos, *Histoire de l'Art Contemporain*, Cahiers d'Art, Paris 1938.

ARTICLES AND PREFACES

J. Baschet : Au Temps des Fauves, *L'Illustration*, Paris 1935. R. Cogniat : Du Fauvisme à l'Après-Guerre, *L'Amour de l'Art*, Paris 1934. V. Costantini : La Pittura dei ' Fauves,' *La Fiera Letteraria*, Milan 1928. G. Diehl : Le Fauvisme, *Beaux-Arts*, Paris 1942. G. Duthuit : Le Fauvisme, *Cahiers d'Art*, Paris, 1929, 1930, 1931. M. Feurring : Henri Matisse und die Fauvisten, *Prisma*, Munich 1946. P. Fierens : Le Fauvisme, *Cahiers de Belgique*, Brussels 1931. W. George : Le Mouvement Fauve, *L'Art Vivant*, Paris 1927. A. Gide : Promenade au Salon d'Automne, *Gazette des Beaux-Arts*, Paris 1905.

R. Huyghe : Le Fauvisme, *L'Amour de l'Art*, Paris 1933. A. Ozenfant : Les Fauves, 1900-1907, *L'Esprit Nouveau*, Paris 1922. G. Rouault : Gustave Moreau, *L'Art et Les Artistes*, Paris 1926. A. Salmon : Les Fauves et le Fauvisme, *L'Art Vivant*, Paris 1927. Le Salon d'Automne, *L'Illustration*, Nov. 4, 1905, Paris ; reprinted in *Cahiers d'Art*, No. 5-6, 1931. L. Vauxcelles : Salon des Fauves, *L'Illustration*, Paris 1905. L. Vauxcelles : Salon des Indépendants, *Gil Blas*, Paris 1906.

GROUP EXHIBITIONS, 1902-1950

1902-08, ' Le Père ' Soulier, Paris *(Vlaminck, Friesz, Matisse, etc.)*. 1903-08, Gal. Druet, Paris *(Matisse, Marquet, Manguin, Van Dongen, Derain, Vlaminck, Friesz, etc.)*. 1907, Gal. Blot *(Manguin, Marquet, Puy)*. 1908, Gal. Ch. Malpel, Toulouse *(The Fauve Painters)*. 1908, Gal. Druet, *(3rd Group : Marquet, Manguin, Puy, Friesz, etc.)*. 1927, Gal. Bing *(Matisse, Marquet, Dufy, Friesz, Derain, Vlaminck : Works 1904-1908)*. 1934, Gal. des Beaux-Arts, Paris *(Matisse, Marquet, Puy, Manguin, Vlaminck, Derain, Dufy, Friesz Van Dongen, etc.)*. 1935, Petit-Palais, Grenoble *(The Fauves)*. 1941, Harriman Gal., New York *(Matisse, Manguin, Vlaminck, Derain, Dufy, Braque, Friesz : Works 1902-1908)*. 1942, Gal. de France, *(The Fauves)*. 1947, Gal. Bing *(The Chatou School)*. 1950, Kunsthalle, Bern. 1950, XXVth Biennale, Venice.

EXPRESSIONISM

GENERAL

Thieme-Becker, *Allgemeines Lexikon der Bildenden Künstler*, Leipzig 1907-42, 35 vol. (detailed bibliography for each painter). W. Kandinsky and F. Marc, *Der Blaue Reiter*, Munich 1912, 2nd edition, 1914. P. Fechter, *Der Expressionismus*, Munich 1914. W. Hausenstein, *Die Bildende Kunst der Gegenwart*, Stuttgart 1914. H. Bahr, *Expressionismus*, Munich 1916. H. Walden, *Einblick in Kunst : Expressionismus, Futurismus, Kubismus*, Berlin 1917. W. Waetzold, *Deutsche Malerei seit 1870*, Leipzig 1918. H. Walden, *Expressionismus, Die Kunstwende*, Berlin 1918. H. Hildebrandt, *Der Expressionismus in der Malerei*, Stuttgart 1919. *Schöpferische Konfession*, Berlin 1920 (contributions by Beckmann, Hölzel, Hoetger, Klee, Marc, Pechstein, etc.). K. Pfister, *Deutsche Graphiker der Gegenwart*, Leipzig 1920. E. von Sydow, *Die Deutsche Expressionistiche Kultur und Malerei*, Berlin 1920. C. Glaser, *Graphik der Neuzeit*, Berlin 1922. P. F. Schmidt, *Kunst der Gegenwart*, Berlin 1923. P. Westheim, *Für und Wider*, Potsdam 1923. H. Hildebrandt, *Die Kunst des 19. und 20. Jahrhunderts*, Potsdam 1924. R. Hamann, *Die Deutsche Malerei vom Rokoko bis zum Expressionismus*, Leipzig 1925. C. Einstein, *Die Kunst des 20. Jahrhunderts*, Berlin 1926. C. Breysig, *Eindruckskunst und Ausdruckskunst*, Berlin 1927. K. Woermann, *Geschichte der Kunst aller Zeiten und Völker*, Leipzig 1927, vol 6 : *Die Kunst... von 1750 bis zur Gegenwart* (with extensive bibliography). E. Waldmann, *La Peinture Allemande Contemporaine*, Paris 1930. A. H. Barr, *German Painting and Sculpture*, New York 1931. L. Justi,

Von Corinth bis Klee, Berlin 1931. H. Read, *Art Now*, London 1933. M. Sauerlandt, *Die Kunst der letzten 30 Jahre*, Berlin 1935. W. Willrich, *Säuberung des Kunsttempels*, Berlin 1937 (Nazi pamphlet attacking modern art ; interesting for its numerous quotations and reproductions). P. Thoene, *Modern German Art*, preface by H. Read, London 1938. F. Schmalenbach, *Grundlinien des Frühexpressionismus*, in : *Kunsthistorische Studien*, Basel 1941. G. F. Hartlaub, *Die Graphik des Expressionismus in Deutschland*, Calw 1947. C. Lorck, *Expressionismus*, Lübeck 1947. P. O. Rave, *Kunstdiktatur im 3. Reich*, Hamburg 1949 (contains invaluable information regarding the fate of Expressionist painters and works of art under the National-Socialist government).

A SELECT LIST OF MAGAZINES BEARING ON THE EXPRESSIONIST MOVEMENT

Die Aktion, Berlin 1911-1933 (most important years : 1911-1919). *L'Amour de l'Art*, Paris 1934 (covering Germany and Central Europe ; contributions by W. Grohmann, F. Schiff, P. Westheim ; detailed bibliography by G. Bazin). *Der Anbruch*, Berlin, J. B. Neumann, 1917-22. *Der Ararat*, magazine issued by the Goltz Gallery, Munich 1919-21. *Neue Blätter für Kunst und Kultur*, Dresden 1918-20. *Der Cicerone*, Leipzig 1909-30. *Genius*, Munich 1919-21. *Jahrbuch der Jungen Kunst*, Leipzig 1920-24. *Deutsche Kunst und Dekoration*, Darmstadt 1897-1932. *Die Kunst*, Munich 1899-1937. *Kunst und Künstler*, Berlin 1903-33. *Das Kunstblatt*, Weimar-Potsdam-Berlin 1917-32. *Der Querschnitt*, Berlin 1921-36. *Der Sturm*, Berlin 1910-32. *Das Wort*, Moscow 1936-39 (conspectus of Expressionism : contributions by B. Balâzs, E. Bloch, H. Walden, B. Ziegler, etc. : 1937, nos. 9, 12 ; 1938, nos. 2-7). *Zeitschrift für Bildende Kunst*, Leipzig 1866-1932, with appendix : Kunstchronik (contains, from 1907 on, regular reports on Expressionist exhibitions, as well as many articles on Expressionism).

DIE BRÜCKE

E. L. Kirchner, Chronik K(ünstler) G(emeinschaft) Brücke, 1913 ; with cuts by Heckel, Kirchner, Müller, Schmidt-Rottluff (privately printed ; reprinted in *Katalog der Ausstellung : Paula Modersohn und die Maler der Brücke*, with contributions by A. Rüdlinger and W. F. Arntz, and an extensive bibliography, Kunsthalle, Bern 1948). P. F. Schmidt, *Blütezeit der Dresdener 'Brücke*,' in *Aussaat*, Lorch 1947. In preparation : an analytic study the 'Die Brücke' group by Prof. Hans Wenzel of Stuttgart.

EXHIBITIONS

1906, Autumn, in the exhibition-hall of the Seifert Lamp Factory, Dresden-Löbtau. 1906-07, Exhibition of black-and-white work, same gallery. 1907,

Kunstsalon Richter, Dresden. 1909-10, Arnold Gallery, Dresden. 1912, Gurlitt Gallery, Berlin. 1912, Kunsthütte, Chemnitz. 1912, Commeter Gallery, Hamburg. 1913, January, Der Neue Kunstsalon, Munich. From 1907 on, Travelling Exhibition : Brunswick, Flensburg, Hamburg, Copenhagen, Leipzig, Solothurn, etc.

NEW ASSOCIATION OF ARTISTS, MUNICH

O. Fischer, *Das Neue Bild, Veröffentlichung der Neuen Künstlervereinigung*, Munich 1912 (containing a narrative account of the society, studies of the artists, and a critique of the defection of Kandinsky, Marc, Kubin and Münter). *Katalog der Ausstellung ' Der Blaue Reiter*,' Munich, September to October 1949 (with an historical study by Ludwig Grothe of art life in Munich from 1900 to the advent of the ' Blaue Reiter ' ; excellently documented).

EXHIBITIONS

1909, December, Thannhauser Gallery, Munich : first exhibition. 1910, September, Thannhauser Gallery, Munich (with works by Braque, Derain, Le Fauconnier, Picasso, Rouault, Van Dongen ; catalogue with contributions by Burljuk, Kandinsky, Le Fauconnier, Redon). 1911, December, Third Exhibition in the same gallery, after the defection of Kandinsky, Kubin, Marc and Münter.

GROUP EXHIBITIONS OF THE EXPRESSIONISTS

1912, First Group Exhibition, Goltz Gallery, Munich. 1913, Second Group Exhibition, Goltz Gallery, Munich. 1918, The Expressionist Woodcut, Goltz Gallery, Munich. 1919, Expressionist Painting, Städtisches Museum, Erfurt. 1919, Expressionist Art, from private collections in Leipzig, Kunstverein, Leipzig. 1920, July-September, German Expressionism, Darmstadt-Mathildenhöhe. 1921, Sept. 11-Oct. 2, Kunsthalle, Basel (184 items). 1922, Liljevalchs Konsthall, Stockholm. 1923, January-February, Goltz Gallery, Munich. 1928, April, Recent German Art, from private collections in Berlin, Nationalgalerie, Berlin ; catalogue with preface by L. Justi (204 items). 1928, July, German Post-Impressionism, Nationalgalerie, Berlin. 1929, June 10-July 8, Contemporary German Painter-Engravers, Bibliothèque Nationale, Paris. 1931, March 13-April 28, Museum of Modern Art, New York. 1937, Summer, ' Degenerate Art ' Exhibition, Munich. 1938, July, XXth-Century German Art, New Burlington Galleries, London (269 items). 1939, Contemporary German Art, Institute of Modern Art, Boston. 1946, Exhibition of the Haubrich Collection, Cologne (138 items). 1948, Kunsthaus, Chur. 1949, Modern Expressionism, Kunsthaus, St. Gall. 1949, Stedelijk Museum, Amsterdam.

GENERAL INDEX